MediaWiki

MediaWiki

Daniel J. Barrett

Beijing · Cambridge · Farnham · Köln · Sebastopol · Taipei · Tokyo

MediaWiki
by Daniel J. Barrett

Published by O'Reilly Media, Inc., 1005 Gravenstein Highway North, Sebastopol, CA 95472.

O'Reilly books may be purchased for educational, business, or sales promotional use. Online editions are also available for most titles (*http://safari.oreilly.com*). For more information, contact our corporate/institutional sales department: (800) 998-9938 or *corporate@oreilly.com*.

Editor: Mike Loukides
Production Editor: Sumita Mukherji
Copyeditor: Emily Quill
Proofreader: Sumita Mukherji

Indexer: Daniel J. Barrett
Cover Designer: Karen Montgomery
Interior Designer: David Futato
Illustrators: Robert Romano and Lesley Borash

Printing History:
    October 2008:   First Edition.

ISBN: 978-0-596-51979-7

[M]   [3/10]

1268000074

Table of Contents

Preface xi

Part I. Getting Started

1. **A First Look** **3**
    What's MediaWiki?   4
    A Typical Day on a MediaWiki Site   4
    When to Use MediaWiki   5
    When Not to Use MediaWiki   6
    Additional Resources   7

2. **Basic Use** **9**
    Quick Tour of a Wiki Page   9
    Articles   12
    Editing Primer   20
    Menu Reference   23
    Getting Help   27

3. **Your User Identity** **29**
    Creating an Account   30
    Logging In and Out   30
    User Pages   31
    Signatures   32
    Watchlists   33
    Tracking Your Contributions   35
    Preferences   35
    User CSS and JavaScript   43

Part II. Writing and Editing Articles

4. **Editing Articles** **47**
Getting Started with Editing   48
Creating an Article   51
Paragraphs and Headings   52
Typestyles and Fonts   54
Links (Briefly)   55
Images and Uploaded Files   56
Lists   61
Tables   68
Mathematical Formulas   70
Escaping Wikitext with <nowiki>   71
Conflicts   72
Beyond the Basics   73

5. **Links** **75**
Internal Links   75
External Links   81
Interwiki Links   84
Interlanguage Links   84
Graphical Links   86
File Links   86
Linking Tips   87

6. **Organizing Articles** **89**
Categories   90
Namespaces   96
Subpages   99
Redirects   101
Disambiguation Pages   103
Renaming Articles   104
Deleting Articles   106

7. **Advanced Article Construction** **107**
Maintaining a Consistent Wiki   108
Variables   109
Templates and Transclusion   112
Logical Parser Functions   122
Dynamic Page List   124
Recipes for Refactoring   132

8. Special Pages **139**
    Maintenance Reports   140
    List of Pages   147
    Login/Sign Up   149
    Users and Rights   150
    Recent Changes and Logs   152
    Media Reports and Uploads   155
    Wiki Data and Tools   157
    Redirects and Random Pages   158
    High-Use Pages   159
    Page Tools   161
    Other Special Pages   163
    Special Pages Grouped by Task   165

Part III.   Running and Administering MediaWiki

9. Installing MediaWiki **173**
    Before You Begin   174
    Installing the Prerequisites   176
    Installing MediaWiki   180
    Important Optional Features   187
    A Tour of MediaWiki's Files   193
    Maintaining the Code   196

10. Practical Wiki Design **203**
    Adopting MediaWiki   203
    Planning   206
    Establishing Standards   210
    Governance   212
    Integrating with Other Websites   213

11. Configuring MediaWiki: An Overview **215**
    Administrative Roles   216
    Advanced Page Constructs   217
    Special Pages for Sysops and Bureaucrats   218
    System Messages   218
    Cascading Stylesheets   223
    JavaScript   223
    Configuration Settings   224
    Extensions   225
    Skinning   225

SQL Programming 225
Maintenance Scripts 226

12. Controlling Wiki Features **227**
Users 227
User Rights and Permissions 229
Article Content 236
Configuring the Editing of Articles 238
Maintaining Articles 241
Configuring Namespaces 245
File Uploads 248
Search 250
Special Page List 252
Database Configuration 252
Email Configuration 253
JavaScript Configuration 253
Logging and Debugging 254

13. Changing Appearances **257**
The Basics 257
Menus 260
Search Box 265
Tables of Contents 266
External Link Appearance 266
Page Credits 266
Overall Look and Feel 267
International Support 269

14. Installing Extensions **271**
Obtaining Extensions 271
Installing an Extension 272
Recommended Extensions 274

15. Creating Extensions **281**
Overview of Extension Types 282
Creating a Variable 289
Creating a Parser Function 291
Creating a Tag Extension 294
Behavior Changes 299
Creating a Special Page 301
Useful Tasks for Extension Writers 307
Creating a Skin 313

Publishing an Extension   316
Other Extension Topics   316
Finding a MediaWiki Programmer   317

16. Wiki Administration **319**
Maintenance Scripts   320
Backups   320
Upgrades   322
Read-Only Wiki   323
Performance and Scaling   323
Security   327
Vandalism   329
Common Maintenance Tasks   330
For More Information   333

Index **335**

Preface

In 2001, Wikipedia changed the world by proving that thousands of strangers could collaborate to produce a valuable information resource. Encyclopedia publishers shuddered. Skeptics scoffed. And in the meantime, users around the world have produced *millions* of Wikipedia articles.

Wikipedia was not the first wiki,* but it's clearly the most successful, largely due to its powerful software, *MediaWiki*.

This book is about making MediaWiki work for you, whether you plan to read wikis, write and edit articles, or install and run your own MediaWiki site.

Who Should Read This Book?

This book serves four audiences:

Wiki readers
    Anyone who reads Wikipedia or other wikis running MediaWiki software.
Wiki authors
    Anyone who writes or edits wiki articles.
Wiki sysops
    Authors with special privileges for maintaining the wiki.
Wiki administrators
    System administrators and programmers who install, configure, and run MediaWiki on a server.

Roadmap

Part I of this book is dedicated to wiki *readers*, explaining how to navigate a MediaWiki site effectively. Part II focuses on *authors*, and discusses how to

---

* That honor goes to WikiWikiWeb, created by Ward Cunningham in 1994.

write and edit wiki articles, beginning with the basics and moving to more complex tasks. Part III is for *administrators and programmers*. We'll cover how to install and maintain a MediaWiki site, how to configure its many settings, and how to program your own features, called MediaWiki extensions.

Conventions Used in This Book

The following typographical conventions are used in this book:

Italic
> Indicates new terms, URLs, email addresses, filenames, and file extensions.

`Constant width`
> Used for program listings, wiki articles, wiki categories, wiki namespaces, as well as within paragraphs to refer to program elements such as variable or function names, databases, data types, environment variables, statements, and keywords.

`Constant width bold`
> Shows commands or other text that should be typed literally by the user.

`Constant width italic`
> Shows text that should be replaced with user-supplied values or with values determined by context.

> This icon signifies a tip, suggestion, or general note.

> This icon indicates a warning or caution.

Using Code Examples

This book is here to help you get your job done. In general, you may use the code in this book in your programs and documentation. You do not need to contact us for permission unless you're reproducing a significant portion of the code. For example, writing a program that uses several chunks of code from this book does not require permission. Selling or distributing a CD-ROM of examples from O'Reilly books does require permission. Answering a question by citing this book and quoting example code does not require permission.

Incorporating a significant amount of example code from this book into your product's documentation does require permission.

We appreciate, but do not require, attribution. An attribution usually includes the title, author, publisher, and ISBN. For example: "*MediaWiki* by Daniel J. Barrett. Copyright 2009 Daniel J. Barrett, 978-0-596-51979-7."

If you feel your use of code examples falls outside fair use or the permission given above, feel free to contact us at *permissions@oreilly.com*.

Safari® Books Online

Safari^{.>} When you see a Safari® Books Online icon on the cover of your
Books Online favorite technology book, that means the book is available online
through the O'Reilly Network Safari Bookshelf.

Safari offers a solution that's better than e-books. It's a virtual library that lets you easily search thousands of top tech books, cut and paste code samples, download chapters, and find quick answers when you need the most accurate, current information. Try it for free at *http://safari.oreilly.com*.

How to Contact Us

Please address comments and questions concerning this book to the publisher:

O'Reilly Media, Inc.
1005 Gravenstein Highway North
Sebastopol, CA 95472
800-998-9938 (in the United States or Canada)
707-829-0515 (international or local)
707 829-0104 (fax)

We have a web page for this book, where we list errata, examples, and any additional information. You can access this page at:

http://www.oreilly.com/catalog/9780596519797

To comment or ask technical questions about this book, send email to:

bookquestions@oreilly.com

For more information about our books, conferences, Resource Centers, and the O'Reilly Network, see our website at:

http://www.oreilly.com

Acknowledgments

As always, I thank O'Reilly Media and my long-time editor, Mike Loukides, for believing in the idea of this book. I also thank members of the O'Reilly Editorial, Production, and Tools team (Karen Crosby, Keith Fahlgren, Abby Fox, Marlowe Shaeffer, and Adam Witwer) for their quick responses to my DocBook typesetting questions and requests, and the illustrators and production team for turning my manuscript and sketches into a finished product. Big thanks to the technical review team (Shannon Bohle, Rob Church, Brion Vibber, JP Vossen, and Jim R. Wilson) for their careful reading and thoughtful suggestions that tangibly improved the book. (Of course we used a wiki to review and discuss the manuscript.)

I'd also like to thank my colleagues at VistaPrint: Jeromy Carriere and Robert Dulaney for permission to work on this project, Wendy Cebula for harping on "people, process, technology," Jim Sokoloff for Subversion tips (notably, externals and vendor branches), Paul Shelman for inspiration, and all my colleagues in Capabilities Development for their many questions and requests that propelled me up the MediaWiki learning curve. In the MediaWiki community, I thank the MediaWiki development team for creating a world-changing tool, readers of `mediawiki-l` who answered my obscure questions about internals (especially Brion), and the writers of some outstanding third-party extensions (Ilya Haykinson, Amgine, Unendlich, Cyril Dangerville, and Gero Scholz for Dynamic Page List; Tim Starling for ParserFunctions; and many others). Thanks also to Robert Strandh for opening my eyes to the distinction between "ease of use" and "ease of learning."

Finally, I thank my family, Lisa and Sophia, for their amazing patience and love.

Getting Started

PART I
Getting Started

## CHAPTER 1

A First Look

"The whole world is singin' this song...wikki-wikki-wikki-wikki...."

—Newcleus, "Jam On Revenge"

A *wiki* is a website that lets people freely create, edit, and link a collection of articles. Now, every website can be considered a bunch of interlinked pages, but wikis allow the content and the structure to be changed by a community. Wikis are a great way for a group of people to coordinate and create content, even if that group is made up of thousands of people in different places.

Here are some typical things you can do on a wiki:

- Create an article on a topic that interests you.
- Make changes to other people's articles, without requiring their permission.
- Create links between articles.
- Group similar articles together into convenient categories.
- View the history of an article to see all the changes, who made them, and when.
- See interesting statistics about the articles: which ones are most popular, which ones probably need updating, and so on.

Wikis are often devoted to a particular topic or theme. Wikipedia (*http://www.wikipedia.org*) is an encyclopedia, videoville (*http://www.videoville.org*) is devoted to music videos, The Aquarium Wiki (*http://www.theaquariumwiki.com*) covers aquatic topics, and so on. Within corporate intranets, wikis serve as documentation systems and help employees share knowledge.

What's MediaWiki?

MediaWiki is the world's most popular wiki software, and with good reason. It's pretty easy to use, has powerful features, is highly configurable, scales up to millions of users, and best of all, it just plain *works*. More than 2,000 wikis are powered by MediaWiki worldwide, including Wikipedia.[*] Thanks to the generosity of its creators, MediaWiki is freely available, so anyone can create wikis with it.

 Wikipedia has some features that aren't standard in MediaWiki. We'll point them out as they come up.

MediaWiki is freely distributable,[†] so you can download, install, run, and share it without cost. It's also open source, so any competent programmer can modify its internal behavior (its source code) if desired.

A Typical Day on a MediaWiki Site

To give you an idea of the workings of a wiki, here's a short story about a nonexistent wiki and its users.

It's a sunny day on the Web, and the hard drives are humming at BongoWiki, a popular wiki devoted to musical instruments. Users from around the world come to *www.bongowiki.org*, log in with a username and password, and create and edit articles. At the moment, user Wackerman is creating a new article about snare drums, and user StrataVarious is updating an older article on violin strings.

Wackerman uses the wiki's built-in search engine to check for an existing snare drum article. Finding nothing, he clicks an Edit link and begins writing: not just words, but additional symbols called *wikitext* that produce headings, bulleted lists, graphical images, and other typesetting effects. His first sentence looks like this:

```
The '''snare drum''' is an essential part of a [[drum kit]].
```

The triple quotes mean "display this word in boldface," and the brackets produce a link to another wiki page, `drum kit`. When finished, Wackerman

---

[*] Source: *http://www.mediawiki.org/wiki/Sites_using_MediaWiki*

[†] Under the GNU General Public License, *http://www.gnu.org/licenses/old-licenses/gpl-2.0.html*.

previews his work, enters a change comment to describe what he's done, and saves the article. It is instantly available for other users to read.

Meanwhile, StrataVarious has browsed to an article on violin strings by following category links. Beginning in the `Instruments` category, she browses to `Stringed instruments`, then `Violins`, then `Violin parts`, and finally to the article called `Violin strings`. Clicking the Edit link, she makes the necessary changes, previews the results, enters a change comment, and saves.

Behind the scenes, a wiki sysop named Scribe is monitoring activity on the site. She visits the Recent Changes page, notices the edits by Wackerman and StrataVarious, and checks that they conform to the wiki's published standards. She fixes a broken link in the `Violin strings` article, enters her comment, and saves. Then she visits the New Pages page to see what articles have appeared today and, to her surprise, discovers that an anonymous user has created hundreds of articles with nonsense names. It's a clear case of wiki vandalism. Using a special page on the wiki, she bans further edits from that user's IP address. Then she heads to a discussion area called a talk page and posts a note for other sysops, proposing that wiki edits should be restricted to logged-in users only. Other sysops disagree, and vigorous debate follows.

Another sysop, Conductor, reads Scribe's note and begins deleting the bogus articles. After several dozen, he gets tired and wishes there were a way to remove all the vandal's articles in one shot. He emails a wiki administrator, explaining the problem. Using the PHP programming language, the administrator creates and installs a MediaWiki extension that deletes all recent articles coming from a given IP address.[‡] Conductor runs the extension and wipes out the bogus articles instantly.

Over many months, BongoWiki grows to be the largest and most trusted repository of musical instrument knowledge on the Web. And yet none of the hundreds of authors have ever met one another in person. This is the power of wikis.

When to Use MediaWiki

As the preceding story demonstrates, MediaWiki is a terrific collaborative tool. It's ideal for:

Informal knowledge-sharing
> With its "anyone can edit anything" philosophy, MediaWiki works well for building a repository of knowledge in bits and pieces. It's far lighter-weight than the big, commercial content management systems.

[‡] There really is an extension like this: Nuke, by Brion Vibber, *http://www.mediawiki.org/wiki/Nuke*.

Quick turnaround

MediaWiki is easy and rapid to use. Not all features are easy to *learn*, but once you know them, you can search, modify, and maintain the content very efficiently.

Communities of like-minded people

MediaWiki is fantastic for rapid, informal sharing of knowledge among company employees, scientists, professors, students, and other groups. It's particularly great for technical communities, like software developers or system administrators accustomed to markup languages like HTML.

Global communities

MediaWiki is built to be multilingual, supporting a range of languages and locales.

Ease of administration

A small number of people can run a wiki fairly efficiently for large numbers of users. Even a single capable sysop/administrator can support hundreds of readers and authors.

Reliability

MediaWiki is stable, solid software. New releases are run for months on Wikipedia before they're packaged as official releases, so most bugs are squashed by then. The software just works.

When Not to Use MediaWiki

MediaWiki software is terrific for a community of geographically distributed, like-minded people producing an information resource. But it's not for every purpose. In particular, it's not for:

Applications that need strict access control

MediaWiki is a public system at its core. Although you can restrict access to individual articles and, to a limited extent, sets of articles, the software is not optimized for this purpose, maintenance gets painful as the wiki grows, and the access control methods are not necessarily secure.

General content management

MediaWiki is not a content management system (CMS). It has no work-flow, its handling of uploaded documents is fairly primitive, it doesn't integrate with popular applications like Microsoft Office, and, as mentioned, its access control model is not very flexible.

Users with limited technical skill

MediaWiki requires its users to learn wikitext, a markup language to indicate bold, italics, links, and so on, which may be a burden for nontechnical users. While you can create articles without wikitext—just by typing paragraphs of plain text—this doesn't take advantage of the wiki's power. Nontechnical users might be happier with a wiki that has a WYSIWYG* editor.

Use MediaWiki for what it does best: facilitating collaboration on a massive scale. We'll speak more about the challenges of rolling out a MediaWiki site to users in Chapter 10.

Additional Resources

MediaWiki is extensively documented online. Most of the material is scattered throughout three sites: Wikipedia, MediaWiki.org, and Meta-Wiki, each organized in its own way. There are also a number of useful mailing lists. Here's a quick reference guide:

Wikipedia
> Wikipedia's extensive help system, *http://en.wikipedia.org/wiki/Help:Contents*, documents wikitext and covers many interesting policies and procedures. These procedures are tailored to Wikipedia's needs, but might be applicable to other wikis as well.

MediaWiki.org
> The official site *http://www.mediawiki.org* documents the MediaWiki software, third-party extensions, wiki configuration, system administration, and much more. This is also where you download MediaWiki software and updates.

Meta-Wiki
> *http://meta.wikimedia.org* is devoted to all the projects of the Wikimedia Foundation, including MediaWiki and Wikipedia. It also includes extensive documentation on MediaWiki's features, though much of it is being migrated to MediaWiki.org.

`mediawiki-l` *mailing list*
> Wiki features are discussed in several mailing lists described at *http://www.mediawiki.org/wiki/Mailing_lists*. You can subscribe or simply read the archives. The most important list for our purposes is `mediawiki-l`, which discusses installing and configuring MediaWiki software; its archives are at *http://lists.wikimedia.org/pipermail/mediawiki-l/*.

---

* WYSIWYG = What You See Is What You Get.

## CHAPTER 2

Basic Use

Wikipedia and thousands of other websites run MediaWiki, and this chapter will teach you how to get started using any of them: finding and reading articles, basic editing, and so forth. Thanks to the software's consistent operation and behavior, once you find your way around one MediaWiki site, you'll feel at home on any of them. In this chapter, we'll introduce:

General look and feel
   The common parts of a MediaWiki page

Navigation
   Moving around from page to page

Articles
   The main content of the wiki

Searching
   Finding articles by keyword

Categories
   Organizing similar articles into groups

Namespaces
   Dividing the wiki into sections

We'll also briefly discuss writing and editing articles, just enough to get you started. Chapter 4 will cover this topic in detail.

Quick Tour of a Wiki Page

On any MediaWiki site, such as Wikipedia, you'll see the same basic components on each page.[*] Some parts might be stylized (or "skinned") differently,

---

[*] A notable exception is the wiki's home page, which likely has an individualized layout, as in Wikipedia's case.

appear in different locations on the page, or be accompanied by additional features, but most of the time they're all present, looking something like Figure 2-1.

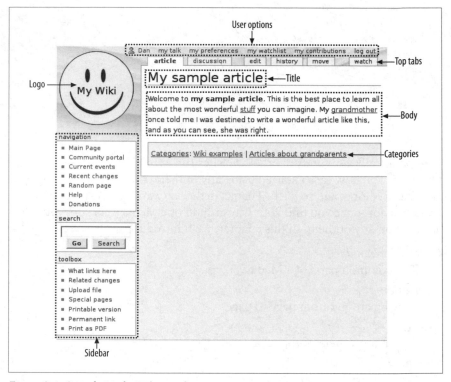

Figure 2-1. Sample MediaWiki article

Here are the major parts:

Logo
    A picture that identifies the wiki. It appears on every page. Click it to return to the wiki's home page at any time.

Article title
    The name of the article, in this case, My sample article.

Article body
    The text and images that make up a wiki article. The text contains links to other wiki articles, depicted here as the underlined words "stuff" and "grandmother."†

---

† MediaWiki links need not be underlined, but underlined links are easier to see in this book.

Categories

Similar articles are grouped into categories for convenient browsing. In this case, the categories are `Wiki examples` and `Articles about grandparents`. All of the category names are links, and clicking on any of them leads to a list of all the articles in that category.

Sidebar

The sidebar contains a collection of navigation tools:

Navigation menu

This menu links to several important pages that make good starting points.

Search box

The Search button operates like a regular search engine, listing the wiki articles that match your keywords. The Go button jumps directly to a relevant article; if it doesn't, you are offered the opportunity to create one.

Toolbox

A menu of tasks that changes as you browse the wiki, displaying links appropriate to the page you're viewing. On an article page, for example, the Toolbox can display a printable version of the article. When a user page is displayed (see "User Pages" on page 31), the Toolbox contains a link for emailing that user.

Language menu

This optional menu (not pictured) contains links to foreign-language translations of the current article. See "Interlanguage Links" on page 84 for more details.

User options

A menu of links about you (i.e., your identity on the wiki), usually at the top of the page. Here's where you log in and out, set preferences, and more. If you are not logged in, this menu will lack most of its links. Chapter 3 covers this menu and its features in detail.

Top tabs‡

Actions for working with articles: viewing, editing, renaming, and more. See Chapter 4 for details.

MediaWiki's menus are a bit arbitrary. For instance, "Donations" (in the Navigation menu) is hardly about navigation, whereas "Special Pages" (in the Toolbox) arguably is. But these are small issues, you'll get used to them, and

---

‡ "Tabs" is a bit misleading because some MediaWiki sites don't display these links as tabs. Most do, however.

wiki administrators can change them if desired. (Wikipedia has a slightly different menu arrangement, for example.)

Articles

MediaWiki content is contained in *articles*, one per topic. When people talk about a "wiki page," they usually mean an article. In this section, we'll cover the various types of articles and how to locate them by searching and browsing.

Every article has a title and a body. Titles come in many styles: a single noun like `Dog`, a proper name like `William Shakespeare`, a verb phrase like `Harvesting wheat in the fall`, or even `Random thoughts that I wanted to share with the world today, so there`. The article body is the content: text, images, or other media. An article titled `William Shakespeare` might include a biography of the famous playwright, a portrait or two, and an audio recording of a famous speech from *Hamlet*.

Articles are written and edited by a community of wiki users. Many MediaWiki sites let anybody edit any article or create new articles. This openness is a core philosophy behind wikis.

Searching for Articles

MediaWiki's search box has two search buttons, labeled Search and Go, rather than the usual single button. Briefly, the Search button produces traditional search results (hits), while Go jumps directly to articles and offers the opportunity to create new ones. (Pressing Enter is the same as clicking Go.)

 The built-in search box of Firefox, IE7, and possibly other web browsers can also search the wiki. When visiting a MediaWiki site, check your browser's list of available search engines, and you'll see your wiki listed as a choice next to Google and the rest. This happens automatically, thanks to a technology standard called OpenSearch.

Enter some text in MediaWiki's search box, click Search, and a page of search results appears: links to wiki articles matching your search text, as shown later in Figure 2-2. An article matches if it contains *all* the words in your search text. Search is case-insensitive: capital and lowercase letters are equivalent.[*] If you

---

[*] Article titles are case-sensitive in other situations, however: see the sidebar "Article Titles and Case-Sensitivity" in "Links to Nonexistent Articles" on page 76 for the gory details.

enclose your search text in double quotes, then an article matches if it contains that exact phrase.[†]

The Go button does much the same thing, with two additional features:

Jumping to an article
If your search text exactly matches the title of a article, the Go button brings you directly to that article, rather than displaying a page of search results. So if you enter Dog and click Go, and there's an article called Dog, that article will be displayed. The search results page is simply skipped. If there is no exact match to your search text, then you'll see a search results page as if you'd clicked Search.

Creating an article
If your search terms don't exactly match an article's title, the search results page asks if you want to create that article. For example, a failed search for dog bicycles produces a message like this:

> There is no page titled "dog bicycles". You can create this page.

By clicking create this page, you'll be led to the MediaWiki edit page to create the article.

A search results page, shown in Figure 2-2, displays two types of results:

Page title matches
Articles whose titles contain all your search terms.

Page text matches
Articles whose content contains all your search terms.

You will also see at the bottom of the page:

- Links for viewing further search results, one page at a time.
- A search area where you can modify your terms and search again. You can also limit the search to certain collections of articles (see "Namespaces" on page 16). For instance, to search only Help pages, clear all checkboxes except for Help.

The search engine ignores some common words (like "the"); the complete list is at *http://dev.mysql.com/doc/refman/5.0/en/ fulltext-stopwords.html*. Also, by default, words of three letters or less are ignored. Both of these behaviors can be changed by the wiki administrator: see "Search Database Tuning" on page 251.

[†] Double quotes work only in MediaWiki 1.12.0 and higher.

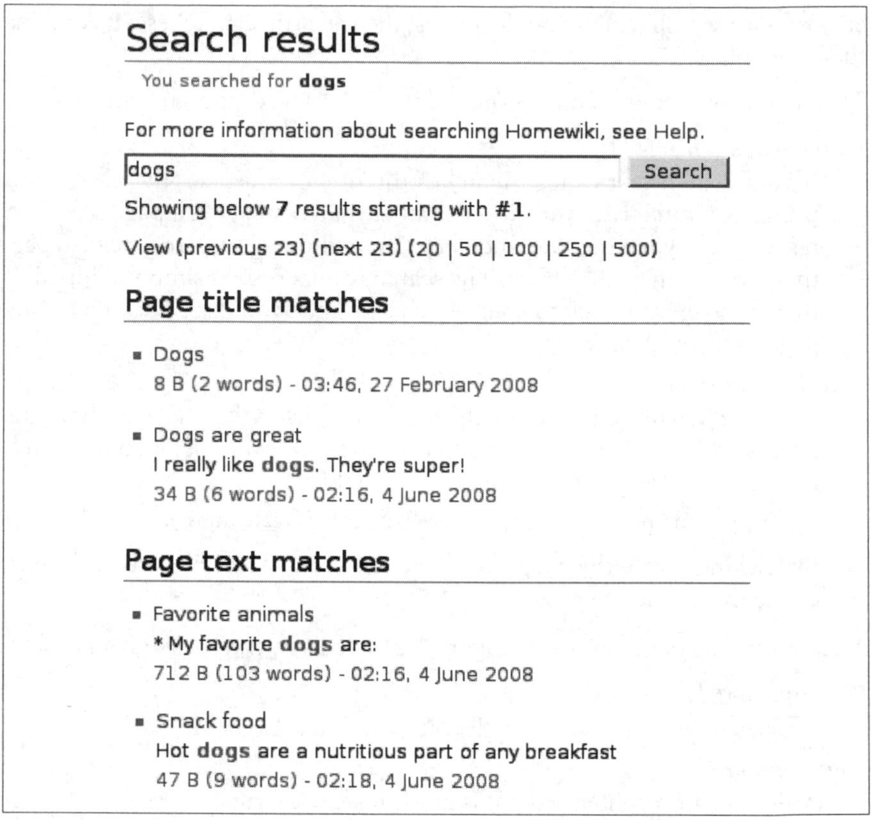

Figure 2-2. A search results page

Browsing by Categories

MediaWiki articles on similar topics are grouped into descriptive categories, which are listed at the bottom of most articles. For example, the article Dog might be in the categories Mammals, Pets, and Carnivores. Each category name is a link that leads to a category page (Figure 2-3) listing all articles in the category, optionally with text at the top describing the category. The list of categories in an article is preceded by a "Categories" link that leads to a page of *all* categories in the wiki.

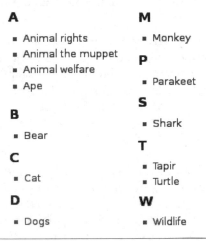

Category:Animals

All about animals.

Subcategories

This category has only the following subcategory.

M

- Mammals

Pages in category "Animals"

The following 13 pages are in this category, out of 13 total.

A

- Animal rights
- Animal the muppet
- Animal welfare
- Ape

B

- Bear

C

- Cat

D

- Dogs

M

- Monkey

P

- Parakeet

S

- Shark

T

- Tapir
- Turtle

W

- Wildlife

Figure 2-3. A category page

The list of all categories is not an article, but a *special page*, a web application within MediaWiki. We'll see many other special pages in Chapter 8 and throughout the book.

Categories provide a path for moving through the wiki. From the article Dog, you could click the Pets category link and see a list of all pets. From here you'd click, for example, Parakeet, and when the Parakeet article loads, you'll see it's in the category Birds. Click Birds to list all bird-related articles in the wiki, and continue.

Categories can have categories, too. The Pets category could be contained in the Hobbies category, which is in the Leisure Activities category, which is in

Activities, which is in Human Behavior, which is in Psychology, and so on. When category *A* is inside category *B*, we call *A* the *child category* or *subcategory*, and *B* the *parent category* or *supercategory*. A single article may be in many categories, and a single category can have many parents and many children.

These parent/child relationships between categories provide yet another path through the wiki. Suppose your company has a MediaWiki site on its intranet, and you're looking for information on company-provided travel insurance. You search for "travel insurance" but find nothing. So, you could visit the Departments category page, which has a subcategory Human Resources, which has a subcategory Policies, which contains an article called Travel Policy, which discusses travel insurance. You notice that the benefit is called "business trip insurance" which is why it didn't show up in your search results. Thank goodness for categories.[‡]

We've been discussing categories purely from a reader's perspective, as if they were always present, perfectly organized, and ready for use. This is ideal, but not always the case. In an active wiki, contributors are constantly shuffling articles into and out of categories, creating categories, and reorganizing parent and child categories. We'll see how to do all that in Chapter 6.

Namespaces

Some wiki page titles begin with a word and a colon, such as Help:Contents or Category:Wiki examples. These prefixes are called *namespaces*, and they divide the wiki into major sections with particular purposes. Help-related articles are found in the Help namespace, for example, and categories are found in the Category namespace. Articles about the wiki's own operation are found in a namespace named after the wiki. That is, a wiki called MyWiki would have a namespace MyWiki, with articles titled MyWiki:About, MyWiki:Privacy policy, and so on. (The standard namespaces can be found in Table 6-1 in the section "Namespaces" on page 96.)

Articles such as Dog, which have no namespace specified, are said to be in the *main namespace* or *article namespace*.

[‡] We'll discuss workarounds for this search problem in "Redirects" on page 101.

To list articles in a given namespace, visit the page `Special:AllPages`.[*] (Type "Special:Allpages" in the search box and click Go.) Then select a namespace and click Go.

For now, you don't need to know much about namespaces. Just be aware that they exist, as we'll refer to them often. We'll cover them in depth in "Namespaces" on page 96.

User Pages

Every registered wiki user has a personal wiki article, called a *user page*. The name is `User:`*username*. If your username is Jsmith, for example, your user page is `User:Jsmith`. That article is in the `User` namespace, which contains all user pages from `User:Aaaaargh` to `User:Zzzzz`.

Talk Pages

Every article has an associated *talk page*, or discussion page, where visitors can write comments. To visit an article's talk page, click the article's Discussion tab.

Talk pages are ordinary wiki articles, but by agreement, they are dedicated to discussions about articles. For example, if the article `Dog` explains what foods are appropriate for dogs, but you disagree with the advice, the place to say so is the article's talk page, `Talk:Dog`. If your comments are deemed worthwhile by the community, they might later move to the `Dog` article.

Talk pages have an additional top tab, labeled "+" or "New Section". Click this tab to append a new section to the talk page rather than editing the whole page. This is the easiest way to add a new discussion topic with its own heading.

As you might guess from the name `Talk:Dog`, all talk pages (for the main namespace) are contained in a namespace called `Talk`. Every other namespace (`User`, `Help`, `Category`, etc.) has an associated talk namespace (`User talk`, `Help talk`, `Category talk`, etc.) that contains its talk pages. For example, the user page `User:Jsmith` has an associated talk page, `User talk:Jsmith`, in the `User talk` namespace. Likewise, the talk page for `Category:Wiki examples` is `Category talk:Wiki examples`.[†]

---

[*] `Special:Allpages` is another "special page" in MediaWiki.

[†] Earlier, we said that article titles in namespaces consist of a word, a colon, and the article name, such as `User:Jsmith`. Now you see that namespace names can include several words, such as `User talk` or `Help talk`.

Many MediaWiki users remain unaware of talk pages, as the little "discussion" tab is easy to overlook. Sometimes, the discussion provides interesting clues to the collaborative process that developed the main article.

Links

MediaWiki articles are filled with *internal links* to other articles in the same wiki. They appear in various colors with different meanings:‡

- Blue means the article is not in your browsing history, meaning you might not have visited it yet.
- Purple means you have visited the article.
- Red means there is no article on the topic. Clicking the link brings you to an edit page to create the article. A red category link means nobody has created a category page of that name.

In addition to internal links, there can also be *external links* to other websites. These are often accompanied by a small icon to distinguish them from internal links. Secure links are followed by a padlock icon, and ordinary nonsecure links have an arrow.*

History

MediaWiki keeps track of every edit made to every article. On any article page, you can see who edited the article, when they did it, and what changes they made, by clicking the top tab labeled History. Each bulleted line of an article's history, as shown in Figure 2-4, represents a *revision* of the article, where someone edited the article and saved the changes.

 This revision control system is one of MediaWiki's great features. You can edit articles without worrying because if you mess things up, the previous revision can be restored easily by clicking an "undo" link.

---

‡ These are the default colors in the default skin; wiki sysops can change them. Also, for a cool trick, see the preference "Threshold for stub link formatting" in "Miscellaneous Preferences" on page 41.

* Again, assuming your sysops have not changed this behavior.

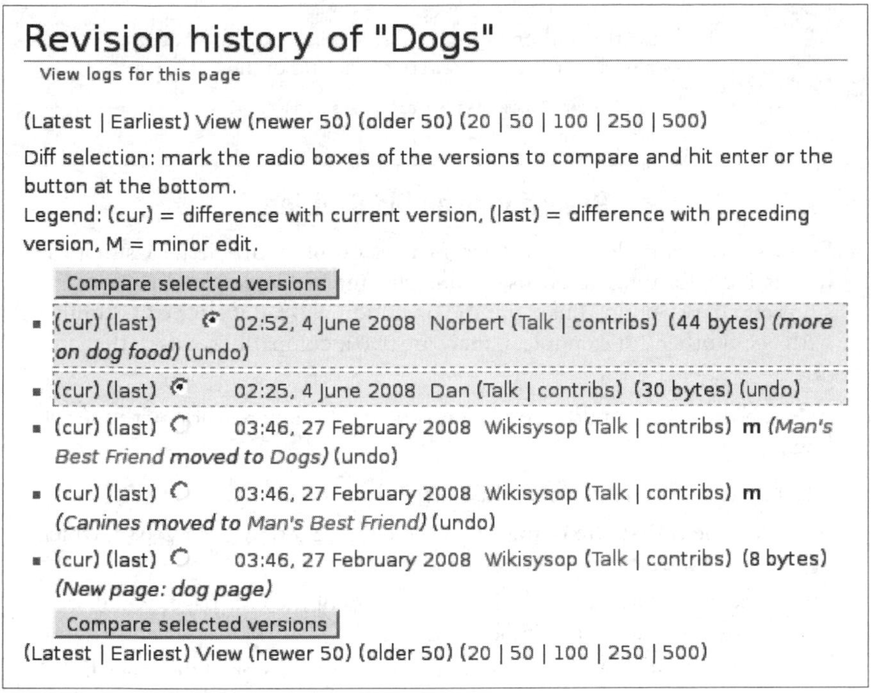

Revision history of "Dogs"

View logs for this page

(Latest | Earliest) View (newer 50) (older 50) (20 | 50 | 100 | 250 | 500)

Diff selection: mark the radio boxes of the versions to compare and hit enter or the button at the bottom.

Legend: (cur) = difference with current version, (last) = difference with preceding version, M = minor edit.

   Compare selected versions

- (cur) (last)   ⦿ 02:52, 4 June 2008   Norbert (Talk | contribs) (44 bytes) *(more on dog food)* (undo)

- (cur) (last) ⦿   02:25, 4 June 2008   Dan (Talk | contribs) (30 bytes) (undo)

- (cur) (last) ⦾   03:46, 27 February 2008   Wikisysop (Talk | contribs) **m** *(Man's Best Friend moved to Dogs)* (undo)

- (cur) (last) ⦾   03:46, 27 February 2008   Wikisysop (Talk | contribs) **m** *(Canines moved to Man's Best Friend)* (undo)

- (cur) (last) ⦾   03:46, 27 February 2008   Wikisysop (Talk | contribs) (8 bytes) *(New page: dog page)*

   Compare selected versions

(Latest | Earliest) View (newer 50) (older 50) (20 | 50 | 100 | 250 | 500)

Figure 2-4. A history page

Here are some interesting things you can do on a history page:

- See who made any revision by examining the username on that line. You can also click the username to visit that user's personal page, the "talk" link to visit her personal talk page, or the "contrib" link to see her other edits on the wiki (all discussed in Chapter 3).

- View previous versions of the article by clicking the date and time of any revision.

- View the changes, or *diffs*, made in revisions:

    —To see the changes made in a particular revision, click its "last" link.

    —To compare an old revision to the most recent one, click its "cur" link.

    —To compare any two revisions, select the radio buttons next to both of them and click "Compare selected versions".

- Undo a revision by clicking the "undo" link if one appears, and if you have permission to do so. If this doesn't work, see the sidebar "Reverting to an Old Revision."

To learn the authorship of any wiki page quickly, add the query parameter `action=credits` to the end of the URL, e.g.:

`http://example.com/wiki/My_article?action=credits`

Reverting to an Old Revision

You can always undo the most recent revision of an article by visiting the history page, locating that revision, and clicking its "undo" link. Earlier revisions also have "undo" links, but the operation will fail if later edits conflict with one another (for example, if there are two incompatible edits to the same line).

As a substitute for "undo", you can revert back to any revision with the following steps:

1. Locate the old revision on the article's history page.
2. Click the timestamp of that revision (e.g., **22:23, 4 June 2008**), which displays the article as it used to be.
3. Click the old article's Edit tab. At the top of the edit page, you'll see a message indicating it's an old revision:

   > WARNING: You are editing an out-of-date revision of this page. If you save it, any changes made since this revision will be lost.

   Nonetheless, you'll soon be saving this old revision.
4. In the Summary area, enter an appropriate change comment like "reverted to revision of 22:23, 4 June 2008."
5. Save.

You have now created a new revision that is a copy of the old one, reverting the article.

Editing Primer

On most MediaWiki sites, any article can be modified by any user. This is accomplished on the *edit page*, available by clicking an article's Edit link. You'll see a main Edit link to edit the entire article, and sometimes Edit links next to each section for editing only that section of the article.

For now, we'll describe just enough editing to get you through the next few chapters. You'll find more details in Chapter 4 and on the Quick Reference card in this book.

Wikitext

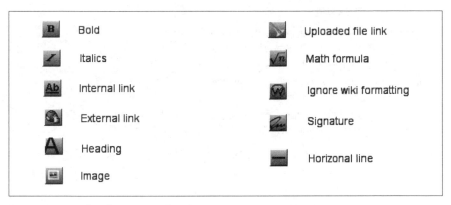

Figure 2-5. Toolbar buttons on the edit page

MediaWiki's edit page has a small button bar, called the *toolbar*, for making words bold, italic, and so on. It has familiar-looking buttons, as shown in Figure 2-5; however, they don't work in the same way as in Microsoft Word or other WYSIWYG editors. Instead, these buttons emit *wikitext*, special symbols that surround your words. When you highlight a word and click the italics button, for example, the editor does not display the word in italics. Instead, it places two single quotes on each side of the word, like this:

```
Here is a ''very important'' message.
```

You can also type the quote marks by hand. When MediaWiki later displays this decorated text, it appears as:

Here is a *very important* message.

Wikitext might seem cumbersome at first, but most likely you'll get used to it quickly. (Fifty zillion Wikipedia authors can't all be wrong, can they?) If you know HTML, you'll find wikitext much simpler for most tasks. Table 2-1 illustrates some common wikitext.

Table 2-1. A few simple wikitext symbols (not complete)

Concept	Wikitext	Example
Paragraphs	Separate paragraphs by blank lines (press Enter two or more times)	This is a paragraph. Isn't it great? Here is another paragraph.
Bold	Place 3 single quotes on each side	'''This is in bold'''
Italics	Place 2 single quotes on each side	''This is in italics''

Concept	Wikitext	Example

Bulleted lists	Precede items with an asterisk at the beginning of the line	`* First item`
		`* Second item`
		`* Third item`

Numbered lists	Precede items with a hash mark at the beginning of the line; items will be consecutively numbered	`# First item`
		`# Second item`
		`# Third item`

Headings	Place 2 equals signs on each side; must be at the beginning of the line	`== This is a heading ==`

Subheadings	Increase the number of equals signs; must be at the beginning of the line	`=== This is a subheading ===`
		`==== This is a sub-subheading ====`
		`===== etc. =====`

Internal links	Place 2 square brackets on each side to link to another wiki article	`Link to the [[dog food]] article.`

Edit, Preview, Comment, Save

Editing an article involves four steps that all wiki authors must commit to memory—this process is an integral part of MediaWiki life:

Edit
> Click an article's Edit button, and change the wikitext to your heart's content.

Preview
> At any time, click the edit page's Show Preview button to examine what the article will look like when saved. You can also click the Show Changes button to see only what you've changed, in a two-column "before and after" format that highlights the changes.
>
> Repeat the Edit and Preview steps as many times as you like.

Comment
> Below the edit box, there is a Summary line to describe the changes you've made. This step is optional but *highly* recommended, as your summary comments will appear in the article's history, helping other readers understand what you did and why.

Save
> Finally, click the Save Page button to make your changes permanent and available to other readers. This creates a new revision of the article. Your summary comment appears on the article history page.

If you have access to a MediaWiki site, take time to practice with wikitext and the edit-preview-comment-save process. One good place to practice is Wikipedia's sandbox, *http://en.wikipedia.org/wiki/Wikipedia:Sandbox*, a wiki article whose sole purpose is to help people learn wikitext.

Menu Reference

Here's a quick overview of all the menus you'll find on a typical MediaWiki page as you saw previously with Figure 2-1 within the section "Quick Tour of a Wiki Page" on page 9.

Navigation Menu

The Navigation menu is completely customizable by wiki sysops; check out Wikipedia for an example of a customized Navigation menu. MediaWiki's default links are listed here:

Main page
> Return to the home page, just like clicking the wiki logo.

Community portal
> Each MediaWiki site can interpret this however it likes. On Wikipedia, it's a collection of wiki-related news.

Current events
> Each MediaWiki can site interpret this however it likes. It's often a list of news articles from media outlets.

Recent changes
> A list of changes on the wiki, from newest to oldest. Each bulleted entry is one change. From each entry, you can jump to the article (click its title), see the change itself (click "diff"), view the article's history (click "hist"), and see information about the author (using the same username, Talk, and contribs links as on the history page). See "Recent Changes" on page 154 for more details.

Random page
> Just like it sounds: jump to a randomly selected article. See "Random Page" on page 158.

Help
> Each MediaWiki site can interpret this however it likes. If present, this article is usually a list of help articles on the wiki.

Donations
> Each MediaWiki site can interpret this however it likes. If present, it's usually an article that solicits charitable donations from visitors for the upkeep of the wiki.

Toolbox Menu

The links in the Toolbox menu vary depending on where you are in the wiki. For a typical article, the links include:

What links here
> Follow links in reverse: that is, find out which other articles link to this one. See "What Links Here" on page 162.

Related changes
> See changes in articles that are *linked from* this one. See "Related Changes" on page 154.

Upload file
> Upload an image or other file for use in the wiki. See "Images and Uploaded Files" on page 56.

Special pages
> View a list of web applications, called special pages, found on the wiki. See Chapter 8 for the full story.

Printable version
> Display the current article in a format more suitable for printing (without the menus).

Permanent link
> Produce a link to this specific revision of this article. If the article is edited later, this link will still lead to the old revision. These links are great for bibliographic references.[†]

Language Menu

MediaWiki is multilingual: articles may exist in many languages if the wiki is set up to support this. Sometimes the articles are straight translations, and other times they say completely different things.

On Wikipedia, if an article exists in multiple languages, an additional "Languages" menu appears in the sidebar. This menu contains a list of every language in which the article exists. Click *Deutsch*, for example, to see the German edition of the article. Other MediaWiki sites may have a similar feature, as explained in "Enabling Interlanguage Link Support" on page 333.

[†] Although the article will be the old revision, any embedded content that can change independently, such as images or templates, might be different.

You can change the language of all menus, buttons, tabs, and system text. Just click "my preferences" in the user options menu, and under the User Profile tab, change your language and click Save. About 300 languages are supported.

User Options Menu

If you're logged in to the wiki, the user options menu contains:

your username
Your personal user page (the link displays your MediaWiki username).

My talk
Your personal talk page.

My preferences
Settings to affect your experience on the wiki.

My watchlist
List of articles you're watching, so you can be alerted when they change.

My contributions
List of your edits.

Log out
Log out of the wiki.

If you're not logged in, you'll see some or all of:

nnn.nnn.nnn.nnn (an IP address)
Because MediaWiki cannot identify you, it lists the IP address (numeric Internet address) that you're coming from. If the site permits anonymous users to have user pages, this will be a link.

Talk for this IP
The talk page for the previously mentioned IP address, if supported by the wiki.

Log in/create account
Log into the wiki or create a new user account.

In some cases, anonymous users can be tracked or identified by their IP address by anyone viewing the wiki. Registered users, on the other hand, do not have their IP addresses displayed except to the wiki's system administrators. An interesting twist on "anonymous."

The features of the user options menu are discussed in detail in Chapter 3.

Top Tabs

The top tabs represent operations on articles. If you're logged in, you'll see:

Article or Page‡
> View the article. This is selected by default when you browse to an article by link or search.

Discussion
> View the article's talk page.

Edit, View Source, or Create
> If the article is editable, the Edit tab will appear, leading to MediaWiki's edit page. If it is not editable, the tab will read View Source, allowing you to see the wikitext of the article but not edit it. If the article doesn't exist and is being edited for the first time, the tab will read Create.

History
> View the history page.

Move
> Rename the article.

Watch
> Be alerted when the article changes. See "Watchlists" on page 33.

If you're not logged in or you have special privileges, you might see more or fewer tabs.

Footer

The footer menu appears at the bottom of every wiki page. Its linked articles may be interpreted differently by each wiki, but their intended contents are the following:

About...
> A description of the wiki's purpose.

Disclaimers
> Legal (or other) disclaimers about the wiki and its contents.

Privacy policy
> The wiki's official policy on information privacy and/or user privacy.

The footer may also display the time of an article's last change. For example, "This page was last modified 01:13, 26 March 2008."

---

‡ This tab changes depending on the namespace of the article. For help pages, for example, it reads "Help".

Getting Help

In the Navigation menu there's a Help link, and on most MediaWiki sites it leads to something useful.* In case you don't find what you need in the local help pages, Table 2-2 lists some good resources.

Table 2-2. Websites with MediaWiki help

Resource	URL	Description
MediaWiki help	http://www.mediawiki.org/wiki/Help:Contents	Basic help for any MediaWiki site
Wikipedia help	http://en.wikipedia.org/wiki/Help:Contents	More in-depth articles; however, many are specific to Wikipedia's policies and practices
Wikimedia Meta-Wiki help	http://meta.wikimedia.org/wiki/Help:Help	Various user guides and more

---

* It depends whether the wiki administrator has installed the standard help pages, or if the wiki's users have written their own.

## CHAPTER 3

Your User Identity

Most MediaWiki sites can be browsed anonymously, but there are advantages to signing up as a *registered user*.* Before you fret, "Oh no! Not another username and password to memorize," consider the benefits of creating an account: tailoring the behavior of the wiki to your liking, keeping track of your edits over months or years, monitoring other people's changes to your articles, and, of course, that warm, fuzzy sense of community. (Assuming the community members are getting along!)

In this chapter, we'll discuss MediaWiki's features for registered users, including the following:

Creating an account
    How to sign up and have an identity on the wiki

Your user page
    A personal wiki page just for you (although anyone else can edit it)

The Toolbox menu for users
    Special links that appear on user pages

Communicating via user talk pages
    Sending messages to other wiki users

Your watchlist
    Monitoring changes to selected articles

Your contributions
    Listing all the edits you've made

Setting preferences
    Tailoring your wiki experience

---

* Sign ups and anonymous use can be disabled by the wiki administrator; see "User Rights and Permissions" on page 229.

User CSS and JavaScript
    Writing custom code to change the behavior of the wiki

Many of these features are reachable from the user options menu found on every wiki page (see "User Options Menu" on page 25).

Creating an Account

To create an account (assuming you aren't logged in already):

1. Click the link "Log in/Create account" on any wiki page.
2. On the login page, click "Create an account".
3. Follow the simple directions. Creating your account will automatically log you in to the wiki.

This assumes that your wiki permits people to create their own accounts. (This feature is sometimes disabled.)

 After you're logged in, you'll no longer see a "log in" link (only "log out"). If you need to visit the login page in this case, say, to create an account for someone else, go to the Toolbox, click "Special pages", and locate and click "Log in/create account" in the list. Alternatively, enter `Special:UserLogin` in the search box and click Go.

Logging In and Out

If you are already a registered user, log in by clicking the same "Log in/create account" link just mentioned. Enter your username and password.

Once you're logged in, the "Log in" link becomes a "Log out" link, available on all pages.

Remember My Login on This Computer

When logging in or creating an account, you can optionally select the checkbox "Remember my login on this computer". This feature creates a cookie on your computer so that the next time you return to this wiki, you won't have to log in again. The cookie lasts for about one month.

User Pages

Every registered user on a MediaWiki site has a *user page*, which is an article devoted to him or herself. The article name is `User:username`. For example, if your username is Dolphin, your user page will be `User:Dolphin`.

To visit your user page, click your username in the user options menu. If the page does not yet exist, you'll be presented with a MediaWiki edit page to create it. You can then edit and save it like any other article, as we saw in "Editing Primer" on page 20.

 Your user page is neither private nor protected. Any other user can edit it, just like any other wiki article.

On some MediaWiki sites, even non-logged-in visitors may have a user page. Its name is based on the visitor's IP address, for example, `User:123.45.67.89`.

Photo on Your User Page

You can place a photograph of yourself on your user page. Here's a quick and easy layout:

1. Upload a small photo, say, *YourPhoto.jpg* (see "Images and Uploaded Files" on page 56).
2. Edit your user page.
3. On the first line, write:

   `[[Image:YourPhoto.jpg|right|frame]]`

This sets your photo on the right side of the page, and the text flows around it.

User Talk Pages

As mentioned in "Talk Pages" on page 17, every namespace has an associated talk namespace, and the `User` namespace is no exception. So, you not only have a user page, but also a *user talk* page, `User talk:username` (e.g., `User talk:Dolphin`).

User talk pages are ordinary articles, but with a twist. Any time someone else writes on your user talk page, you'll be alerted. Therefore, user talk pages are a means for users to communicate with one another. There are two types of alerts when someone edits your user talk page:

- Next time you hit a wiki page, you'll see an alert at the top of the browser, as in Figure 3-1. The alert remains until you visit your user talk page.
- If you set your email preferences to do so (see "Email Preferences" on page 37), you'll receive an email message.

 If you edit your own user talk page, no alert occurs.

You have new messages (last change).

Figure 3-1. User talk page alert

User Toolbox

Because a user page is an article, its Toolbox menu contains the usual links for articles: "What links here", "Upload file", and so on. But it also adds several user-related links:

User contributions
Same as "my contributions" (see "Tracking Your Contributions" on page 35), but displaying that user's contributions instead of yours.

Logs
A list of recent actions by that user, such as uploading files and renaming and deleting articles. See "Recent Changes and Logs" on page 152.

E-mail this user
Send email to the user, assuming that an email address is set in that user's preferences.

Signatures

All registered users have a *signature*: a compact display of the username and related information. When you write on a talk page, it's traditional to "sign" your comment with wikitext. There are several styles of signatures, as shown in Table 3-1.

Table 3-1. Wikitext signatures

Signature	Meaning
~~	Your username or nickname alone, linked to your user page.
~~	Same as above, but with the addition of a timestamp. This is the recommended signature for talk pages. Sometimes people precede it with two dashes (--~~~~), especially if on a line by itself.
~~	Just a timestamp, no username or nickname.

For example:

```
Yes, I completely agree! ~~~~
```

appears something like this:

Yes, I completely agree! Jsmith 03:21, 4 June 2008 (UTC)

Signatures are controlled by several preferences: see "User Profile Preferences" on page 35.

Watchlists

Suppose you've worked hard on an article and want to know when anyone else changes it. Simply add it to your *watchlist*—your personal list of articles of interest—by clicking its "watch" tab. To remove an article from your watchlist, click its "unwatch" tab. You can watch any article, not only those you've edited.

 Watching an article also watches its talk page, and vice versa.

Viewing Your Watchlist

To see your watchlist, click the link "my watchlist" in the user options menu. This displays the most recent changes to your watched articles, organized by date. A typical change looks like this:

22:04 My article (diff; hist) . . (+9) . . Dan (Talk | contribs)

The parts are:

22:04
    Time of the edit (the date is listed as a heading)

My article
    The article title

diff
> Link to a diff page displaying the change

hist
> Link to the article's history page

+9
> Number of characters added (+) or removed (–) in the change

Dan
> Name of the user who made the change: a link to a user page

Talk
> Link to the user's talk page

contribs
> Link to the user's contribution list

You might also see an "m" next to an entry, indicating a minor edit, or an exclamation point, indicating that the change has not yet been marked as "approved" (patrolled) yet by someone in charge (see "Patrolling Articles" on page 243).

Email Notifications

Want to receive emails when your watched articles are modified? Visit your preferences page (see "Preferences" on page 35) and under the User Profile tab, check, "E-mail me when a page I'm watching is changed". This feature is disabled by default.

Also by default, you will not be emailed about minor edits. To receive email notifications for minor edits, check, "E-mail me also for minor edits of pages".

> If you edit an article on your watchlist yourself, MediaWiki does not send you an email about it. (New users commonly "test" the email notification feature by editing a page on their own watchlist, then wonder why no email arrives. Now you know.)

Other Watchlist Preferences

Your preferences page has a number of other settings for tailoring your watchlist. See "Watchlist Preferences" on page 40 for further discussion.

Changing Your Watchlist

To update your watchlist, return to the link "my watchlist" in the user options menu. Several of the views on this page are for modifying your watchlist:

View and edit watchlist
> Lists all watched articles, and lets you remove them by clicking checkboxes.

Edit raw watchlist
> Lists all watched articles in a traditional edit box, where you can add and remove titles.

Tracking Your Contributions

Want to see all the articles and edits you've made on the wiki? In the user options menu, click the link "my contributions". You'll see a bulleted list of your edits, looking much like a history page:

> 22:04, 1 April 2008 (hist) (diff) My article

This line is almost exactly like the ones that appear in your watchlist, except it includes the date and skips your name, talk page link, and contributions link. You'll also see a bunch of widgets to control the output. You can choose to view contributions:

* From other users, or from new accounts only
* In particular namespaces
* From particular years and months

Preferences

Now that you're a registered user, you can tailor your MediaWiki experience by changing your *preferences*. To begin, click "my preferences" in the user options menu, or visit `Special:Preferences` via the search box. You'll see several collections of settings that affect how MediaWiki works for you. Let's cover each collection.

User Profile Preferences

The user profile preferences section is for basic information about yourself.

Real name
> If you fill in your real name here, it will appear instead of your username or nickname (see below) on Credits pages. It will not appear anywhere else (e.g., history pages, my contributions, etc.).

Email
> This address is used in several situations:
> - When someone visits your user page and clicks "email this user"
> - When the MediaWiki software contacts you for some reason, such as a watchlist notification
>
> Sending email will reveal your email address to the recipient.

Nickname
> Overrides your username for signatures. This does not affect your username as displayed on history pages, the Recent Changes page, and so on.

Raw signatures (without automatic link)
> When enabled, *anything* you've entered as your nickname—including wikitext—will be displayed instead of a link to your user page. For example, the nickname [`http://example.com` `'''Joe Example'''`] produces an external link to *example.com* labeled "Joe Example" in bold. Avoid putting images or templates (Chapter 7) in signatures: this is considered bad wiki etiquette.

Language
> Your choice of (human) language for MediaWiki's user interface (menus, messages, etc.). On some wikis, the choice affects language for the articles as well.

Changing your nickname or signature style will not affect any previous signatures in articles, only future signatures.

Change Password

No surprises here: to change your login password for the wiki, enter your old password, then the new one twice, then save. Additionally, the checkbox "Remember my login on this computer" sets a cookie to keep you logged in, just as on the login page (see "Remember My Login on This Computer" on page 30).

If you want to change your username, you're out of luck: MediaWiki does not have this feature. So, pick a good one!†

Email Preferences

These checkboxes control how you are notified by MediaWiki. You must have entered your email address preference for these to work. (See "User Profile Preferences" on page 35.)

Email me when a page I'm watching is changed
> When you're watching an article and it changes, MediaWiki notes this in your watchlist, but it does not email you unless you've checked this box.

Email me when my user talk page is changed
> Normally when your user talk page is changed, a notice will appear at the top of each wiki page. If you additionally want an email about the change, check this box.

Email me also for minor edits of pages
> For the previous two settings, if the edit is minor (i.e., the checkbox "This is a minor edit" is checked on the edit page), you won't be emailed. This checkbox overrides this behavior, so you are emailed even for minor edits.

Enable e-mail from other users
> This permits other users to email you via MediaWiki, e.g., from the Toolbox on your user page. If this is unchecked and another user tries to email you, they'll see a message that you've "chosen not to receive email from other users."

Send me copies of emails I send to other users
> Any email you send via the wiki will be cc'ed to your address.

Skin Preferences

MediaWiki's *skin* determines the look and feel of all its wiki pages. It sets the colors, fonts, positioning, and other attributes of the page.

The default skin (and the most popular, and the most actively maintained) is called MonoBook, and all examples in this book are based on it. Nevertheless, you can change the skin for your account on this preferences page.

To preview skins without changing your account, click the Preview link next to each skin. If you find one you prefer, select it, and click Save.

---

† A sysop can change your username, however: see "Renaming Users" on page 228.

Uploaded Files Preferences

These preferences control the display of uploaded images and other files, discussed in "Images and Uploaded Files" on page 56:

Limit images on file description pages to...
> When viewing an image page (e.g., `Image:File.jpg`), this setting determines the maximum display size of the image.

Thumbnail size
> When using the "thumb" option on images, as in `[[Image:File.jpg|thumb]]`, this setting determines the width of the displayed image.

Date and Time Preferences

These preferences control date and time display throughout the wiki: in the footer, on history pages, on the Recent Changes page, and more:

Date format
> Your preferred way to see dates and times displayed.

Time zone
> If you are geographically located in a different time zone from the wiki server, use this setting to make dates and times correct for your local time, rather than the server time. The easiest method is to click the "Fill in from browser" button, which calculates your time difference from GMT (Greenwich Mean Time).

Editing Preferences

These preferences affect the behavior of the edit page for articles:

Rows
> The height (number of lines) of the editing area.

Columns
> The width of the editing area, in characters. The default skin, MonoBook, ignores this setting and always stretches the edit box to the full browser width.

Enable section editing via [edit] links
> If enabled, edit links are placed next to each section heading, so you can edit a section at a time.

Enable section editing by right-clicking on section titles (JavaScript)
> If enabled, and you right-click on a section heading, the edit page will be displayed with that section loaded. (In some browsers, you'll also see your usual right-click menu, which is annoying.)

Edit pages on double-click (JavaScript)
If enabled and you double-click anywhere in an article's title or body, the edit page will be displayed with that article loaded.

Edit box has full width
In some skins, this preference stretches the edit box to the full width of the browser window. The default skin, MonoBook, ignores this preference.

Show edit toolbar (JavaScript)
When enabled (it's the default), the edit page has a button bar above the edit box for bold, italics, linking, and other wikitext features.

Show preview on first edit
Normally when you visit the edit page, the original article text is not displayed. When this checkbox is enabled, the edit page displays the article text, as if you'd pressed the Show Preview button.

Show preview before edit box
When enabled (the default), previews are shown near the top of the edit page. When disabled, previews are near the bottom of the page.

Mark all edits minor by default
When enabled, the checkbox "This is a minor edit" will be checked automatically when you visit the edit page. This is a time-saver if most edits you make are minor.

Use external editor by default, Use external diff by default
These preferences allow you to edit wiki pages and perform diffs (comparisons) using external programs. At press time, this is quite difficult to set up. Although MediaWiki can do the sending, setting up a receiver is complicated, and pretty much beyond the ability of nonprogrammers. For more details see:

> *http://en.wikipedia.org/wiki/Help:External_editors*
> *http://help.wikia.com/wiki/External_editors*
> *http://en.wikipedia.org/wiki/Wikipedia:Text_editor_support*

Prompt me when entering a blank edit summary
This tries to prevent users from skipping the edit summary (change comment) by printing a warning when it's blank:

> Reminder: You have not provided an edit summary. If you click Save again, your edit will be saved without one.

Recent Changes Preferences

These settings affect the behavior of the Recent Changes page, reachable via the Navigation menu or as `Special:RecentChanges` (see "Recent Changes" on page 154).

Days to show in recent changes
Limit the number of days' worth of entries to display.

Number of edits to show in recent changes
Limit the total number of entries to display.

Hide minor edits in recent changes
By default, do not display edits marked as "minor" by their authors.

Enhanced recent changes (JavaScript)
A more compact display with one line per article, rather than one line per change. If an article has multiple changes, you can expand the list with a click. Try it out!

Watchlist Preferences

These preferences affect the behavior of your watchlist:

Days to show in watchlist
Limit the length of the watchlist display.

Expand watchlist to show all applicable changes
Normally, if an article was changed several times, it will appear in your watchlist only once. This preference causes your watchlist to display all the changes, one per line. Multiple changes may be rolled together into a single line, with a clickable icon that expands the display to show all lines.

Maximum number of changes to show in expanded watchlist:
Limit the number of entries displayed if you've selected the previous preference ("Expand watchlist...").

Hide my edits from the watchlist
Don't display your own edits.

Hide bot edits from the watchlist
Don't display edits made by bots (software applications that modify the wiki).

Hide minor edits from the watchlist
Don't display edits marked as minor by their authors.

Add pages I create to my watchlist
Automatically add articles that you create to your watchlist.

Add pages I edit to my watchlist
> Automatically add articles that you edit to your watchlist.

Add pages I move to my watchlist
> Automatically add articles that you rename to your watchlist.

Search Preferences

These preferences control the behavior of the search results page, `Special:Search`:

Hits per page
> Limit the number of search results displayed.

Lines per hit
> Limit the number of matching lines displayed for each matching article. So, if an article has 10 lines that match your search keywords, and this preference is set to 3, only 3 of those lines will be displayed.

Context per line
> Limit the length of the matching lines displayed (in characters).
>
> As an example, if the preceding 3 values are 10, 1, and 30, respectively, then the search page will list up to 10 matching articles, displaying at most one matching line from each, where the line is at most 30 characters long. If there are more than 10 hits, the search page will display a "next 10" link, leading to the next page of 10 results.

Search in these namespaces by default
> At the bottom of the search page is a list of namespaces to be searched by your query. This preference determines which of these namespaces is included by default; you can always change it on the search page for a given search.

Miscellaneous Preferences

These preferences control a variety of features:

Threshold for stub link formatting (bytes)
> This handy feature displays links in a different color if the linked article is short. Now you can glance at a link and quickly judge whether the linked article is long enough to bother clicking on. You provide the threshold value: if you enter 50, then links to any article containing 49 characters or fewer will be colored differently. Wikitext and whitespace count toward the length, so an article containing `'''A'''` is considered to be seven characters long, even though it displays only one (bold) letter.

Underline links

> Links are not underlined by default; you can change this behavior here. The choices Never and Always are self-explanatory; Browser Default allows the browser to determine the link style.

Format broken links like this

> Set the appearance of links that point to nonexistent wiki articles. If the checkbox is enabled, these links appear in a different color, usually red. If not, the links appear with a question mark appended.

Justify paragraphs

> Force paragraphs in articles to be right-justified, if you prefer that look.

Auto-number headings

> Number the headings and subheadings in articles.

Show table of contents (for pages with more than 3 headings)

> Automatically display a table of contents in any article that has more than three headings at any level. Individual articles can override this setting with the magic words __TOC__ and __NOTOC__, as explained in "Table of Contents" on page 53.

Disable page caching

> Always read articles directly from MediaWiki's database, not from the cache. This is an advanced feature that may significantly slow down your wiki experience, but guarantees that all pages you are viewing are current. In practice, though, you shouldn't need this.

Enable "jump to" accessibility links

> Display several links for scrolling quickly to the navigation menu and the search box. These jump links are intended for text-only web browsers; otherwise, the only two skins that support them at press time— MonoBook and Modern—hide the links. If you're desperate to see these links in a traditional browser, use custom CSS containing this line:
>
> ```
> #jump-to-nav { display:block; }
> ```

Don't show page content below diffs

> When doing a diff operation, as described in "History" on page 18, the article content is normally displayed below the diffs. This preference suppresses this behavior.

Finally, if any third-party wiki extensions (Chapter 14) have user-configurable preferences, they will usually appear in this preferences section.

User CSS and JavaScript

If you're an advanced user and want to customize MediaWiki's appearance with JavaScript or cascading stylesheets (CSS), check out the User CSS and User JavaScript features. If enabled by the wiki administrator,‡ two special subpages beneath your user page let you add JavaScript or CSS to all pages you view.

User:*YourName*/monobook.js
> User-supplied JavaScript, added to every wiki page you view.

User:*YourName*/monobook.css
> User-supplied CSS, added to every wiki page you view.

 After modifying one of these articles, force-refresh your browser to ensure that the changes take effect. That's Ctrl-F5 in Internet Explorer, or Shift-Refresh in Firefox.

For example, to display links in italics within every article body, put in User:*YourName*/monobook.css:

```
#bodyContent a { font-style: italic; }
```

To add a button to the edit page that inserts a smiley face into the edit box, upload a 16×16 pixel image for the button, locate its path (see "File Path" on page 155), and add to User:*YourName*/monobook.js:

```
mwCustomEditButtons[mwCustomEditButtons.length] = {
    "imageFile": '/w/images/some/path/smiley.jpg',
    "speedTip": "insert a smiley",
    "tagOpen": ":-)",
    "tagClose": "",
    "sampleText": ""
};
```

We'll talk more about this particular JavaScript code from a sysop's point of view in "Adding buttons to the edit page" on page 239.

To make the most of custom CSS, you'll need to know the CSS class and ID names on the page so you can override them. You can see them by doing a View Source operation on any wiki page in your browser.

---

‡ See "JavaScript Configuration" on page 253 and "CSS for All Pages" on page 267.

To learn more about cascading stylesheets, see:

http://www.w3schools.com/css/
http://www.w3.org/Style/CSS/
http://en.wikipedia.org/wiki/Cascading_Style_Sheets

For more on JavaScript, see:

http://www.w3schools.com/JS/
http://www.javascript.com/
http://en.wikipedia.org/wiki/JavaScript

## PART II

Writing and Editing Articles

## CHAPTER 4

Editing Articles

MediaWiki articles are written not in plain text, but with *wikitext*, a special language for typesetting we saw briefly in "Editing Primer" on page 20. Table 4-1 gives a quick preview of wikitext's special symbols that change the appearance of the text. For example, a bold word is surrounded by three single quotes `'''like this'''`, and an internal link is surrounded by double square brackets `[[like this]]`. Wikitext is a type of *markup language*, which simply means that you "mark up" ordinary text with these symbols. (HTML, the language of web pages, is another example of a markup language.)

Table 4-1. Types of wikitext

Special symbols	Examples	Purpose
Single quotes, two or more	`'''bold words'''`, `''italic phrase''`	Bold, italics, and other typestyles
Square brackets	`[[link]]`, `[http://example.com]`	Create links
Equals signs	`== Hello world ==`	Headings and subheadings
Symbols at the beginning of a line	`*`, `***`, `#`, `{|`, `|,⊠!`	Lists and tables
Angled brackets	`<tagname>Text here</tagname>`, `<hello/>`	XML-like tags with many purposes; similar to HTML, but full HTML is not supported
Curly braces	`{{stuff inside curly braces}}`	Many purposes, including variables, templates, and parser functions
Double underscores	`__TOC__`	Many purposes, usually an overall effect on one wiki page

In this chapter, we'll cover:

The edit page
> The appearance and mechanics of the MediaWiki edit page, a web-based tool for writing wikitext.

Creating and editing articles
> Starting new articles and modifying existing ones.

Formatting articles with wikitext
> Paragraphs, headings, typestyles, images, lists, tables, and mathematics (links are covered more fully in Chapter 5).

Suppressing wikitext
> Using the <nowiki> tag to display special symbols literally, "escaping" them so they're not treated as typesetting commands.

Edit conflicts
> When two people try to change an article simultaneously.

No Private Articles

Wikipedia and many other MediaWiki sites permit nearly anyone to modify nearly any article. Users cannot create "private" articles. Even your personal user page can be edited by others.[*] If you are concerned about privacy, try the following:

- Create subpages below your user page (see "Subpages" on page 99), which other users traditionally leave alone.

- Add articles of interest to your watchlist (see "Watchlists" on page 33) and set up email alerts (see "Email Preferences" on page 37), so if someone changes an article, you'll know.

Also, remember that public wikis are indexed by Google and other search engines. Not only are articles public on the wiki, but they may also be found in search results and copied to other websites. Keep this in mind when choosing your words.

Getting Started with Editing

To modify an article, click one of its Edit links:

- The main Edit link, which edits the entire article at once.

---

[*] A wiki administrator can implement limited privacy by configuring user rights (see "User Rights and Permissions" on page 229) and installing some third-party extensions, but overall, MediaWiki's working model favors public access to everything.

- Individual Edit links next to each section heading, which edit only that section (and any subsections).

Any Edit link takes you to MediaWiki's *edit page*, shown in Figure 4-1, with the article's wikitext loaded and ready to be modified.

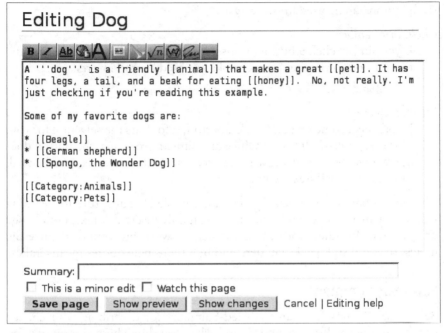

Figure 4-1. Edit page for the article "Dog"

The Edit Box

On the edit page, the *edit box* is an ordinary text area for adding, removing, and modifying wikitext. It is a standard text area as found on many other websites.

A few editing tips:

- Undo is Ctrl-Z and redo is Ctrl-Y.
- Need a spellchecker? Do your editing in Firefox, which has a built-in spellchecker for all text areas. Suspicious words become highlighted (usually underlined in red). Right-click on a word to correct it or add it to Firefox's spelling dictionary.

The Toolbar

The *toolbar* or "button bar" above the edit box contains convenient buttons to insert wikitext symbols for boldface, italics, links and more. To see the purpose of any button, check out Figure 2-5 within the section "Wikitext" on page 21, or hover your mouse over any button and a tool tip will pop up.

Each button can be used in two ways:

Click, then replace
    If you simply click a button, it inserts wikitext containing some dummy text for you to change. For example, the bold button inserts:

        '''Bold text'''

Select, then click
    If you select some text and click a button, it formats the selection for you. However, unlike Microsoft Office and similar programs, the button does *not* remove the formatting when clicked a second time. A second click will just insert the wikitext again.

The button bar is convenient but cannot completely substitute for learning wikitext. This is because the button bar can only insert wikitext, not change or remove it. In other words, it can italicize a word but cannot remove the italics, so you'll still need to understand that two single quotes means italics.

Summary Comment

Below the edit box is an area labeled Summary for describing your change briefly, so other wiki users understand what you did. These summary comments appear on an article's history page, providing a quick rundown of everything that's been done to the article during its lifetime.

Previewing and Saving

Below the edit box is an array of buttons and links for taking the next action:

Save page
    Save your changes, creating a new revision of the article. Remember to first preview your changes and enter a summary comment.

Show preview
    Display how the article will look, but without saving it. The edit box will remain on the page so you can continue editing.

Show changes

> Display a two-column "before and after" view of the article, showing only your changes. As with Show Preview, the edit box will remain on the page for further editing.

Cancel

> Give up. Return to the article without saving your changes. (Alternatively, just leave the edit page.)

This is a minor edit

> If your change is trivial, click this checkbox before saving, and on the article's history page your change will be marked with an "m" to indicate it was minor.

Watch this page

> If selected before saving, this checkbox adds the article to your watchlist (see "Watchlists" on page 33).

 If two people edit the same article simultaneously and both try to save it, only one will succeed. See "Conflicts" on page 72 for more information.

For more information on the edit page, see *http://meta.wikimedia.org/wiki/Help:Editor*.

Creating an Article

Don't look for a button labeled "create article" in MediaWiki: there isn't one. To create an article, first search for it: enter an article name in the search box and click Go. If the article exists, you'll jump right to it (so you needn't create it). But if there's no such article, you'll be offered the opportunity to create it.

Suppose you search for "dog food" and no such article exists. On the search results page, you'll see these two lines:

> You searched for <u>dog food</u>

> There is no page titled "dog food". You can <u>create this page</u>.

The links "dog food" and "create this page" lead you to the edit page to create the article.

Paragraphs and Headings

To create a *paragraph*, just start typing. A blank line indicates the end of a paragraph:

```
This is a paragraph.  What fun!
This is the third sentence of the same paragraph.

This is a new, second paragraph.
```

Blank lines are significant: the more you add, the more space there is between the paragraphs.

To create a *heading*, surround a line of text with equals signs:

```
== This is a heading ==
```

The first equals sign *must* be at the beginning of a line with no leading spaces. The number of equals signs indicates the level of heading, subheading, sub-subheading, and so on.

```
= Level 1 heading =
== Level 2 heading ==
=== Level 3 heading ===
==== Level 4 heading ====
```

As a rule, avoid level 1 headings: they are too large, the same size as the page title, which can be confusing for readers. It's a standard to start with level 2.

To break a paragraph in the middle, use the <br> or <br/> tag:

```
This is a paragraph<br>broken in the middle
```

Here's a larger example containing several paragraphs and headings:

```
== All about wikis ==

The MediaWiki edit page has many interesting features.

Read on to learn them.

=== A button bar ===

The button bar contains buttons that are helpful for typesetting
your text.  Try clicking a few of them.

=== The edit box ===

The edit box is where you type your wikitext.

== For more information ==

See "MediaWiki" from O'Reilly Media for more details.
```

Table of Contents

If a wiki article has more than three headings, a *table of contents* of links automatically appears above the first heading. The table of contents displays all headings in order, each linking to the corresponding article section.[†]

There are several ways to control the table of contents:

Force it
> If an article has too few headings but you want a table of contents anyway, place the word `__FORCETOC__` (two underscores on each side) anywhere in the article. This "magic word" forces a table of contents to be produced.[‡]

Move it
> The magic word `__TOC__`, when placed in an article, causes the table of contents to appear at that exact location instead of the default location above the first heading.

Suppress it
> Place the magic word `__NOTOC__` anywhere in an article to prevent a table of contents from appearing.

Suppress it just for you
> In your preferences (`Special:Preferences`), under Misc, uncheck "Show table of contents (for pages with more than 3 headings)" to suppress all tables of contents for yourself.

[†] Each heading becomes an anchor (see "Anchors" on page 80), and the table of contents links to those anchors.

[‡] Magic words are discussed in Chapter 7.

Indenting

To indent a paragraph, place a colon at the beginning of the first line:

```
:This paragraph will be indented. The colon is
placed only in the first line.
```

The more colons, the greater the indenting:

```
:::::Very far indented indeed!
```

To produce a preformatted text box, suitable for computer programming examples or any verbatim text, precede each line (including blank lines) by a single space:

```
[space here]function dog_catcher($name, $truck) {
[space here] ...
[space here]}
```

Similarly, use the `<pre>` tag:

```
<pre>
function dog_catcher($name, $truck) {
 ...
}
</pre>
```

which produces the same visual effect as leading spaces but ignores wikitext and HTML formatting. So with leading spaces, `'''hello'''` displays as **hello**, but inside a `<pre>` region it displays literally as `'''hello'''`.

Indenting on Talk Pages

When responding to a comment on a talk page, (see "Talk Pages" on page 17) indent your words one level further than the original comment. Also remember to sign your name (see "Signatures" on page 32).

```
: Here is a comment.
:: Here is somebody's response
::: Here is your response to the response. ~~~~
```

Typestyles and Fonts

Italic text is produced by enclosing words in two single quotes:

```
''this is italics''
```

For bold text, use three single quotes:

```
'''this is bold'''
```

And for bold italics, use five quotes:

```
'''''this is bold italics'''''
```

These "single quote" styles do not span multiple lines—they end at the first line break (when you press Enter):

```
''these italics will end here<ENTER>
and not continue on this second line''
```

Underlined text is produced by the `<u>` tag:

```
This is <u>underlined</u> text.
```

For monospaced text, use the `<code>` tag:

```
<code>This is monospaced</code>
```

which is great for presenting computer code within a sentence.

To change the color or size of small amounts of text, use the HTML tags `<big>`, `<small>`, `<font>` or `<span>`:

```
Here's some <big>large text</big> and some
<small>little words</small>.

<font color="red">Here is red text</font>

<font size="+3">Here is big text</font>

<span style="color:green">Here is green text</span>
```

For controlling the style of a paragraph, use the HTML `<div>` tag:

```
<div style="color:purple">
Here is a long paragraph in purple, blah blah blah....
</div>
```

Links (Briefly)

Links are a rich subject covered in detail in Chapter 5, but here's a quick peek. To create a link to another wiki article—an internal link—simply enclose its title in double square brackets:

```
For more information, see [[dog food]].
```

If the article dog food doesn't exist, that's fine: the link will automatically point to the edit page for dog food, encouraging others to create the article! To use different text for the link, append the desired text after a pipe symbol:

```
For more information, see [[dog food | my article about dog food]].
```

This link displays "my article about dog food" but points to the article dog food.

To link to an external website, just type the URL and MediaWiki turns it into a link:

```
http://www.oreilly.com/
```

Or, if you want alternate text for your link, use single square brackets, followed by a space, followed by the link text:

```
Visit [http://www.oreilly.com/ O'Reilly Media, Inc.] for a good time.
```

Images and Uploaded Files

MediaWiki articles can contain images (and other files) that have been uploaded to the wiki. That is, any file must first be "copied into" the wiki via uploading before it can appear in an article.[*]

The 10-second tutorial on images is:

- Upload the image (say, *myfile.jpg*)—if it's not already in the wiki—by clicking the "upload file" link in the Toolbox and following the instructions.
- To display the image in your article, add an image tag, i.e., `[[Image:myfile.jpg]]`.
- If your wiki is configured to display external images (which is *not* the default behavior), then any URL of an image, such as `http://example.com/picture.gif`, will be transformed into the image itself.[†]

Armed with this knowledge, you can do simple things with images, and this might keep you happy for a long time. Nevertheless, we'll now go into more depth so you can have a thorough understanding of uploaded files.

 In MediaWiki jargon, every uploaded file lives in the `Image` namespace, even nonimages like PDFs and Microsoft Office files (if these file types are permitted by the wiki administrator).

Working with Uploads

There are two ways of working with uploaded files:

Embed, then upload
Create image links like `[[Image:myfile.jpg]]`, save the article, and later click the (now red) links to visit the upload page. This is a good method

---

[*] Unless the wiki administrator has tailored MediaWiki to permit "external" images—located on another website—to be embedded in articles.

[†] See "External Images" on page 236 to configure this behavior.

when you're writing an article at high speed and don't want to interrupt your work to upload files.

Upload, then embed

Visit the upload page to upload your files, remember their names, and later edit articles to add image links. This is a good method when you have lots of images to upload, but aren't sure where you'll use them yet.

Images Explained

Suppose *myfile.jpg* is a graphics file on your local PC. After you upload it to MediaWiki, assuming you keep the same name, the following features become available:

Image:Myfile.jpg

An image page. This is a wiki article, located in the `Image` namespace, devoted to your image. Here, you can document your image (by editing the article), view the revision history of the image, and more.

Image talk:Myfile.jpg

Yes, image pages have associated talk pages, just like articles in other namespaces.

[[Image:Myfile.jpg]]

An image link that accomplishes two things when placed into a wiki article. First, it displays (embeds) the image in the article. Second, the displayed image becomes a link to the associated image page, `Image:Myfile.jpg`.

[[:Image:Myfile.jpg]]

An inline link to the image page that does not display (embed) the image. It works like any other internal link: you can supply alternate text (`[[:Image:Myfile.jpg|my alternate text]]`), and so on.

[[Media:Myfile.jpg]]

A media link, linking to the actual uploaded file, not the image page. Clicking it will download or display the file. As with other links, you can supply alternate text (`[[Media:Myfile.jpg|my alternate text]]`) and so on.

Uploading a File

Assuming your wiki permits uploads (not all do), look in the Toolbox menu and click Upload File. The upload page (`Special:Upload`) appears as in Figure 4-2.

Upload file

Use the form below to upload files. To view or search previously uploaded files go to the list of uploaded files, uploads and deletions are also logged in the upload log.

To include a file in a page, use a link in the form **[[Image:File.jpg]]**, **[[Image:File.png|alt text]]** or **[[Media:File.ogg]]** for directly linking to the file.

```
┌─ Upload file ──────────────────────────────────────────────────────────┐
│                                                                         │
│      Source   ┌────────────────────────────────────────┐  ┌──────────┐ │
│    filename:  │C:\Temp\mypicture.jpg                    │  │ Browse...│ │
│               └────────────────────────────────────────┘  └──────────┘ │
│                                                                         │
│               Maximum file size: 2 MB                                   │
│               Permitted file types: png, gif, jpg, jpeg.                │
│                                                                         │
│  Destination ┌──────────────────────────────────────────────────────┐  │
│   filename:  │Mypicture.jpg                                         │  │
│              └──────────────────────────────────────────────────────┘  │
│   Summary:   ┌──────────────────────────────────────────────────────┐  │
│              │Any comments you wish to write...                     │  │
│              │                                                      │  │
│              │                                                      │  │
│              │                                                      │  │
│              │                                                      │  │
│              └──────────────────────────────────────────────────────┘  │
│                                                                         │
│               ☐ Watch this page  ☐ Ignore any warnings                  │
│                                                                         │
│              ┌──────────────┐                                           │
│              │ Upload file  │                                           │
│              └──────────────┘                                           │
└─────────────────────────────────────────────────────────────────────────┘
```

Figure 4-2. The Special:Upload page

From the `Special:Upload` page, do the following:

1. Click the Browse button to locate and select your desired file.

2. Take note of the name that appears as the "Destination filename". This will be the filename within the wiki, i.e., [[`Image:NameGoesHere`]]. Modify it here as needed. If a file of this name exists in the wiki already, you'll be warned to change the name or overwrite the file.

3. Add a brief description of the file in the Summary box. Consider adding category tags to categorize the file, described in "Adding an Article to a Category" on page 90.

4. Click Upload File.

If the upload is successful, you can now embed the file in articles.

If you're in the middle of an editing session, Shift-click the Upload File link rather than simply clicking it. This opens a new window for the upload. If you merely click the link, you'll navigate away from the edit page and possibly lose your edits.

Embedding an Uploaded Image

Any uploaded image can be embedded in a wiki article by referring to its name in the `Image` namespace, creating an image tag:

```
[[Image:NameOfFileHere]]
```

For example:

```
[[Image:Myfile.jpg]]
```

If you can't remember the name of an uploaded image, visit the special pages `Special:NewImages` and `Special:ImageList` to locate it.

Remember that the image link has two purposes:

1. It embeds the image in the article.
2. It makes the image a link to its image page, a wiki article that documents the image.

Image links may have options following the name and separated by pipe symbols. These options are listed in Table 4-2. For example, the following link displays an image scaled to 100 pixels wide with a border around it and alternate text of "Hi there":

```
[[Image:Myfile.jpg|Hi there|100px|border]]
```

Table 4-2. Image options

Option	Meaning
left	Left-align the image
right	Right-align the image
center	Center the image
none	Default alignment
thumb	Display a thumbnail image with a caption and an enlarge button, and allow text to flow around the image
thumbnail	Same as thumb
frame	Same as thumb, but no "enlarge" button
frameless	Ordinary image (the default)
border	Draw a box around the image; ignored for thumb
*NNN*px	Scale the image to width *NNN* pixels

Option	Meaning
(Anything else)	Anything unrecognized as an option is treated as an image caption; if the image is a thumbnail, the caption is displayed near it; otherwise, the caption appears when the mouse is hovered over the image

Image Pages

Image tags lead to an *image page*, a wiki article dedicated to that image, as shown in Figure 4-3. These articles can be edited (to add explanatory wikitext and categories) just like any other, and they list the file's revision history and other information.

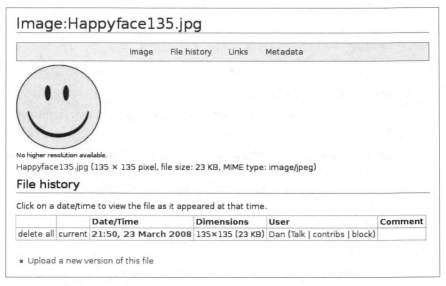

Figure 4-3. An image page

Linking to an Uploaded File

To produce a link to an uploaded file, refer to it using the Media namespace:

```
[[Media:Myfile.jpg]]
[[Media:Document.pdf|Click to download]]
```

The full URL path to an uploaded file can be displayed and manipulated using the filepath parser function, so you can produce an "external" style link to the file:‡

‡ Available in MediaWiki 1.12.0 or later.

```
My image, which is located at {{filepath:myimage.jpg}},
may be [{{filepath:myimage.jpg}} downloaded here].
```

This produces:

My image, which is located at http://wiki.example.com/w/images/5/5a/my-image.jpg, may be downloaded here.

External Images

It's easy to link to an external image with an ordinary external link:

```
[http://images.example.com/myfile.jpg My favorite picture]
```

Displaying an external image within a wiki article is another matter, as this operation is not permitted by default. The wiki administrator can change this with a configuration setting (see "External Images" on page 236).

Lists

Wikitext provides three kinds of lists:

- Bulleted lists
- Numbered lists
- Definition lists

These lists are discussed in the following sections.

Bulleted Lists

To make a bulleted list, simply begin each line with an asterisk, and end each line with a newline (pressing the Enter key):

```
* Dog
* Cat
* Cute little bird
```

The results look like:

- Dog
- Cat
- Cute little bird

The asterisk must begin the line: no leading space is permitted.[*] Any space between the asterisk and its text is ignored, however, so you could equivalently write:

---

[*] Leading space would produce a preformatted text box; see "Indenting" on page 54.

```
*Dog
*Cat
*       Cute little bird
```

but not:

```
* Dog
* Cat
* Cute little
bird
```

because the linebreak after "little" ends the bullet, leaving "bird" in the next paragraph:

- Dog
- Cat
- Cute little

bird

You can insert linebreaks with the **
** tag:

```
* Dog
* Cat
* Cute little bird<br>Tweet<br>Tweet
```

which produces:

- Dog
- Cat
- Cute little bird
  Tweet
  Tweet

Bullets can be nested at multiple levels:

```
* This is a bulleted item
* Here is another!
** This is a level 2 bullet
*** Here is a level 3 bullet
** Now we're back at level 2
* And now back at level 1
```

which appears as:

- This is a bulleted item
- Here is another!
  - This is a level 2 bullet
    - Here is a level 3 bullet
  - Now we're back at level 2
- And now back at level 1

The list ends when it reaches a nonbulleted line (or the end of the article). This means that if you insert a nonbulleted item in the middle of a list, you'll end the list, which might not be what you want. For example, this broken list:

```
* My favorite dogs are:
** Fido
** Spike
(My neighbor's dog)
** Rover
```

produces a misplaced "Rover" with a broken-looking double bullet:

- My favorite dogs are:
  - Fido
  - Spike

(My neighbor's dog)

- •Rover

because "(My neighbor's dog)" ends the list. To indicate that "(My neighbor's dog)" should be considered part of the list, place bullet symbols in front of it—the right number for the indent level—and add a colon:

```
* My favorite dogs are:
** Fido
** Spike
**: (My neighbor's dog)
** Rover
```

This produces:

- My favorite dogs are:
  - Fido
  - Spike

    (My neighbor's dog)
  - Rover

To insert a preformatted text box into a nested, bulleted list, use a `<pre>` tag explicitly:

```
* First item
** Nested item
*: <pre>here's the preformatted text</pre>
** Another nested item
```

because you can't have a leading bullet (continuing the list) and a leading space (for preformatted text) at the same time.

Numbered Lists

Numbered lists have the same rules as bulleted lists, but instead of asterisks, you use hash marks:

```
# Dog
# Cat
# Cute little bird
```

This produces:

1. Dog
2. Cat
3. Cute little bird

Numbered lists can also be nested at multiple levels:

```
# This is a numbered item
# Here is another!
## This is a level 2 item
### Here is a level 3 item
## Now we're back at level 2
# And now back at level 1
```

which produces:

1. This is a numbered item
2. Here is another!
    1. This is a level 2 item
        1. Here is a level 3 item
    2. Now we're back at level 2
3. And now back at level 1

Notice that every level begins with the number 1. There is no way in wikitext to substitute letters, Roman numerals, or any other format instead.

When you insert a nonnumbered item in the middle of a list, you need the same continuation trick as for bulleted lists, but using hash marks:

```
# My favorite dogs are:
## Fido
## Spike
##: (My neighbor's dog)
## Rover
```

In this author's opinion, numbered lists in wikitext are frustrating, limiting, and just plain badly implemented. Using a numbered list to document the steps of a complicated process, full of embedded examples and images, will make you tear your hair out. For a list of any complexity, break the "no HTML" rule and use the <ol> tag instead:

```
<ol>
<li>First item</li>
<li>Second item</li>
 <ol type="a">
 <li>First subitem</li>
 This inserted text will '''not''' break the numbering,
 and nor will this image:

[[Image:Myfile.jpg]]

 <li>Second subitem</li>
 </ol>
<li>Third item</li>
</ol>
```

For more on HTML numbered lists, see *http://www.w3schools.com/tags/tag_ol.asp*.

Definition Lists

Definition lists are a convenient format for documenting a set of terms (words or phrases). Sandwich your term between a leading semicolon and a colon, followed by a paragraph:

```
; Dog
: A cuddly canine

; Cat
: A furry feline
```

or equivalently:

```
; Dog: A cuddly canine
; Cat: A furry feline
```

both of which produce:

Dog
　　　A cuddly canine
Cat
　　　A furry feline

A term can have multiple paragraphs, each preceded by a colon:

```
; Dog
: A cuddly canine
: Man's best friend
```

which appears as:

Dog
> A cuddly canine
>
> Man's best friend

Definition lists do not suffer from the same "broken list" problems as numbered lists, because leading colons cause indenting anyway. So, other wikitext can be inserted without a problem into the middle of the definition:

```
; Dog
: A cuddly canine
WOOF WOOF
: Man's best friend
```

Combining List Types

Here's a numbered list inside a bulleted list:

```
* Bullet one
* Bullet two
*# Numbered item 1
*# Numbered item 2
*# Numbered item 3
* Bullet three
```

which produces:

- Bullet one
- Bullet two
  1. Numbered item 1
  2. Numbered item 2
  3. Numbered item 3
- Bullet three

How about a bulleted list inside a numbered list?

```
# Numbered item one
# Numbered item two
#* Bullet 1
#* Bullet 2
#* Bullet 3
# Numbered item three
```

which produces:

1. Numbered item one
2. Numbered item two
   - Bullet 1
   - Bullet 2

- Bullet 3
   3. Numbered item three

A definition inside a numbered list:

```
# Numbered item one
# Numbered item two
#; Term
#: Definition
# Numbered item three
```

which produces:

1. Numbered item one

2. Numbered item two

   Term
      Definition

3. Numbered item three

A numbered list as part of a definition:

```
; Term 1
: Definition 1
:# Numbered item 1
:# Numbered item 2
:## Numbered subitem 1
:##: <pre>A preformatted text box in subitem 1</pre>
:## Numbered subitem 2
: Definition 1 continued
; Term 2
: Definition 2
```

which produces:

Term 1
   Definition 1

   1. Numbered item 1

   2. Numbered item 2

      1. Numbered subitem 1

```
: A preformatted text box in subitem 1 :
```

      2. Numbered subitem 2

   Definition 1 continued

Term 2
   Definition 2

For more information on lists, see *http://en.wikipedia.org/wiki/Help:List*.

Tables

MediaWiki articles can contain tables with rows, columns, and headings. The syntax for creating tables is perhaps the most complicated "basic" wikitext. We'll cover a useful set of features; the full documentation can be found at *http://www.mediawiki.org/wiki/Help:Tables*.

Simple Table Syntax

Tables begin with this character sequence at the start of a line:

```
{|
```

They contain one or more rows, separated by this sequence (again at the start of a line):

```
|-
```

and end with this sequence (at the start of the line):

```
|}
```

Here's a small example:

```
{|
| dog
| woof
|-
| cat
| meow
|-
| bird
| tweet
|}
```

which produces this three-row, two-column table:

dog	woof
cat	meow
bird	tweet

Within a row, each table cell begins with a pipe (|) at the start of a line:

```
| This is a table cell
```

To throw a border around the table and each cell, add `border="1"` to the top line:

```
{| border="1"
| dog
| woof
|-
| cat
| meow
```

```
|-
| bird
| tweet
|}
```

Of course, cells can contain other wikitext such as links, boldface, and so on:

```
{| border="1"
| [[dog]]
| '''woof'''
|-
...
```

An alternative table syntax places each row on a single line, with cells separated by double pipe symbols, a format that is sometimes easier to read:

```
{|
| dog || woof
|-
| cat || meow
|-
| bird || tweet
|}
```

That's all you need to create simple tables. Read on for more details.

Table Headings

To create optional headings over each column, add them as the first table row, replacing the pipes with exclamation points:

```
{|
! Animal
! Sound
|-
| dog
| woof
|-
...
```

Table Captions

A table may have an optional caption preceded by the sequence:

```
|+
```

For example:

```
{|
|+ Animals and Their Sounds
! Animal
! Sound
|-
| dog
```

```
| woof
|-
...
```

Table Styles

Tables can be stylized using the same attributes as in HTML tables, including the `style` attribute for cascading stylesheet (CSS) directives. To stylize an entire table, the attributes go in the first row:

```
{| align="center" border="1"
```

To stylize a row, the attributes appear just after the |- sequence:

```
|- valign="top"
```

And to stylize a cell, the attributes come immediately after the pipe and must be separated from the cell text by another pipe:

```
| style="color:green" | this is a lovely green cell
```

You can even stylize the table caption, for instance, moving it to the bottom of the table:

```
|+ align="bottom" | Animals and Their Sounds
```

 To provide custom table styles for all wiki users, the wiki administrator may write them in CSS and add them to `Media Wiki:Common.css`, described in "CSS for All Pages" on page 267.

Sortable Tables

If you can't decide on a good order for your table rows, make them sortable and let the reader decide instead. Add the attribute `class="sortable"` to your table definition:

```
{| class="sortable"
...
```

Now each column contains an icon that, when clicked, sorts the rows of the table according to that column.

Mathematical Formulas

MediaWiki can optionally display complicated mathematical formulas. If your wiki is configured for this feature, place the formula inside a `<math>` tag:

```
<math>\sqrt{x^2 + y^2}</math>
```

and MediaWiki will display it beautifully, as in Figure 4-4.

$$\sqrt{x^2 + y^2}$$

Figure 4-4. Math example

The math typesetting system is rich and complex. It uses a powerful, third-party software package called LaTeX (*http://www.latex-project.org*) with its own syntax. We won't teach you LaTeX here (it's large enough for its own book), but for a reasonably quick overview of math mode, check out:

> *http://en.wikipedia.org/wiki/Help:Displaying_a_formula*
> *ftp://ftp.ams.org/pub/tex/doc/amsmath/short-math-guide.pdf*

> When reading a traditional LaTeX guide to learn its math syntax, mentally substitute MediaWiki's `<math>` tag where the documentation uses LaTeX's usual symbols. For example, the traditional LaTeX formula for the square root of two, `$\sqrt{2}$`, would be written for MediaWiki as `<math>\sqrt{2}</math>`.

Escaping Wikitext with `<nowiki>`

Wikitext is full of symbols with special meaning for typesetting. For example, a leading asterisk like this:

```
* Here is a bullet
```

produces a bullet like this:

- Here is a bullet

But what if you need to produce a symbol literally, and not have it interpreted as wikitext? Suppose you want a line to begin literally with an asterisk, and not have it turned into a bullet. This is the purpose of the `<nowiki>` tag. Anything appearing between `<nowiki>` and `</nowiki>` is displayed literally. To produce a leading asterisk, you'd write:

```
<nowiki>*</nowiki> Here is a leading asterisk, not a bullet
```

which would appear as:

* Here is a leading asterisk, not a bullet

`<nowiki>` is particularly useful for writing about MediaWiki's features, when you must display literal wikitext symbols. For example, to produce this paragraph about wikitext syntax:

> Internal links use square brackets [[like this]]. A bold internal link looks '''[[like this]]'''. And then there's the mysterious <nowiki> tag, which is always followed by </nowiki>.

you'll need a liberal application of the `<nowiki>` tag:

```
Internal links use square brackets
<nowiki>[[like this]]</nowiki>.
A bold internal link looks
<nowiki>'''[[like this]]'''</nowiki>.
And then there's the mysterious <nowiki><nowiki></nowiki> tag,
which is always followed by <nowiki><</nowiki>/nowiki>.
```

Yikes—what's going on with the final `</nowiki>` display? Its first character "<" is escaped by surrounding it with `<nowiki>` and `</nowiki>`, so the remainder of the tag, `/nowiki>`, is not interpreted as anything special.

Conflicts

As you know, MediaWiki permits multiple people to edit the same article. But what if two users edit the same article at the same time? In this case, the first one to save the article will succeed. The second one to save will encounter an *edit conflict*. The second save cannot succeed until the second author manually merges the two authors' changes.

Conflicts are rare in practice, but you need to know how to resolve them.

Suppose you're editing the article dog food:

```
'''Dog food''' comes in many shapes and sizes. The most
popular brands are...
```

and you make a change, adding "and flavors":

```
'''Dog food''' comes in many shapes, sizes and flavors. The most
popular brands are...
```

Meanwhile, as you work within the edit page, another wiki user, Dora, quickly edits the same article, adds a sentence, and saves her changes behind your back:

```
'''Dog food''' comes in many shapes and sizes. It is eaten by canines
all over the world. The most popular brands are...
```

When you try to save your changes, you see this message:

> Edit conflict: Dog food

MediaWiki has blocked your save operation, preventing you from blindly overwriting Dora's changes. Below this message, MediaWiki displays all the information you need to make things right:

1. Dora's version of the article (the currently saved version) in the edit box
2. A comparison (diff) of your changes and Dora's changes
3. Your version of the article (not saved)

It also prints these instructions:

> Someone else has changed this page since you started editing it. The upper text area contains the page text as it currently exists. Your changes are shown in the lower text area. You will have to merge your changes into the existing text. Only the text in the upper text area will be saved when you press "Save page".

In other words, your job now is to examine Dora's changes and your changes, and figure out the best way to merge your changes into her version of the article, which is in the edit box. (If you do nothing, or just click Save Page, Dora's changes will remain and yours will be lost.) In this case, you decide on:

```
'''Dog food''' comes in many shapes, sizes and flavors. It is eaten by
canines all over the world. The most popular brands are...
```

Now when you save the article, the save succeeds.[†]

Edit conflicts might be annoying, but they're arguably better than the alternatives: blindly overwriting other users' changes (definitely bad), or allowing only one writer at a time, locking out all others, possibly for a long time (the model used by some other systems).

Beyond the Basics

This chapter only scratches the surface of MediaWiki's editing capabilities. Chapter 7 will cover more advanced topics such as templates, dynamic lists, and parser functions.

[†] Of course, if *another* edit and save happens while you're merging, you'll get another conflict. This rarely happens though.

## CHAPTER 5

Links

Any web page can have links, but on a wiki, links are critical. Much of the power, expressiveness, and utility of wikis comes from effective linking, leading the reader efficiently from topic to topic. A wiki article without links is like a room without exits.

In this chapter, we'll discuss:

- Internal links within a single wiki
- External links to other websites
- Interwiki links between wikis
- Interlanguage links between translations of the same article
- Graphical links that use graphics instead of text
- File links to files on a local computer
- Linking tips for effective wiki articles

Internal Links

An *internal link* leads to another page on the same wiki. It's simple to create an internal link: just type the name of the target page surrounded by double square brackets:

```
[[like this]]
```

Here's an example of an internal link placed conversationally within a sentence:

```
It's cheaper to purchase [[dog food]] in bulk.
```

This displays a link to the wiki article Dog food.

The links [[dog food]] and [[Dog food]] are equivalent, pointing to the same article. The link [[Dog Food]] with a capital "F" refers to a different article, however. MediaWiki's rules of case-sensitivity are quirky, but they make sense when you're used to them. The sidebar "Article Titles and Case-Sensitivity" explains these rules in detail.

 MediaWiki article titles are generally plain, conversational text, like dog food or building a dog house. Some other wikis prefer "camel-case" article titles, like DogFood or BuildingADogHouse. This is not recommended for MediaWiki sites.

Links to Nonexistent Articles

A terrific feature of MediaWiki is that you can link to articles that don't exist yet. If article Dog contains a link [[Dog food]] but there is no such article, the link displays in red, and clicking it leads the reader to the edit page, encouraging him to write the article. When someone eventually does create the Dog food article, every article containing [[Dog food]] automatically links to it.

This manner of "linking in advance," sometimes called *lazy linking*, allows authors to refer to articles (by merely linking to them) without interrupting their train of thought to create them. Additionally, all these lazy links are collected and displayed on the special page Special:WantedPages (see "Wanted Pages" on page 146), so interested authors can create the articles most wanted by other community members.

Article Titles and Case-Sensitivity

One of the most confusing things for new MediaWiki authors is the case-sensitivity of article titles. For example, the links [[hello world]] and [[Hello world]] refer to the same article, but [[Hello World]] does not. Nevertheless, a search for hello world finds both articles. What's going on here?

These are the rules:

- When *searching*, search terms are case-insensitive.
- When *editing*, internal links are case-sensitive except for the first letter.
- When *displaying* an article, MediaWiki automatically:
  — Capitalizes the first letter of the title, in both the article title and the URL.
  — Converts spaces to underscores in the URL.

Now you might be thinking, "Whaaaat?? The first letter behaves differently from the rest? Underscores?? What madness is this?" In regular use, however, these quirky rules make sense. Let's take them one at a time.

Search is case-insensitive. This is clearly desirable. A reader who searches for "dog food" should find both upper- and lowercase matches.

Internal links are case-sensitive except for the first letter: This is natural for authors, who might link to [[dog]] in the middle of a sentence or [[Dog]] at the beginning, both leading to the same article. However, it is *arguable* that [[DOG]] in all capitals should link to a different article, as an acronym for (say) "Department of Oil and Gas" or "Digital Onscreen Graphic." Therefore, only the first letter is case-insensitive. When this rule causes problems (e.g., both [[dog food]] and [[Dog Food]] should link to the same page but don't due to the capital "F"), create a redirect from one title to the other (see "Redirects" on page 101).

Display rules. MediaWiki displays a title with its first letter capitalized because it looks nicer than using all lowercase. As for spaces and underscores, MediaWiki treats them equivalently in titles, but chooses underscores in URLs to make them simpler, since space characters would get "encoded" and appear as %20. This space/underscore behavior can lead an author to mistakes and misunderstandings about link syntax, perhaps best illustrated with an example:

```
Beginners sometimes [[Lead with]] an unnecessary capital, rather than
[[lead with]] the equivalent lowercase, because they don't understand the
rule. You also see them [[include_the_underscore]] in links, not realizing
spaces are equivalent and easier to work with; so please don't [[include
the underscore]].
```

Alternate Text

Normally your link text is the same as the article name. If you write:

```
Walk your [[dog]] twice a day.
```

the link appears as "dog". To provide different text for the link, use a pipe symbol:

```
[[article | alternate text]]
```

For example, this wikitext:

```
Walk your [[dog | terrier]] twice a day.
```

displays "terrier" but still links to dog. This style is called a *piped link*.

You can also change the hover text displayed when the mouse is placed on the link. By default, it's the same as the link text, but you can change it with a <span> tag:

```
Walk your [[dog | <span title="my favorite breed">terrier</span>]] twice
a day.
```

When the mouse is placed on the "terrier" link, the hover text "my favorite breed" will pop up.

The Plural Trick

If any letters immediately follow the closing brackets with no space in between, they become part of the link text. So:

```
[[dog]]s
```

displays the link text "dogs" but still links to dog. It's the same as:

```
[[dog | dogs]]
```

but shorter to type. This shorthand is great for forming plural links, but it is not limited to plurals. For instance:

```
I like [[jump]]ing on the sofa.
```

displays the link text "jumping" but links to jump, as if you'd written:

```
I like [[jump | jumping]] on the sofa.
```

This trick works only for trailing letters, not numbers or symbols:

```
[[abc]]123              Link is still "abc"
[[upside]]-down         Link is still "upside"
[[Rock and roll]]!!!    Link is still "Rock and roll"
```

 The plural trick is particularly effective if your wiki maintains a standard that all titles are singular. This is helpful not only for making plural links, but also for linking while writing, so authors never need to wonder, "Hmmm, was that other article name singular or plural?"

Links to Other Namespaces

When linking to an article outside the main namespace, the syntax is again the name of the article inside double square brackets:[*]

```
[[Namespace:Article]]
```

For example:

```
For help, see [[Help:Contents]].
```

To suppress the namespace from the displayed link text, use the pipe trick (see the sidebar "The Pipe Trick"):

```
[[Help:Contents|]]
```

---

[*] Except for category links and inline image links, as we'll see.

The Pipe Trick

When working with namespaces, a common linking style is, "link to the article, but don't display the namespace name." While you can do this with alternate text:

```
[[Namespace:Article | Article]]
```

MediaWiki provides a shortcut called the *pipe trick*. Simply place a pipe symbol (vertical bar) immediately before the closing braces:

```
[[Namespace:Article |]]
```

This produces exactly the same effect as `[[Namespace:Article | Article]]`. The pipe must be adjacent to the closing braces. The following attempts don't work due to whitespace between the pipe and the closing braces:

```
[[Namespace:Article| ]]
[[Namespace:Article | ]]
```

The pipe trick will also remove any words in parentheses at the end of the title. That is:

```
[[namespace:article name (parenthetical remark) |]]
```

resolves to "article name". For example, if your article is named:

```
Help:Linking to an article (or not)
```

then the pipe trick:

```
[[Help:Linking to an article (or not) |]]
```

produces the link text, "Linking to an article".

The pipe trick also works with interwiki links (see "Interwiki Links" on page 84):

```
[[Prefix:Article name |]]
```

The pipe trick differs from all other wikitext in an important way. Most other wikitext produces its visual effect at *display* time. When you surround text with triple quotes `'''like this'''`, it displays as bold, but when you edit the article again, the triple quotes remain. Not so with the pipe trick: it "works" just once, when the article is saved, permanently changing the link. When you edit the article again, the pipe trick has been replaced by a traditional "alternate text" link. To see this in action, edit an article, and include this link:

```
[[Help:Linking to an article (or not) |]]
```

Save the article, then edit it again. The wikitext has been changed:

```
[[Help:Linking to an article (or not) | Linking to an article]]
```

Also, because the pipe trick expands at save time, it won't work when the article name is produced dynamically. For example, this won't work as expected:

```
[[{{FULLPAGENAME}} |]]
```

In this case, magic words like FULLPAGENAME expand when displayed, not when saved; so at save time, the article name will be unknown and the pipe trick won't work. In fact, this example doesn't even produce a link. (Try it.)

Links to Category Pages

To link to a category page, you must precede the category name with a colon:

```
[[:Category:My category]]
```

If you forget the colon, you'll produce a category tag, placing the article into that category (see "Adding an Article to a Category" on page 90).

```
[[Category:My category]]
```

Links to Image Pages

Image pages, like category pages, require a leading colon for inline links:

```
[[:Image:MyImage.jpg]]
```

Otherwise you'll embed the image in the article, as described in the sidebar "Images Explained" within "Working with Uploads" on page 56.

Anchors

When an article has headings, each may be treated as an *anchor* for linking. (These are sometimes called *section links*.) Links with anchors cause the browser to scroll down to the desired heading automatically. Anchors are preceded by a hash sign, #. For example, if an article Terrier has a heading Care And Feeding, you can link to it within the article as:

```
[[#Care And Feeding]]
```

or from another article as:

```
[[Terrier#Care And Feeding]]
```

which here represents the URL *http://wiki.example.com/wiki/Terrier#Care_And_Feeding*.

The link text appearing on the wiki page will display the hash sign and the anchor text, which can look ugly, so consider using alternate link text:

```
[[Terrier#Care And Feeding | feeding terriers]]
```

External Links

Most wiki links are internal links, but it's also common to link to external sites. There are several ways to do this, as discussed in the following sections.

The Plain Method

Simply type a URL, and it magically becomes a link:

```
http://www.example.com
```

The displayed link text is simply the URL itself.[†]

 To remove the icon following an external link, wrap the link in a `<span>` of class `plainlinks`:

```
<span class="plainlinks">http://example.com</span>
```

The Fancy Method

The full syntax for external links differs from internal links in the following respects:

- External links use a single square bracket, instead of double
- Alternate text is preceded by whitespace, instead of a pipe

So, a link to *www.example.com* would be:

```
[http://www.example.com/   Example web site]
```

producing the link text "Example web site". The alternate text can include wikitext; to add some boldface, try:

```
[http://www.example.com/   Example '''web''' site]
```

Along with changing the link text, you can also change the hover text that displays when the mouse is placed on the link. By default, the hover text equals the link text. To replace it, use the same `<span>` trick as in "Alternate Text" on page 77:

```
[http://www.example.com/   <span title="Hi!">Example '''web''' site</span>]
```

Your URL may include query string arguments, as in:

```
[http://www.example.com/dog.cgi?a=1&b=2&c=3 A link with a query string]
```

This is commonly done for "mailto" links to include a subject line:

[†] Exception: if the URL points to an image file, and if external images are enabled for the wiki, the image will be embedded in the page (see "External Images" on page 236).

```
[mailto:nuts@oreilly.com?Subject=Another%20fine%20book Mail O'Reilly]
```

Notice that the subject line must be URL encoded, because MediaWiki will interpret any whitespace as ending the URL.

The Reference Method

Surround a URL with single square brackets, but don't include any alternate text:

```
Please visit my site [http://example.com].
```

and it becomes a numbered link:

Please visit my site [1].

where "1" links to *http://example.com*.

Supported Protocols

By default, MediaWiki supports the following types of external links:

```
http://
https://
ftp://
irc://
gopher://
telnet://
nntp://
worldwind://
mailto:
news:
```

A wiki administrator can change this list: see "URL Protocols for External Links" on page 236.

External Links to Yourself

Sometimes, you need to refer to your wiki server by an external link instead of an internal one. For instance, if your server at *wiki.example.com* is running other applications besides the wiki, you might be tempted to link like this:

```
-- Don't do this!
[http://wiki.example.com/other/page.html My other page]
[ftp://wiki.example.com/ My FTP site]
```

In these situations, don't hardcode your server name (*wiki.example.com*). Instead, use the magic words **SERVER** and **SERVERNAME**, supplied by MediaWiki, which expand to the server's base URL and name, respectively:

```
[{{SERVER}}/other/app.html My other page]
[ftp://{{SERVERNAME}}/ My FTP site]
```

Another case is linking to certain special pages that accept query parameters, such as a history page:

```
[http://wiki.example.com/wiki/index.php?title=My_Article&action=history
 History page for My Article]
```

Avoid hardcoding by using the magic word `fullurl`, which produces the full URL of an internal wiki article. The same history page URL is represented by:

```
[{{fullurl:My Article|action=history}} History page for My Article]
```

The syntax is:

```
{{fullurl:article name here | optional_querystring}}
```

Linking Errors Quiz

Can you spot the mistakes in the following links?

1. `[[http://www.example.com]]`
2. `[http://www.example.com|my page]`
3. `[[my_article_name]]`
4. `[[my_article_name | my article name]]`
5. `[[My article name | my article name]]`
6. `[http://example.com http://example.com]`
7. `[file:///C:/myfile.txt my file]`

Answers:

1. `[[http://www.example.com]]` is an external URL, but double square brackets are for internal wiki articles. Here is the proper syntax: `[http://www.example.com]` or `[http://www.example.com my link text]`.

2. `[http://www.example.com|my page]` uses a pipe between the URL and the alternate text "my page," but pipes are for internal links. External links use a space character as the separator. This mangled link actually points to http://www.example.com|my with the alternate text of "page". The correct link would be `[http://www.example.com my page]`.

3. `[[my_article_name]]` is not wrong, but bad style. Underscores are equivalent to space characters, so use spaces instead: `[[my article name]]`.

4. `[[my_article_name | my article name]]` truly shows that the writer doesn't understand link syntax. It's equivalent to `[[my article name]]`.

5. `[[My article name | my article name]]` indicates that the writer doesn't know that the link's first letter is case-insensitive. This link is equivalent to `[[my article name]]`.

6. `[http://example.com`   `http://example.com]`   is   equivalent   to `http://example.com` alone, with no brackets. Solitary URLs get turned into links. So use the simpler format.

7. `[file:///C:/myfile.txt my file]` has two problems: it's a file link, which some browsers will refuse to display for security reasons, and it points to a local file on the *reader's* PC, which is ridiculous on a multiuser wiki.

Interwiki Links

An *interwiki link* is an external link—often to another wiki—that behaves like an internal link. For example, on many wikis, the link:

```
[[wp:Dog]]
```

is an interwiki link to Wikipedia, pointing to its `Dog` article at:

```
http://www.wikipedia.org/wiki/Dog
```

`wp` looks like a namespace, but it's not. It's a prefix that stands for:

```
http://www.wikipedia.org/wiki/Article_Title_Here
```

In a displayed article, an interwiki link is styled exactly like an internal link. And when you write an article, an interwiki link has the same wikitext format as an internal link with a namespace:

```
[[Prefix:Article name]]
```

Interwiki links have several advantages over external links:

- They're shorter to type.
- They look like internal links when displayed, which might be to your taste for (say) local sites on your company's intranet.
- Your wiki administrator can change the meaning of the interwiki prefix internally, automatically repointing all those links to the new site. You can't do that with handwritten external URLs.

Some interwiki prefixes are included with MediaWiki; `wp` is a common one. A MediaWiki administrator can define others; they work best for sites with a flat, predictable link structure. See "Creating Interwiki Links" on page 332 for more details.

Interlanguage Links

An *interlanguage link* is a link from an article—say, `Dog`—to a translation of that article in another language—say, `Chien` in French. Translation doesn't happen automatically: both Dog and Chien must be written by someone. Interlanguage links just relate the articles automatically for any of MediaWiki's 300+ languages.‡

If your wiki supports interlanguage links, as Wikipedia does, there are two types:

- Links from the Language menu, which appears when an article has been translated
- Links within an article's text

Otherwise, see "Enabling Interlanguage Link Support" on page 333 to learn how to enable support.

Language Menu Links

You can place interlanguage links into any article, such as Dog:

```
[[fr:Chien]]
[[es:Perro]]
```

These French and Spanish interlanguage links will cause MediaWiki's language menu (see "Quick Tour of a Wiki Page" on page 9) to appear in the sidebar on the Dog page, reading:

Français
Español

These link to the two translated articles. The links are not symmetric: if you view the Chien article, no language menu will appear unless the French article contains interlanguage links as well.*

Interlanguage Links in Articles

If you'd rather link directly to a foreign-language translation within an article, prepend a colon onto an interlanguage link:

```
For a French translation, see [[:fr:Chien]].
```

much as you would for a category link.

---

‡ See all 300+ languages and their two-letter codes on your preferences page in the Languages drop-down list ("User Profile Preferences" on page 35). For programmers, see the source file *languages/Names.php*.

* This makes sense because translations are themselves not symmetric. Just because "Foo" in one language means "Bar" in another doesn't make the reverse always true: "Bar" could have other meanings.

For more information on interlanguage links, see:

http://en.wikipedia.org/wiki/Help:Interlanguage_links

Graphical Links

In traditional web pages, you'll commonly see pictures that are links: buttons, arrows, photos, etc. MediaWiki does not support graphical links by default, but you can still create them in several ways.

Graphical Links with Spans

If your wiki administrator lets you embed external images by URL (see "External Images" on page 236):

```
http://example.com/mypicture.gif
```

then create an external link using this image as the "alternate text," enclosing it in a `<span>` of class `plainlinks` (see "External Link Appearance" on page 266):

```
<span class="plainlinks">[http://example.com
 http://example.com/mypicture.gif]</span>
```

This displays the image *mypicture.gif* linked to *http://example.com*.

Graphical Link Extensions

Various third-party extensions produce graphical links (see "ImageMap" on page 276). Also, the custom tag `extimg` from "Creating a Tag Extension" on page 294 could be adapted to produce links.

File Links

A *file link* points to a disk file on the computer running your web browser. It begins with `file://`, such as:

```
file:///home/oreilly/myfile
```

which on a Linux computer is *home/oreilly/myfile*, or:

```
file:///C:/Temp/myfile.txt
```

which on a Windows computer is *C:\Temp\myfile.txt*. File links in a multiuser environment like a wiki make more sense for shared files on remote filesystems, such as Windows shares, *\\sharename\myfile.txt*:

```
file://///sharename/myfile.txt
```

By default, MediaWiki does not support file links, and it takes several steps to make them work:

- A wiki administrator must permit the `file://` protocol in MediaWiki's configuration file, as explained in "URL Protocols for External Links" on page 236.
- Your browser must support them. (Firefox does not, for security reasons, but for workarounds, see *http://www.techlifeweb.com/firefox/2006/07/how-to-open-file-links-in-firefox-15.html*.)

Once this is set up, file links are simply external links to MediaWiki:

```
[file:///mnt/share/myfile My local file]
```

Linking Tips

Every word in a wiki article has the potential to be a link, but a "link everything" philosophy is not always helpful for the reader. What are good strategies for deciding when and where to link? Wikipedia provides sensible advice at:

http://en.wikipedia.org/wiki/Wikipedia:Manual_of_Style_%28links%29

http://en.wikipedia.org/wiki/Wikipedia:Build_the_web

http://en.wikipedia.org/wiki/Wikipedia:Only_make_links_that_are_relevant_to_the_context

Here are some brief guidelines to get you started.

Link Related Terms

Provide links to related articles, not vaguely relevant ones. If an article about dog-walking contains the sentence:

```
Always keep your dog on a leash so she does not
chase butterflies as they fly into a neighbor's yard.
```

some relevant links would be [[dog]] and [[leash]]. Links to [[fly]] or [[yard]] would be less relevant, since the articles are unlikely to focus on dogs.

Link More Than Once

If an important term appears several times in an article, turn more than one of them into a link. A single link is fragile, easily removed by a careless editor, losing the only connection to a related article.

On a related note, make sure that the *first occurrence* of any linked term in an article is itself a link. The following example would be bad style:

```
Once a dog, always a [[dog]].
```

because the first occurrence of dog is not a link, while the second is.

Avoid Adjacent Links

Don't link two adjacent words with different internal links:

```
I bought some [[dog]] [[food]] yesterday.
```

because the reader can't visually distinguish the two links [[dog]] [[food]] from the single link [[dog food]]. Instead, rewrite the sentence to place non-linked words between the links:

```
I bought [[food]] for my [[dog]] yesterday.
```

Include a "See Also" Section

To refer to related articles that don't come up naturally in the text, add a "See Also" section at the end of the article. Make it a bulleted list of links:

```
== See also ==
* [[Dog feeding habits]] - How and when they like to eat
* [http://dogs.example.com The Dog House] - Official site
```

## CHAPTER 6

Organizing Articles

As a MediaWiki site grows, it's important to keep it organized. Otherwise, a previously helpful wiki starts to look like a confused book written by a hundred authors who have never met one another. Good writing, well-chosen article titles, and careful linking can help keep things in order, but MediaWiki also provides several powerful features specifically for organizing articles. In this chapter, we'll cover:

Categories
> Collecting articles into named groups

Namespaces
> Partitioning the wiki into broad areas

Subpages
> Creating a hierarchical article

Redirects
> Creating synonyms or aliases for wiki articles

Disambiguation pages
> Pages that distinguish articles with similar or identical names

Renaming
> Changing the title of an article

Deleting
> Removing an article

We'll talk more about designing an effective wiki in Chapter 10, including planning for a good organization. Even after this planning, wikis may need to be rearranged (*refactored*) on a regular basis to serve their community most efficiently.

MediaWiki's special pages (Chapter 8) are helpful for keeping the wiki organized. See "Administration" on page 168.

Categories

A *category* is a collection of articles that includes:

- A name
- Zero or more members of the category, including:
  —Articles
  —Other categories, called *subcategories*
- A category page, named `Category:NameOfCategory`, which lists the members and can be edited like an article

Authors can create categories, add and remove articles from categories, and even create parent-child relationships between categories. For example, a category named `Mammals` might contain the articles `Dog`, `Cat`, and `Otter`, plus the subcategories `Big Mammals`, `Small Furry Mammals`, and `Mammals That Make Appropriate Pets`. Its category page would be `Category:Mammals`.

It's important to distinguish between the category itself (e.g., `Mammals`) and the category page that lists the members (e.g., `Category:Mammals`). A category is just the set of members. The category *page* is an article that documents the category, with the special property that it lists all members automatically.

Just as a category can have many members, a single member can be in many categories.

Adding an Article to a Category

To place an article into a category, edit the article, not the category page. Anywhere in the article text, add a *category tag*:

```
[[Category:NameOfCategory]]
```

and save the article. For example, to add the article `Dog` to the categories `Mammals` and `Pets`, edit `Dog` and enter anywhere in the article:[*]

```
[[Category:Mammals]]
[[Category:Pets]]
```

 A category is not an external thing to which you add articles. Rather, articles are "tagged" with the names of categories.

Adding a category tag has two complementary effects:

- The article displays a link to the category page, usually at the bottom
- The category page displays a link to the article in an alphabetical list of members

So the `Dog` article will have three links at the bottom:

```
Category: Mammals | Pets
```

`Mammals` and `Pets` link to their respective category pages, and the word `Category` links to the list of all categories, `Special:Categories` (see "Categories" on page 148).

Likewise, the `Mammals` category page will display a `Dog` link, alphabetized under "D".

Listing All Members of a Category

To see a list of all the members of a given category, simply visit the category page, `Category:NameOfCategory`, e.g., `Category:Mammals`.[†]

Creating a Category

Creating a category is simple: just insert a category tag into any article and save. If the category doesn't exist, it's created automatically.

Suppose you want to start a new category, `Carnivores`, and add the `Dog` article to it. Simply pretend the category exists and add this tag to `Dog`:

```
[[Category:Carnivores]]
```

---

[*] Yes, *anywhere* in the article. It's best to standardize on one place, say the top or the bottom, but this flexible system permits cool tricks like transcluding category tags via templates (see "Conditional Transclusion" on page 116).

[†] Advanced authors can list all members of a category with a Dynamic Page List tag, described in "Dynamic Page List" on page 124.

Save the article, and MediaWiki automatically creates the `Carnivores` category, placing a category link at the end of the `Dog` article, as expected. The link will be red, however, signifying that no category page exists.

 MediaWiki creates categories automatically, but not their category *pages*. That's up to you.

Before creating a category, visit `Special:Categories` to see if there's already an existing category that might be appropriate. Wikis with similar or redundant categories become sloppy and inconsistent. (Imagine an author trying to choose among categories named `Dogs`, `Dog`, `Canines`, `Canine`, and `Woofing Mammals`. Aaargh.)

Creating a Category Page

After creating a category, you should create the associated category page. In our previous example, the category page for `Carnivores` would be `Category:Carnivores`. Whenever this category appears in an article, such as `Dog`, it is displayed in red, indicating that the category page does not exist.

 Even if a category page doesn't exist, the list of members is still displayed at `Category:NameOfCategory`.

To edit the category page, click the red category link to visit the edit page. (Just like clicking a red article link when an article does not exist.) Add some text briefly explaining the purpose of the category. For example, on `Category:Carnivores`, you might write:

```
This category is about [[animal]]s that eat [[meat]].
```

Category pages are much like articles: you can edit them, view their history, make comments on the associated talk page, and so on. Here are the differences:

- There's an automatically generated list of all articles and subcategories located below the text.
- There's no "move" tab to rename a category.

Subcategories

Categories can be related to each other as subcategories (child categories) and supercategories (parent categories). These relationships are created by editing category pages. To make category *A* the parent of category *B*:

1. Edit the "child" category page, `Category:B`.
2. Add the parent's tag, `[[Category:A]]`, and save.

So, to make `Mammals` a subcategory of `Animals`, edit the page `Category:Mammals` and insert:

    [[Category:Animals]]

As with articles, you can add multiple category tags to a category page. That is, a category can have multiple parents. So the `Mammals` category could be the child of `Animals`, `Hairy Things`, and `Warm-Blooded Objects`. Likewise, a category can have multiple children. For example, `Mammals` could have child categories `Big Mammals`, `Small Mammals`, and `Gazelles`. To achieve these relationships, you'd edit the three subcategory pages and insert `[[Category:Mammals]]`.

 In computer science terminology, the MediaWiki category structure forms a directed graph, not a tree, and may contain loops.

Renaming a Category

Renaming a category is a nontrivial exercise in MediaWiki: you must switch all the member articles from one category to another. This means visiting every article that references the category and changing the old category link to use the new name. For example, to rename the category `Dogs` to `Canines`, you could:

1. Visit the category page `Category:Dogs`.
2. For each article and subcategory in the category `Dogs`:
   a. Shift-click the link to open a new window
   b. Click Edit
   c. Edit the category link and save
   d. Close the window

When finished with all the articles, complete the renaming by:

- Copying any wikitext from the old category page to the new one
- Deleting the old category page

What a pain, right? Fortunately, there are alternatives that reduce the effort, though they require some technical knowledge:

- Export all articles in the category using `Special:Export` ("Export Pages" on page 161), and edit the resulting XML file to change `Category:Dogs` to `Category:Canines`. Add a note to the edit summary to document that you did this. Then, have a wiki sysop import the XML file (see "Import Pages" on page 162).

- Install the pywikipedia bot, which can rename a category in a single operation. See *http://meta.wikimedia.org/wiki/Pywikipedia*.

Deleting a Category

To delete a category:

1. Remove the category tag from all members. (The pywikipedia bot can help with this, too.)

2. Delete the category page as you would any other article. (Deletions might be limited to sysops on your wiki.)

Deleting the category page alone does not delete the category; all its articles will still be members.

Hidden Categories

Category links, as we've seen, appear automatically within their member articles. You can suppress this behavior for a category, creating a hidden category, by placing the magic word `__HIDDENCAT__` anywhere in its category page.

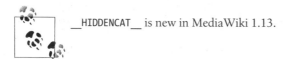 `__HIDDENCAT__` is new in MediaWiki 1.13.

For example, if you want the category `Sneaky` to be hidden, edit `Category:Sneaky` and insert the magic word `__HIDDENCAT__`. This has two effects:

- All articles in the `Sneaky` category will not list `Sneaky` among their categories, and will not contain a link to `Category:Sneaky`.

- `Sneaky` is made a subcategory of `Hidden categories`, which is an automatically maintained category. View this category (at `Category:Hidden categories`) to see a list of all hidden categories.

Hidden categories are useful to wiki sysops for tracking user behavior. Imagine you have a template called "Under construction" (i.e., `Template:Under construction`) to display a message that an article is a work in progress. If you want to keep track of all articles that are under construction, you could add a category tag to the template:

```
[[Category:Articles under construction]]
```

so that every article using the template will be in the category `Articles under construction`. However, you might not want this category tag appearing in the articles, so make it a hidden category by editing `Category:Articles under construction` and inserting the magic word `__HIDDENCAT__`.

Linking to a Category Page

The annals of wiki history are filled with failed attempts to link to a category page. The most natural guess:

```
See a list of all [[Category:Dogs | dogs]]
```

is wrong. `[[Category:Dogs]]` is a category tag, not a link. It adds the article to the category `Dogs` when placed *anywhere* in the article, even in the middle of a sentence as above.

Here's the secret. To link to a category page, add a colon (:) just before the word `Category`:

```
[[:Category:NameOfCategory]]
```

So, to fix our example, use:

```
See a list of all [[:Category:Dogs | dogs]]
```

Controlling Sorting on Category Pages

In an article such as `Dog`, an ordinary category tag:

```
[[Category:Mammals]]
```

will make `Dog` appear on the `Mammals` category page, alphabetized by its first letter, "D". This placement is not always ideal, however:

- If the article name begins with a nonessential word like "The", you might want it alphabetized differently. For example, the article `The Dogs of War` might be better alphabetized under "D" rather than "T".

- For articles in other namespaces (say, `Help:Contents`), you might want to alphabetize by the article name (under "C") rather than the namespace name (under "H").

You can control this behavior by providing a *sort key* in the category tag:

```
[[Category:Something | sort key]]
```

Now, on the category page, the article title will appear at the position of *sort key*. For example, in the article The Dogs of War, if you write:

```
[[Category:Books | Dogs of War]]
```

then The Dogs of War is placed under "D" where "Dogs of War" would be. For articles in other namespaces, you can take a shortcut using MediaWiki's built-in PAGENAME variable (see "Article Name Variables" on page 111) as the sort key, causing the article title to sort without its namespace. To make Help:Contents sort under "C" as if it were "Contents", write:

```
[[Category:Help | {{PAGENAME}}]]
```

 A blank sort key forces an article into the first position on the category page. Wikipedia uses this trick to make the main article stand out in a large category list. For example, on the Dogs category page, the article Dog is placed first by tagging Dog with:

```
[[Category:Dog | ]]
```

If you do this trick for multiple articles in the same category, they'll all appear "first," but in sorted order.

Namespaces

Namespaces are high-level groupings of wiki articles with a similar purpose. For example, the Help namespace contains help pages, the Image namespace contains uploaded files, and the Category namespace contains all category pages.

When an article is in a namespace, its title consists of the namespace name, a colon, and the title proper.‡ Here are some examples:

```
Help:Contents
Category:Mammals
Image:My photo.jpg
Talk:Walking a dog
User:Jsmith
```

---

‡ Some pages and links look like they contain namespaces, but they don't. One example is interwiki links like [[wp:Dog]] for Wikipedia's Dog article (see "Interwiki Links" on page 84). These names don't show up on Special:AllPages or other lists of namespaces.

If you're familiar with namespaces from other areas of technology, such as computer programming, MediaWiki's namespaces are similar. Just as programming languages can have classes of the same name but in different namespaces, so it is with articles in MediaWiki. The article `Dog` is different from `Talk:Dog`, which is different from `Help:Dog`.

MediaWiki supplies 16 namespaces and two "virtual" namespaces by default, listed in Table 6-1. Wiki administrators can also create their own namespaces: see "Creating Namespaces" on page 246.

Table 6-1. MediaWiki's standard namespaces

Namespace	Description	Namespace	Description
The main namespace *(no name)*	Ordinary articles. *Special feature*: has no visible namespace name. Articles created with "no namespace" are here.	Talk	Discussion of articles in the main namespace.
User	User pages. *Special feature*: associated with a real user; toolbox contains additional links to email the user, see user contributions, etc. See "User Pages" on page 31.	User talk	Discussion of user pages. *Special feature*: any edit automatically alerts the user in question. See "User Talk Pages" on page 31.
Project	Articles about the wiki itself. *Special feature*: the wiki name (e.g., Wikipedia) is an alias: on Wikipedia, `Project:Example` is identical to `Wikipedia:Example`.	Project talk	Discussion of project pages. *Special feature*: the wiki name is again an alias, e.g., `Project talk:Example` is identical to `Wikipedia talk:Example` on Wikipedia.
Image	Uploaded files. *Special feature*: `[[Image:...]]` links embed the image in the article. See "Images and Uploaded Files" on page 56.	Image talk	Discussion of uploaded files.
MediaWiki	System messages. Only sysops can edit. *Special feature*: contains the infrastructural text of the wiki. See "System Messages" on page 218.	MediaWiki talk	Discussion of system messages.
Template	Templates. *Special feature*: easy transclusion. See "Templates and Transclusion" on page 112.	Template talk	Discussion of templates.
Help	Online help for using the wiki.	Help talk	Discussion of help articles.
Category	Categories. *Special feature*: automatic list of all articles in the category.	Category talk	Discussion of categories.

Namespace	Description	Namespace	Description
Media	Direct access to uploaded files. A "virtual" namespace: users cannot create articles here. See "Linking to an Uploaded File" on page 60.	Special	Special pages. A "virtual" namespace: users cannot create articles here. See Chapter 8.

Namespaces are more rigid, less powerful, and less convenient than categories, but they have features that categories do not. See Table 6-2 later in this chapter for details.

Talk Namespaces

Every "regular" namespace has an associated "talk" namespace, as seen previously in Table 6-1. The main namespace has `Talk`, the `Image` namespace has `Image talk`, the `User` namespace has `User talk`, and so on.

As a result, every "regular" article has an associated talk page for discussing the article. For example, the help page `Help:Contents` has a talk page `Help talk:Contents` where you can ask questions, complain that the help page stinks, or, better yet, offer suggestions for improvement. The talk page is accessible from the article's Discussion tab.

Adding an Article to a Namespace

To place an article into a namespace, simply rename the article using its Move tab. For example, to move the article `Dog` into the `Mammal` namespace, rename the article as `Mammal:Dog`. To remove an article from a namespace, rename it without the namespace prefix.

Listing All Articles in a Namespace

To list all articles in a namespace, visit `Special:AllPages` (see "All Pages" on page 147), select the desired namespace, and click Go.

Creating a Namespace

Wiki administrators can create custom namespaces by adding a few lines of custom PHP programming code to the file *LocalSettings.php*. See "Creating Namespaces" on page 246.

Subpages

A *subpage* is a wiki article that sits "beneath" another article. To create a subpage of article XYZ, name it XYZ/*something*: the article title, a slash, and the subpage title. When a subpage is displayed, it automatically contains a link back to its parent.

 An article with a slash in its title is not necessarily a subpage. Real subpages contain an automatic link back to their parent page.

By default, the User namespace and all talk namespaces support subpages. Wiki administrators may change this behavior: see "Namespace Subpages" on page 247.

Subpages may themselves have subpages. If the article Dog has a subpage Dog/Training, then Dog/Training could have a subpage Dog/Training/Tricks with a rubber ball. An article can have many subpages.

Subpages are also a convenient way to keep a collection of personal articles "under" your user page. Simply create an article of the form:

    User:*username*/*articlename*

where *articlename* is any article name. These subpages are not private, nor are they protected from edits by others, but at least they're organized.

Table 6-2 shows how subpages differ from categories and namespaces for organizing articles.

Table 6-2. Categories versus Namespaces versus Subpages

Feature	Categories	Namespaces	Subpages
Creation	Anyone can create	Administrators only (via PHP)	Anyone can create, if subpages are enabled
Adding members	Add category tag to the article	Rename article to have namespace as a prefix	Put a slash in the article name, in a namespace that supports subpages
Removing members	Delete category tag from the article	Rename article to have a different namespace	Rename article without the slash, or as a subpage of a different article
Renaming	Difficult for authors: manually change	Easy for administrators (via PHP); impossible for authors	Easy as renaming an article

Feature	Categories	Namespaces	Subpages
	category tags in all member articles		
One article can be...	In many categories	In one namespace	The subpage of only one other article
Hierarchy and relationships	Subcategories (parent/child): a directed graph	n/a	Strict tree structure: one article, multiple subpages, which may themselves have subpages
Visibility	Category links appear at end of article	Namespace name appears in page title, URL	None in articles (subpages are not listed); subpages link to their parent; third-party extensions can help
Documentation	Category page can document a category	No standard for documenting a namespace; often an article *Name space*:About or *Name space*:Contents is created	No standard: subpages might be documented in their parent article
Access control	n/a	$wgNamespaceProtection setting can make a namespace read-only to a user group; see "Namespace Security" on page 247	Same as for articles
Transclusion control	n/a	$wgNonincludableNamespaces setting enables or disables transclusion; see "Namespace Security" on page 247	n/a

Limitations of Subpages

The main problem with subpages is their lack of visibility. If you're viewing the article Dog, there's no immediate way to see what subpages it has. Several third-party extensions address this problem, if your wiki administrator will install one. The simplest is SubPageList2 (*http://www.mediawiki.org/wiki/Extension:SubPageList2*), which lets you place a simple tag in any article:

```
<subpages/>
```

that expands to a bulleted list of the article's subpages. More powerful extensions include SubPageList3 (*http://www.mediawiki.org/wiki/Extension:SubPageList3*) and the mighty Dynamic Page List (see "Dynamic Page List" on page 124).

Another concern is that users might create subpages when categories would be better. This is a matter of opinion. Categories have more flexibility for navigation and they scale better. On the other hand, subpages are useful for small tasks—say, breaking an article into a few small pieces—where a category might be too heavyweight.

 Is a talk page getting too long? Create a subpage called "Archive" beneath it, and move the older content there. Repeat as needed.

Redirects

A *redirect* is an alternative title for an article. If your wiki has an article called Dog, but people constantly search for it by the name "Canine", you can create a redirect called Canine that redirects to the Dog article. Redirects help to organize a wiki by making articles findable under different names.[*]

Here is the syntax for a redirect:

```
#REDIRECT [[page name]]
```

For example, you could have an article Canine that contains the single line:

```
#REDIRECT [[Dog]]
```

Now, when a wiki user enters "Canine" and clicks Go, she'll be taken directly to Dog. Below the title, she'll see a note indicating that she's been redirected:

```
Dog
   (Redirected from Canine)
```

and the URL of the article will say "...Canine" rather than "...Dog".

Redirects are for internal links only. This will not work:

```
#REDIRECT [http://www.oreilly.com]        (wrong)
```

Common Uses of Redirects

MediaWiki redirects are most useful when an article title has well-known synonyms, as in our earlier Canine example. For each synonym, create an article whose only line is a redirect to the "real" article. An article may have many redirects pointing to it. Our Dog article could have redirects called Canine, Fido, Poodle, and Man's best friend, each containing the same line:

```
#REDIRECT [[Dog]]
```

---

[*] MediaWiki redirects are not HTTP redirects (code 301 or 302); they report HTTP 200.

Another use for redirects is to support alternate capitalizations. Thanks to MediaWiki's case-sensitivity rule (see the sidebar "Article Titles and Case-Sensitivity" within "Links to Nonexistent Articles" on page 76), similar titles such as `German Shepherd` and `German shepherd` refer to different articles because of the "S". If you want both names to point to the same article, bypassing the case-sensitivity rule, create a redirect from one to the other. Assuming `German shepherd` is the real article, edit the second article `German Shepherd` and insert:

```
#REDIRECT [[German shepherd]]
```

A quick way to create a case-sensitivity redirect is to edit the URL directly in the browser:

1. Visit the article in question, `German shepherd`.
2. In your browser, edit the URL in the address bar, capitalizing the "s" in "shepherd", and press Enter.
3. The browser visits `German Shepherd`, which does not exist, and MediaWiki offers you an edit link.
4. Click the edit link and insert `#REDIRECT [[German shepherd]]`.

Yet another use of redirects is to support plurals. If the article is `Dog`, it's common for `Dogs` to be a redirect.

Modifying a Redirect

Sometimes people scratch their heads over how to modify a redirect. After all, if you visit a redirect, it transports you to the target article. That is, if `Poodle` redirects to `Dog`, and you try to visit `Poodle`, you end up at `Dog`. How do you edit `Poodle`? Here's what to do:

1. Visit `Poodle` and get redirected to `Dog`.
2. Notice the note, "Redirected from Poodle", where "Poodle" is a link. Click "Poodle".
3. You're now on the `Poodle` redirect page, so click Edit, make changes, and save.

At this point, you can redirect `Poodle` elsewhere, or remove the `#REDIRECT` line and write an article about poodles.

Another way to edit a redirect page is to add the query parameter `redirect=no` to its URL, which prevents the redirect from occurring so you can edit the article.

Redirecting to a Redirect

Redirects cannot be chained. Suppose article *A* redirects to article *B*, and article *B* redirects to article *C*. If you visit article *A*, you'll be redirected only to article *B*, not to *C*. This situation is called a *double redirect*.

Double redirects are considered errors in MediaWiki because they can lead to loops, where an article eventually redirects back to itself. Double redirects can be tracked down and fixed on the page `Special:DoubleRedirects` (see "Double Redirects" on page 141).

Redirects and Categories

If an article is in a category (see "Categories" on page 90), any redirects to that article are not considered to be in the category. Suppose article `Dog` is the target of a redirect `Poodle`, and `Dog` is in the category `Mammals`. When you view the `Mammals` category page (`Category:Mammals`), you'll see an entry for `Dog`, but not for `Poodle`. This is correct behavior: the article `Dog` contains the category link (`[[Category:Mammals]]`), but the redirect article does not.

Redirects can be explicitly categorized, however. In this case, edit the `Poodle` redirect and add a category tag:

```
#REDIRECT [[Dog]]
[[Category:Mammals]]
```

Now `Poodle` has been added to the `Mammals` category.

Disambiguation Pages

A *disambiguation page* is a wiki article that distinguishes multiple meanings of the same word or phase. It helps to organize a wiki by preventing clashes between topics with similar or identical titles.

For example, the Wikipedia article for `Hot`, *http://en.wikipedia.org/wiki/Hot*, is a disambiguation page, indicating that the word may refer to:

- "High temperature"
- "Lust [or] Physical attractiveness"
- "Jargon used to describe radioactivity..."
- "Amphoe Hot, a district of Chiang Mai province, Thailand"
- ...and more

Disambiguation page support is sort of, but not exactly, built into MediaWiki. To make it work effectively, you need to create a *template*—a reusable piece of wikitext—to append to disambiguation pages. We'll introduce templates in Chapter 7, so for now we'll just use cookbook-style instructions to make this work.

To create the infrastructure for disambiguation pages, create the article `Template:Disambig`, a template to be placed into every disambiguation page. In fact, this template *defines* an article as a disambiguation page. Typical content is:

```
''This [[disambiguation page]] lists articles associated with
the same title.''
<includeonly>[[Category:Disambiguation]]</includeonly>
```

(See `Template:Disambig` on Wikipedia for a fancier style.) Thereafter, to create a disambiguation page, simply put this line at the end of every disambiguation page:

```
{{disambig}}
```

This produces the following beneficial effects when the disambiguation page is displayed:

- It displays whatever message you placed inside `Template:Disambig`, alerting the reader.
- It adds the article to the category `Disambiguation`, aiding sysops in locating these articles.
- It instructs the special page `Special:Disambiguations` to flag any articles that link to our disambiguation page, as they should link to a more specific article instead. (This is the only disambiguation effect provided by MediaWiki out of the box.)

Many wikis have a standard presentation for disambiguation pages. Wikipedia's is a bulleted list of links to the articles in question.

Renaming Articles

Another way to reorganize a wiki is to change the names of articles. When a well-intentioned author creates a poorly named article like `Miscellaneous tips on how to feed a dog that you have`, you can rename it to `Feeding a dog` fairly simply by clicking the article's Move tab. At the prompt, enter the new article name and a change comment, and save. This does the following:

- Renames the article and its associated talk page (if any).
- Retains the article's history under the new name.
- Creates a new revision of the article, noting in the history that the rename occurred.

- Creates a redirect from the old name to the new article, so the old name continues to work (i.e., backward compatibility).
- Optionally updates all other redirects that point to the old name, repointing them at the new article. (MediaWiki 1.13 and later.)
- Makes an entry in the Move log (see "Logs" on page 152).

Another reason to rename articles is to make them fit your wiki's naming standards. See Wikipedia's conventions at *http://en.wikipedia.org/wiki/Wikipedia:Naming_conventions*.

Double Redirects from Multiple Moves

If an article is renamed twice or more, this may create a double redirect (see "Double Redirects" on page 141) which you should fix. So, when you move `Miscellaneous tips on how to feed a dog that you have` to the new name `Feeding a dog`, but later move it to `Dog food`, a double redirect may be created from the first name to the second to the third. (In MediaWiki 1.13 and later, you'll be prompted to "update any redirects that point to the original title," which avoids this problem.) Double redirects can be found and fixed at `Special:DoubleRedirects`.

Undoing a Rename

If you rename an article and change your mind later, you can undo the renaming by visiting the Move log:

1. Visit `Special:Log` ("Logs" on page 152) and locate your move in the Move log.
2. Click the Revert button.

You can also undo a move manually by moving it back to the old name:

1. Visit the new article.
2. Click the Move tab.
3. Enter the old name and click "Move page".

Each of these methods not only restores the article to the original name, but also leaves the new name in place as a redirect back to the original.

Deleting Articles

Deletion, by default, is limited to wiki sysops. This may be changed by the wiki administrator. If you're able to delete an article, you'll see a Delete tab on the article page. Simply click it and follow the directions.

Deleting does the following:

- Makes the article unavailable.
- Releases the article name so it can be reused. However, if you try to create a new article with that name, you'll see a warning that you're re-creating a deleted article.
- Adds an entry to the deletion log.

After you delete an article, all links to it will now display in red, as the article is no longer accessible.

Before You Delete

Deleting an article is a significant change, especially because other articles may still link to it. In the Toolbox on the article page, use "What links here" (see "What Links Here" on page 162) to see how widely used the article is. Even if no wiki articles link to it, other external sites still might, and this deletion will break all of those outside links.

Sometimes, it's more appropriate to redirect rather than delete. If there are two similar articles (say, Dog and Dogs), combine them into Dog and make Dogs redirect to it.

Undeleting

When you delete an article, it still remains within the wiki: it's just not accessible. A wiki sysop can undelete the article, restoring any or all deleted revisions.

To undelete an article, visit Special:Undelete (see "View Deleted Pages" on page 162) and search for the article name. If you don't remember the name, locate it in the deletion log (Special:Log) and click "Restore". Either way, follow the directions in "View Deleted Pages" on page 162.

 You can also find the deletion log entry for an article by trying to recreate the article. On the edit page, you'll see a warning that you're re-creating a previously deleted article, plus the deletion log entry for the article.

## CHAPTER 7

Advanced Article Construction

So far, we've looked at wiki articles as individual documents, constructed from familiar parts like paragraphs, formatted text, bulleted lists, tables, and so on. In this view, the goal is to turn ideas into articles and to write and typeset them effectively. But of course, a wiki is more than a bunch of independent articles. The collection serves a common purpose, whether it's an encyclopedia, a taxonomy of pets, or a corporate knowledge system. That's why we use categories and namespaces to organize articles: to make the information findable and serve this common purpose. In this chapter, we'll continue to take this "larger" view of the wiki and construct sets of articles that share information among themselves.

Suppose you're writing a series of 50 wiki articles about pet illnesses, and every article contains the same link to a popular veterinary website. You could simply copy and paste the link into each article, but if the URL ever changed, you'd need to update all 50 articles. This kind of annoyance is called a maintenance problem, and it gets worse as wikis grow. With MediaWiki, you can avoid this problem by writing the URL in only one article and automatically making it appear in all 50, by way of a feature called transclusion. This is just one of MediaWiki's sharing features we'll discuss in this chapter. Others include:

Consistency maintenance
> Why share content among articles?

Variables
> Special words that stand for (and expand into) common values

Templates and transclusion
> Displaying the text of one article inside another, and a whole lot more

Logical parser functions
> Creating if/then/else logic within articles to display content conditionally

Dynamic Page List (DPL)
A powerful, third-party extension that generates lists and tables dynamically from other articles

Advanced recipes
Applying what you've learned to solve common problems and reduce redundancy in your wiki

 Variables, templates, parser functions, and parser tags are collectively known as *magic words*. We've seen some magic words already, such as:

- Table of contents control words, like __FORCETOC__ (see "Table of Contents" on page 53)

- HTML-like tags, such as <code> (see "Typestyles and Fonts" on page 54)

- Words in curly braces, such as {{fullurl:}} (see "External Links to Yourself" on page 82)

More information on magic words can be found at *http://www .mediawiki.org/wiki/Magic_words*.

Maintaining a Consistent Wiki

On an active wiki, with articles constantly changing under the hands of many authors, content can get out of control. You could see:

- Multiple articles on the same topic

- Inconsistent articles on similar topics, where one gets updated regularly and the other doesn't

- Misplaced content in one article that would fit better in another

- Single articles that cover several topics, which should be split into separate articles

These situations illustrate a problem called *consistency maintenance*: how to keep a wiki's articles consistent and correct over time. On an ideal wiki, each fact should be written in exactly one place, and *referenced*—not copied—by other articles that need it. Whenever there are two copies of a fact, one might change while the other doesn't, producing a consistency maintenance problem.

Articles should share content, not repeat it. The simplest form of sharing we've seen is linking. If the article Bird needs information contained in the article Parakeet, then Bird should link to Parakeet rather than copy the information.

In this chapter, we'll see other forms of sharing such as transclusion and dynamic list generation.

Consistency maintenance is easy to talk about, and wiki sysops are often sensitive to it, but the average wiki author does not think about it. He or she will blissfully create duplicate articles, copy and paste wikitext between articles, and insert irrelevant text, all in an attempt to write a "good" individual article. This redundancy seems to be a fact of wiki life. Even worse, there's "near redundancy," with similar articles saying slightly different things, causing confusion.

Sigmund Freud, the famous psychoanalyst, argued that there's a tension between what's good for the individual and what's good for the group. Wiki authors, for the most part, think about their individual needs when they write. Most do not plan up front, "Hmmm, I'm about to write three articles on similar topics. How shall I structure them to minimize redundancy?" No, they click "Edit", and away they go.

Great wiki authors do not just write great articles, they also structure those articles to be maintainable. Borrowing a term from the software community, we say that these maintainable articles are *well-factored*. When you move content between articles to make them more maintainable, this is called *refactoring* the content. Great wiki authors refactor while they write!

This chapter aims to convince you to write well-factored articles by:[*]

- Eliminating redundancy by identifying common content
- Consolidating the common content in a single place
- Referencing that single place wherever it is needed

Variables

We'll begin our study of sharing and good factoring with *variables*, the simplest type of MediaWiki magic word. A variable is merely a word that stands for a common value. For example, {{SITENAME}} stands for the name of the wiki, such as "Wikipedia" or "MyWiki":

```
Welcome to {{SITENAME}}! Please enjoy this wiki.
```

{{REVISIONDAY}}, {{REVISIONMONTH}}, and {{REVISIONYEAR}} become the day, month, and year (respectively) of an article's most recent revision:

```
This article was last modified on
{{REVISIONMONTH}}/{{REVISIONDAY}}/{{REVISIONYEAR}}.
```

---

[*] And "Ownership" on page 208 explains how to set up a well-organized wiki from the start.

To use a variable in an article, surround it with double curly braces:

```
{{variable name here}}
```

Variables reduce the need to copy (or "hardcode") common values into your articles. If an article uses {{SITENAME}} instead of the wiki's name, for instance, that article can be moved to another MediaWiki site and display the new wiki's name without modification. Or, if the wiki's name changes in the future, that article will not need to be changed.

The article *http://meta.wikimedia.org/wiki/Variable* documents all MediaWiki variables. We'll go into detail about a few useful ones.

The Wiki's Name

Avoid writing the wiki's name in articles, in case the name ever changes. There are several ways to do this:

In the text of articles
Use {{SITENAME}}, a variable that stands for the wiki's name.

```
Welcome to {{SITENAME}}!
```

As a namespace
MediaWiki creates a namespace with the same name as your wiki; for example, the wiki AnimalWiki would have an AnimalWiki: namespace. This namespace is known as the *project namespace*. Rather than hardcode this name in links, e.g., [[AnimalWiki:Contents]], use the name Project, which automatically resolves to the real name (e.g., Animal Wiki), making it more portable and maintainable:

```
See [[Project:Contents]] for more details
```

The syntax {{ns:project}} has the same effect as Project, but is more wordy. This technique uses the magic word ns (namespace).

Server Variables

{{SERVER}} is the base URL of the wiki, e.g., *http://wiki.example.com*, and {{SERVERNAME}} is just its fully qualified hostname (*wiki.example.com*). {{SCRIPTPATH}} is the virtual path to the PHP scripts that make up MediaWiki.

You might be tempted to construct URLs with these components in articles:

```
{{SERVER}}{{SCRIPTPATH}}/index.php
```

but resist the urge and use {{fullurl:}} instead (see "External Links to Yourself" on page 82).

Article Name Variables

You can refer to the current article name within an article by using the variable {{PAGENAME}} and other variables. While this variable can be used simply within articles:

```
Welcome to the "{{PAGENAME}}" article!
```

it will become more helpful later when you create templates in "Templates and Transclusion" on page 112. There are two such variables:

{{PAGENAME}}
> The article name alone, without its namespace

{{FULLPAGENAME}}
> The article name with its namespace

As an example, the following wikitext in the article Help:Dog:

```
Full name {{FULLPAGENAME}}, page name {{PAGENAME}}.
```

displays as:

> Full name Help:Dog, page name Dog.

Two related variables are used with subpages (introduced in "Subpages" on page 99):

{{SUBPAGENAME}}
> The name of the current subpage. (If not a subpage, then it's the same as {{PAGENAME}}.)

{{BASEPAGENAME}}
> The parent page of the current subpage. (If not a subpage, then it's the same as {{PAGENAME}}.)

So, the following wikitext in the subpage Help:My dog/Bark/Woof:

```
On {{FULLPAGENAME}}, we have a page named {{PAGENAME}},
with subpage {{SUBPAGENAME}} contained within {{BASEPAGENAME}}.
```

will display as:

> On Help:My dog/Bark/Woof, we have a page named My dog/Bark/Woof, with subpage Woof contained within My dog/Bark.

By convention, append an "E" to the variable name to encode its value for use in URLs. So if {{FULLPAGENAME}} is Help talk:Walk the dog, then {{FULLPAGE NAMEE}} is Help_talk:Walk_the_dog, and likewise for PAGENAMEE, SUBPAGENAMEE, and BASEPAGENAMEE.

Namespace Variables

Namespaces are always in pairs: an "article" namespace (such as User) paired with a "talk" namespace (User talk). The following variables hold namespace names:

{{SUBJECTSPACE}} *or* {{ARTICLESPACE}}
   The current "article" namespace, e.g., User

{{TALKSPACE}}
   The current "talk" namespace, e.g., User talk

{{NAMESPACE}}
   The namespace of the current page, regardless of whether it's a regular namespace or a talk namespace

You can see these variables in action here:

```
Welcome to this article in the {{NAMESPACE}} namespace.
The associated article namespace is {{SUBJECTSPACE}} and its
talk namespace is {{TALKSPACE}}.
```

Again by convention, append an "E" to the variable name to encode its value for use in URLs. So if {{TALKSPACE}} is User talk, then {{TALKSPACEE}} is User_talk, and so on.

Templates and Transclusion

Suppose you have three wiki pages about three kinds of dogs—Poodle, Collie, and Beagle—and you want each to begin with a common introduction:

```
This article is one in a series on dogs.
See [[:Category:Dogs]] to read the rest of these wonderful articles.
```

You could copy and paste this introduction into each of the dog articles, but this produces a consistency maintenance problem. As each page is edited in the future, each copy of the paragraph could change independently, and eventually they'll differ. You can avoid this inconsistency by writing the paragraph in a single wiki page and automatically making it appear wherever you need it. This process is called *transclusion.*[†]

MediaWiki provides a namespace devoted to transclusion, called Template. Articles in the Template namespace, known as *templates*, are designed to be transcluded into other articles. In our example, we could create a template (say, Template:Dog intro) and transclude it into each of our dog articles:

[†] Many programming languages have a similar feature: the #include statement in C and C++, the require statement in PHP, and so forth.

```
{{Dog intro}}
```

The double curly braces surround the name of the template, so in general the syntax is:

```
{{name of template here}}
```

To solve our earlier "three dog page" problem, we could create the article `Template:Dog intro` containing the introduction, and then place `{{Dog intro}}` at the top of our three articles. This example shows that templates are great for reusing wikitext in multiple articles. They not only save work but also keep the articles consistent with one another. Even better, if you modify the template, the change automatically applies to every article that transcludes it. So, modifying `Template:Dog intro` changes our three dog articles in one shot.

Templates are marvelously powerful. Wikipedia is filled with templates that display informational boxes, add superscripts and subscripts, mark articles for deletion, and much more. See *http://en.wikipedia.org/wiki/Wikipedia:Template _messages* for details. A good set of templates goes a long way toward setting up and enforcing wiki standards quite effectively.

Here's an example template that produces a black and yellow "Under Construction" box in an article. Place the following into `Template:Under construction`:

```
<div style="border:2px solid black; background-color:yellow">
This article is '''under construction'''.
Please do not rely on any information it contains.
</div>
```

Now, if you transclude it into any other article:

```
{{under construction}}
```

the box will appear.

Transclusion is a fundamental part of MediaWiki and is documented in detail at:

> *http://meta.wikimedia.org/wiki/Help:Template*
> *http://meta.wikimedia.org/wiki/Help:Embed_page*

Template Parameters

A template can be static, appearing identically each time it's transcluded. You can make templates more dynamic with *parameters*: values that you pass to a template to display or process. In this manner, the same template can serve multiple purposes, similar to a fill-in-the-blanks form letter.

Suppose that many of your articles have important notes that the reader should pay attention to, such as:

```
'''Note:''' Never feed cat food to your dog.
'''Note:''' Llamas are larger than frogs.
'''Note:''' Duck overpopulation is a serious problem.
```

If you want all these notes to have a consistent look, create a template for them, say, `Template:Note`. The word "Note" is constant but the message may vary, so define a template parameter. This is easy—just pick a name (say, "message") and surround it with *triple* curly braces in the template:

```
{{{message}}}
```

So, you'd create `Template:Note` as:

```
'''Note:''' {{{message}}}
```

Now you've defined a `Note` template with a single parameter: `message`. To transclude this template into another article, write:

```
{{Note | message=Never feed cat food to your dog.}}
```

assigning a value to the `message` parameter. Here is the general syntax for using a template:

```
{{name of template
| parameter1=value1
| parameter2=value2
| parameter3=value3
...
}}
```

This layout, with the template name on a line by itself and each parameter on a subsequent line, is quite common and considered good style. Our `Note` template in this layout would look like:

```
{{Note
| message=Never feed cat food to your dog.
}}
```

Parameters can also be *positional*, referenced by number rather than by name, The first parameter is `{{{1}}}`, the second is `{{{2}}}`, and so on. For example, you could write `Template:Note` as:

```
'''Note:''' {{{1}}}
```

Templates with positional parameters are transcluded by providing their values in order, separated by pipe symbols:

```
{{Note | Never feed cat food to your dog.}}
```

Positional parameters are concise but rigid: their values must be supplied in order when transcluding. Named parameters are clearer for documentation, however, and their values can be provided in any order. This book uses named parameters in all future examples.

Nesting Templates

Templates can transclude other templates. For instance, if `Template:One` contains `{{two}}`, `Template:Two` contains `{{three}}`, and `Template:Three` contains "woof", then `{{one}}` becomes "woof", as each template transcludes the next.

As a more practical example, we'll create `Template:Notable` to generalize the `Template:Note` we created earlier. `Template:Notable` has a `message` parameter just like `Template:Note`, but makes the bold heading a parameter as well:

```
'''{{{heading}}}:''' {{{message}}}
```

So, for example:

```
{{notable
|heading=Warning
|message=Dogs may bite and cats may scratch!
}}
```

displays:

Warning: Dogs may bite and cats may scratch!

Because templates can nest, we can redefine `Template:Note` in terms of `Template:Notable`, as:

```
{{notable
|heading=Note
|message={{{message}}}
}}
```

with the benefit that modifying `Template:Notable` will also change `Template:Note`. In fact, with `Template:Notable` we can define a whole family of similar messages such as `Template:Warning`:

```
{{notable
|heading=Warning
|message={{{message}}}
}}
```

and `Template:Tip`, which adds an attribution after the message, telling us which user suggested the tip:

```
{{notable
|heading=Tip
|message={{{message}}} (Submitted by [[User:{{{username}}}]].)
}}
```

So, transcluding `Template:Tip` would look like:

```
{{tip
|message=Don't bathe your parakeet in cold water.
|username=Jsmith
}}
```

which displays as:

> **Tip:** Don't bathe your parakeet in cold water. (Submitted by <u>User:Jsmith</u>.)

All of these different templates defined in terms of `Template:Notable` not only have a consistent look and feel, but can also be changed together by redefining `Template:Notable`. For instance, `Template:Notable` could box the messages:

```
<div style="border:1px solid black">
'''{{heading}}}:''' {{{message}}}
</div>
```

Or, if you're a wiki sysop, you could define a CSS style "notable" for the wiki and have `Template:Notable` use it:

```
<div class="notable">
<span>{{{heading}}}:</span> {{{message}}}
</div>
```

placing the CSS in `MediaWiki:Common.css` (see "CSS for All Pages" on page 267):

```
div.notable { border: 1px solid black; }
div.notable span { font-weight: bold; }
```

Default Values for Parameters

If you don't supply a value for a parameter, the template will display the parameter name. So, `{{note}}` alone would display:

Note: {{{message}}}

You can change this behavior by providing default values for parameters. In the template, instead of defining a parameter as:

{{{*parametername*}}}

add a default value after a pipe symbol:

{{{*parametername* | *default value*}}}

If no such parameter is passed to this template, the default value will display instead. For a blank default value, put nothing after the pipe symbol. For example, in `Template:Notable`, to supply a default heading of "Hey you" and a default blank message, change the template to:

'''{{{heading|Hey you}}}:''' {{{message|}}}

Conditional Transclusion

Within a template, you can designate parts of the wikitext *not* to be transcluded via several tags:

`<noinclude>`

Don't transclude this text. Display it only when the containing article (e.g., `Template:Notable`) is viewed directly.

`<includeonly>`

Don't display this text on the containing page (e.g., `Template:Notable`). Display it only when transcluding.

`<onlyinclude>`

Transclude only the contents of this tag, suppressing all other wikitext in the article. Inside the `<onlyinclude>` tag, any nested `<noinclude>` and `<includeonly>` tags behave normally.

For example, for `Template:Dog intro`:

```
This article is one of a series on dogs. See
[[:Category:Dogs]] to read the rest of these wonderful articles.
```

suppose you want to document the template's purpose, but not have the documentation show up when transcluded. Just use `<noinclude>`:

```
<noinclude>Place this template at the top of each Dog article.
== The template ==
</noinclude>This article is one of a series on dogs. See
[[:Category:Dogs]] to read the rest of these wonderful articles.
```

When you view `Template:Dog` intro, it appears as:

Place this template at the top of each Dog article.

The template

This article is one of a series on dogs. See Category:Dogs to read the rest of these wonderful articles.

but when it's transcluded, you see only:

This article is one of a series on dogs. See Category:Dogs to read the rest of these wonderful articles.

`<noinclude>` is also great for categorizing the template without categorizing the transcluding page:

```
<noinclude>[[Category:Article introductions]]</noinclude>
```

This category, if placed in `Template:Dog intro`, gets applied to `Template:Dog intro`, but to not the articles that transclude it.

`<includeonly>` is helpful for categorizing every article that includes a template. For example, if we place this into `Template:Dog intro`:

```
<includeonly>[[Category:Articles that use the dog intro]]</includeonly>
```

it will tag every transcluding article with the category, but will not tag `Template:Dog intro` itself.

Table 7-1 summarizes the conditional transclusion tags.

Table 7-1. Conditional transclusion tags

Tag	Visible in original article	Visible when transcluded	Useful for
`<noinclude>`	Y	N	Categorizing templates; documenting templates
`<includeonly>`	N	Y, if there's no `<onlyinclude>` tag	Categorizing the transcluding articles
`<onlyinclude>`	Y	Y, and suppresses *all* wikitext in the article *outside* of `<onlyinclude>` tags	Quickly overriding all other content in an article; nested `<noinclude>` and `<includeonly>` tags work as expected

Transcluding Whitespace

Watch out for whitespace when transcluding templates. Innocent-looking linebreaks in a template can lead to unsightly gaps in their transcluding articles, especially around `<noinclude>` tags. If you transclude this template:

```
<noinclude>
Don't include me
</noinclude>
Include me
```

the result is *not* "Include me". You get "Include me" preceded by a newline, which causes a paragraph break in the transcluding article. You want:

```
<noinclude>
Don't include me
</noinclude>Include me
```

Intentional whitespace inside of tags is fine:

```
<noinclude>
Don't include me
la la la
lots

and
lots of

space!!
</noinclude>Include me
```

The problem is whitespace *surrounding* the tags, including newlines, that shows up unexpectedly in transclusion. A classic example is categorizing a template. Suppose that `Template:Phone` contains a phone number:

```
555-1212
```

and you want to categorize the template without categorizing the transcluding pages:

```
555-1212
<noinclude>[[Category:Phone numbers]]</noinclude>
```

Looks innocent, but when you transclude it:

```
Call {{Phone}} for more information
```

you'll get an unwanted line break after the phone number. To avoid this problem, remove the surrounding whitespace:

```
555-1212<noinclude>[[Category:Phone numbers]]</noinclude>
```

or for clarity, since whitespace inside the tag won't cause problems, use:

```
555-1212<noinclude>
[[Category:Phone numbers]]
</noinclude>
```

Categorizing Templates

Templates are articles, so they may contain all the features of articles, including category tags. If you simply add a category tag, however:

```
This is a fun template.
[[Category:Fun templates]]
```

you will categorize not only the template, but also any article that transcludes it, as the category tag gets transcluded, too. To categorize only the template, use:

```
<noinclude>[[Category:Fun templates]]</noinclude>
```

To categorize only the transcluding articles, use:

```
<includeonly>[[Category:Fun articles]]</includeonly>
```

This last case is great for automatically categorizing articles that use the same template. For example, in our Dog intro template from "Templates and Transclusion" on page 112, we could add:

```
<includeonly>[[Category:Dogs]]</includeonly>
```

and any article that transcludes Template:Dog intro will automatically be added to the Dogs category. Consistency maintenance indeed!

Transcluding Any Article

Articles in other namespaces—not only the Template namespace—can be transcluded, too, as long as the wiki administrator permits it. In general, to transclude one page into another, surround the entire page name with double curly braces:

```
{{namespace:article name}}
```

If the article is in the main namespace, omit the namespace, but include the colon:

```
{{:article name}}
```

If you omit the colon, the article is assumed to be in the `Template` namespace, which is one reason the `Template` namespace is so convenient for transclusion:

```
{{my template name}}
```

The `Template` namespace is the preferred source of transcludable articles and snippets of wikitext. Although you can transclude articles from other namespaces, most full articles are not designed with transclusion in mind, and so can produce unwanted side effects. For instance, article authors don't usually think about enclosing their category tags in `<noinclude>`.

For example, if article `Dog` transcludes article `Cat`, and `Cat` is in the category `Felines`, then `Dog` will automatically be placed in `Felines` as well (because the `[[Category:Cat]]` gets transcluded into `Dog`). You can easily get around these issues, but most article authors do not think about them when writing, whereas template authors learn to do so.

Transcluding Subpages

Transclusion with subpages is not that different from transclusion with regular articles. Suppose you have an article `Dog` with subpages `woof` and `bark`. From another article, you can transclude `Dog/woof` with:

```
{{:Dog/woof}}
```

From within the `Dog` article, you can transclude the `woof` subpage as above, but it's simpler to write:

```
{{/woof}}
```

In the other direction, from within the `woof` subpage, you can transclude the parent article using the `BASEPAGENAME` variable:

```
{{ {{BASEPAGENAME}} }}
```

or with Linux-like `..` syntax:

```
{{../}}
```

Finally, from within `Dog/woof`, you can transclude your sibling subpage `Dog/bark` with:

```
{{../bark}}
```

A great example of transcluding subpages is found on Wikipedia in `Template:Documentation`, a template for documenting other templates:

http://en.wikipedia.org/wiki/Template:Documentation

In the following example, we'll mimic Wikipedia's documentation system for templates, much simplified. Usage instructions for any template *T* are kept in a subpage, `Template:T/doc`, and are automatically displayed when you visit the template; however, the instructions do not appear when the template is transcluded. This has the nice effect that the template's "code" and instructions are kept separate.

 This example requires that the `Template` namespace support subpages, which requires the wiki administrator to enable this feature in *LocalSettings.php*:

```
$wgNamespacesWithSubpages[NS_TEMPLATE] = true;
```

Create the article `Template:Documentation`:

```
<div style="border:1px solid black; background-color:#aaffaa">
== Documentation ==
{{ {{BASEPAGENAME}}/doc }}
</div>
```

Notice that this template transcludes a subpage named **doc** relative to the current article, whatever that article might be. If transcluded in an article (say) `Template:Dog food`:

```
{{documentation}}
```

this template transcludes and displays `Template:Dog food/doc` in turn. Moreover, if we transclude the `Documentation` template within a `<noinclude>` tag:

```
<noinclude>{{documentation}}</noinclude>
```

the instructions in `Template:Dog food/doc` are displayed only when we view the `Template:Dog food` article directly, not when it's transcluded. This is the secret behind `Template:Documentation`.

Let's apply this method to document the "under construction" template we created in "Templates and Transclusion" on page 112:

```
<div style="border:2px solid black; background-color:yellow">
This article is '''under construction'''.
Please do not rely on any information it contains.
</div><noinclude>{{documentation}}</noinclude>
```

This transcludes the Documentation template, which, by referring to the *current article* as BASEPAGENAME, transcludes in turn the current article's /doc subpage, if it exists. Therefore, when you view Template:Under construction directly, the contents of Template:Under construction/doc is transcluded and displayed.‡

Don't like the heading "Documentation" appearing at the top? Let's modify Template:Documentaion to pass a heading as a parameter, but keep "Documentation" as the default:

```
<div style="border:1px solid black; background-color:#aaffaa">
== {{{heading|Documentation}}} ==
{{ {{PAGENAME}}/doc }}
</div>
```

Now, we write:

```
<noinclude>{{documentation | heading=About this template}}</noinclude>
```

and the supplied heading is used instead of the default.

Logical Parser Functions

A *parser function* is a magic word with dynamic behavior in a wiki article. Parser functions can display text and images, produce fill-in-the-blanks forms, retrieve data from remote systems, send email, and do pretty much anything else a web page can do. We've already seen one parser function, fullurl, that emits URLs of wiki pages (see "External Links to Yourself" on page 82).

Now we'll look at a third-party extension, with the overly generic name ParserFunctions, that adds logical if/then/else functionality to wiki articles via parser functions. ParserFunctions is installed on Wikipedia and is available for other MediaWiki sites (see "Parser function extensions" on page 279).

 We'll see other parser functions later in this chapter: #dpl and #tag. We'll also create custom parser functions in Chapter 15.

ParserFunctions provides the following logical functions:*

---

‡ If the doc subpage does not exist, Template:Under construction will display a link to it. We'll improve this behavior in "Logical Parser Functions" on page 122 by displaying a warning message in undocumented templates.

* As well as other functions not discussed here: #expr, #switch, #time, #rel2abs, #titleparts, and #iferror.

#ifexist
> Test if a wiki article exists

#if
> Test if a string has a nonempty value

#ifeq
> Test if two strings or numbers are equal

#ifexpr
> Test an arithmetic expression

Each of these is used similarly:

```
{{#function: expression
| wikitext displayed if expression is true
| wikitext displayed if expression is false
}}
```

The "false" or "else" case is optional and can be omitted:

```
{{#function: expression
| wikitext displayed if expression is true
}}
```

The simplest of these parser functions is #ifexist, which tests whether an article exists. For example, this function call:

```
{{#ifexist: my page
| My page does exist
| Sorry, it does not exist
}}
```

will print "My page does exist" if the article my page exists, and the "Sorry" message otherwise. As a practical example, extend Template:Documentation, from "Transcluding Subpages" on page 120", to display a warning if a template is undocumented:

```
<div style="border:1px solid black; background-color:#aaffaa">
== Documentation ==
{{#ifexist:{{PAGENAME}}/doc
| {{ {{PAGENAME}}/doc }}
| No documentation exists. Please [[{{PAGENAME}}/doc|create it]].
}}
</div>
```

The #if function merely tests if a string has a nonempty value, which is useful for avoiding errors when another magic word returns nothing:

```
{{#if: {{my fancy template}}
| The template produced something!
| No it didn't.
}}
```

The #ifeq function is useful for testing variables. Here, we print a message that depends on SITENAME (the wiki's name):

```
{{#ifeq: {{SITENAME}} | AnimalWiki
| Welcome to the Animal Wiki!
| Welcome to the unknown wiki site
}}
```

or, more compactly:

```
Welcome to the {{#ifeq: {{SITENAME}} | AnimalWiki
| Animal Wiki!
| unknown wiki site
}}
```

The string comparison is case-sensitive. To make it case-insensitive, use MediaWiki's built-in parser function uc to convert strings to uppercase:

```
{{#ifeq: {{uc:{{SITENAME}}}} | ANIMALWIKI
| Welcome to the Animal Wiki!
| Welcome to the unknown wiki site
}}
```

The #ifexpr function evaluates arithmetic and Boolean expressions. For example, to display a message on odd days of the month, we use the mod operator on the day of the month variable:

```
{{#ifexpr: {{CURRENTDAY}} mod 2 = 1
| I am feeling rather odd today!
}}
```

All of these logical functions can be nested, of course, to produce complex if/then/else structures:

```
{{#if: condition1
| {{#if: condition2
|   {{#if: condition3
|     true block 3
|     false block 3
|   }}
|   false block 2
| }}
| false block 1
}}
```

See *http://meta.wikimedia.org/wiki/ParserFunctions* for documentation on all the parser functions in this extension.

Dynamic Page List

Dynamic Page List (DPL) is perhaps the most powerful, flexible, and downright useful MediaWiki extension ever made. Period. It is the Swiss army knife of MediaWiki, with a million household uses. Here's how it works:

1. You hand DPL a set of criteria.
2. DPL locates all articles that match those criteria.
3. DPL hands you a list of those articles, typeset however you request.

For example, you could ask DPL, "Please give me all articles written by user Joe in either the Mammals or Reptiles categories, but not the Cats category, typeset as a numbered list of links, sorted by the article's last edit date, most recent first." In technical terms, DPL lets wiki authors query the MediaWiki database and return arbitrary subsets of articles in various formats (lists, tables, etc.), embedding them in an article.

DPL is a third-party extension. For further discussion, see "Dynamic Page List" on page 278. You won't find it on Wikipedia (at least, not at press time), but a wiki administrator can download and install it easily.

 Getting started with DPL is easy, but for anything complex, expect to keep the (huge) DPL manual onscreen while you work. There are nearly 100 optional parameters, some with complicated syntax. The results are worth the effort, though!

Basic DPL Lists

The simplest DPL example is to display all items in a category as a bulleted list. If your category is Stuff, write:

```
<dpl>
category = Stuff
</dpl>
```

 `<dpl>` is an example of a parser tag extension; see "Creating a Tag Extension" on page 294.

You can split the list into multiple columns with the columns parameter:

```
<dpl>
category = Stuff
columns = 3
</dpl>
```

If you never go any farther than this with DPL, you're still reaping the benefits. But you can do so much more. DPL will display other list formats selected by the mode parameter, such as numbered lists:

```
<dpl>
category = Stuff
```

```
mode = ordered
</dpl>
```

plain lists with no decorations, one item per line:

```
<dpl>
category = Stuff
mode = none
</dpl>
```

inline lists, with all items on the same line, separated by any text or symbols you like (determined by the `inlinetext` parameter, here set to a comma):

```
<dpl>
category = Stuff
mode = inline
inlinetext = ,
</dpl>
```

or a format very similar to category pages:

```
<dpl>
category = Stuff
mode = category
</dpl>
```

DPL can also include and exclude articles based on many criteria, control the sort order of the items in over a dozen ways, include data about authorship and edit times, suppress duplicates, and much more. Want to see all articles in the `Stuff` category except those in the `Talk` namespace, along with the name of the last user to edit it, sorted by last modified date, most recent first?

```
<dpl>
category = Stuff
notnamespace = Talk
addlasteditor = yes
ordermethod = lastedit
order = descending
</dpl>
```

DPL has a second syntax as a parser function, `#dpl`, for times when a parser tag won't do (see the sidebar "Parsing Order and #tag"). All the parameters remain the same; you just write them in parser function syntax. The preceding example would be:

```
{{#dpl:
| category = Stuff
| notnamespace = Talk
| addlasteditor = yes
| ordermethod = lastedit
| order = descending
}}
```

Parsing Order and #tag

The software that turns wikitext into displayable HTML is called the *parser*. As the parser reads the various symbols and magic words in an article, it considers them in a particular order, called the *parsing order*. For example, this wikitext:

```
'''[[dog]]]'''
```

is turned into a bold link by the parser because it first processes the link and then makes it bold. This similar wikitext, however:

```
[[''' 'dog''']]
```

is merely the bolded word "dog" inside double square brackets, as the parser processes the bolding first, which makes "dog" no longer an article name, but simply a bolded word. So, parsing order is very important, though usually, most wiki authors don't need to think about it.

Parsing order becomes apparent and tricky with templates, parser functions, and parser tags. Some combinations work and some simply don't. For example, suppose you'd like to pass some DPL output to `Template:Note` (from "Template Parameters" on page 113):

```
{{Note
| message=My favorite animals are <dpl>category=favorite animals</dpl>
}}
```

In this case, the MediaWiki parser treats the entire message as wikitext and never recognizes `<dpl>` as a parser tag, displaying:

Note: My favorite animals are <dpl>category=favorite animals</dpl>

This is why some extensions like Dynamic Page List include tag (`<dpl>`) and parser function (`{{#dpl:}}`) syntax, so the feature works in a variety of contexts. The following will work as expected:

```
{{Note:
| message=My favorite animals are {{#dpl:category=favorite animals}}
}}
```

For the many parser tags that do not support parser function syntax, MediaWiki defines a special parser function called **#tag** that converts a parser tag into a parser function call. Instead of:

```
<mytag attr1="one" attr2="two">Here is my body</mytag>
```

you write:

```
{{#tag:mytag
| Here is my body
| attr1=one
| attr2=two
}}
```

which evaluates correctly in a parser function context. Use #tag when mixing parser tags and parser functions in ways that don't work, like passing a template as a tag attribute:

```
<mytag attr1="{{my template here}}">my body</mytag>
```

This passes the literal string "{{my template here}}" as the attribute value, which is not what was intended. Work around the problem by using #tag:

```
{{#tag:mytag
| my body
| attr1={{my template here}}
}}
```

Intermediate DPL: Custom Formats

In addition to the basic list formats shown earlier, DPL lets you define custom layouts using the format parameter. The format specification consists of four wikitext values separated by commas:

```
format = ListStart,ItemStart,ItemEnd,ListEnd
```

where the values are displayed as follows:

ListStart
> Wikitext displayed at the beginning of the entire list

ItemStart
> Wikitext displayed before each list item

ItemEnd
> Wikitext displayed after each list item

ListEnd
> Wikitext displayed at the end of the entire list

Whitespace is significant. Always provide all four values (i.e., include all three commas), even if the values are empty. Here's an artificial example to illustrate the roles of each value. Suppose your category has three articles called page1, page2, and page3. This DPL tag:

```
<dpl>
Category = Stuff
format = Begin, XX,YY ,End
</dpl>
```

produces a list starting with Begin and ending with End, with each element surrounded by XX and YY:

Begin XXpage1YY XXpage2YY XXpage3YY End

As a more concrete example, to produce a numbered list of articles with any namespaces removed, use:

```
format = ,\n#[[%PAGE%|%TITLE%]],,
```

In this case, we precede each entry with a newline (\n) and a hash mark (for numbering). The entry itself is a link to %PAGE%, which represents the article's full title, with alternate text %TITLE%, which is the article name with no namespace. See, the syntax gets complicated. Pull up the DPL manual and have fun.

Advanced DPL: Metadata

In this section, we'll use dummy templates to attach metadata to a set of articles, and then use DPL to extract and display the metadata. This technique has so many possibilities that you'll need to refer to the DPL manual for full details.

Suppose you have a category called Mammals that contains the articles Dog, Cat, Mouse, and Wombat. From them, you'd like to produce a list or table of mammals automatically, containing the mammal name (a link to the article) and a brief sentence describing the animal. DPL is capable of extracting and displaying text from articles with its include option:

```
<dpl>
category = Mammals
include = %0[100]
format = ,\n\n[[%PAGE%]]: ,,
</dpl>
```

In this example, we display each link preceded by two newlines and followed by a colon (thanks to format), and then the first 100 characters of the article (thanks to include). For our purposes, this might work, but more likely the first 100 characters of each article will be too inconsistent to produce a useful list. If only each article had a single sentence describing each animal briefly, so we could extract and print it! But restructuring all those articles to contain those sentences might be time consuming, and could produce awkward-looking articles.

One solution is to use *metadata*: pairs of keywords and values embedded in an article. Metadata is implemented using a template. Let's invent one called mammal info, which we transclude in each article in the Mammals category. Here's what it would look like in the Dog article:

```
{{mammal info
| description = A friendly and intelligent mammal that barks.
| habitat = land
| legs = 4
| ...
}}
```

At first glance, this looks like an ordinary use of a template. But here's the funny part: your template *doesn't have to do anything*. The contents of `Template:Mammal info` can be completely blank, and it needn't use its parameters (e.g., `description`). As metadata, this template is simply a convenient container for parameter names and their values; its own body is irrelevant. The DPL tag, however, can access those parameters and values in every `Mammals` article and achieve the result we're looking for. An `include` value like this:

```
include = {mammal info}:description
```

means "from each article, within its `mammal info` template, grab the parameter `description`." When paired with an appropriate `format` value:

```
<dpl>
category = Mammals
include = {mammal info}:description
format = ,* [[%PAGE%]]: ,\n,
</dpl>
```

this produces a bulleted list (thanks to the * and \n) of descriptions, preceded by the article link (`[[%PAGE%]]`):

- <u>Cat</u>: A feline pal that meows.
- <u>Dog</u>: A friendly and intelligent mammal that barks.

 Our template body is empty, but you *could* do fancy tricks inside it. For example, you could insert a `Mammals` category tag to categorize each article automatically.

Our example accesses only one metadata value, `description`, and displays it simply. To access multiple parameters (say, `description` and `legs`) and display them in a more interesting manner, we'll demonstrate DPL's ability to use a second template for layout.[†]

Define a second template that represents your desired display of the metadata:

```
- {{{description}}} (Has {{{legs}}} legs.)
```

(There's a leading space before the dash.) This second template must adhere to a few rules for this technique to work:

- Its parameters must be the same as the original's (e.g., `description`, `habitat`, `legs`).

[†] At press time, DPL version 1.7.4 has no way to access multiple parameters directly in the `format` value, so we are forced into this more complicated implementation. We're able to do it using the `tablerow` option, however, as we'll see later in the section.

- Its name must be identical to the first one (`Template:Mammal info`) followed by additional characters, traditionally `.dpl`. Ours will be called `Template:Mammal info.dpl`.

Now create this deceptively simple-looking DPL tag:

```
<dpl>
category = Mammals
include = {mammal info}.dpl
</dpl>
```

and lo and behold, you get:

- <u>Cat</u> - A feline pal that meows. (Has 4 legs.)
- <u>Dog</u> - A friendly and intelligent mammal that barks. (Has 4 legs.)

The `include` line `{mammal info}.dpl` means "get values from `mammal info` and pass them to `mammal info.dpl`."

Let's review the general method to display articles of interest with metadata:

1. Pick your articles of interest. Suppose they are all in a category C. (You can use any DPL features to select these articles; a category is the easiest.)

2. Invent your metadata: a set of named parameters related to articles in your category C.

3. Create a template, T. Its contents do not matter. It's just going to be a dumb container for your metadata.

4. In every article of interest, transclude template T, setting values for your metadata parameters:

```
{{T
| param1 = A
| param2 = B
| ...
}}
```

5. Create a second template, T.`dpl`, to illustrate how your metadata parameters should be displayed:

```
- My {{param1}} ate my {{param2}}.
```

6. In some article, create a DPL tag that selects your articles of interest (using the template T):

```
<dpl>
category = C
include = {T}.dpl
</dpl>
```

7. Your list of articles gets displayed!

- article1 - My dinosaur ate my bird.

- article2 - My horse ate my cow.
- ...

This technique of using templates for metadata has many variations. For example, you can use DPL's `table` and `tablerow` parameters to typeset the metadata as a table:

```
<dpl>
category = Mammals
include = {mammal info}:habitat:description
table = style="border:1px solid black",Animal,Home,About
tablerow = %%,%%
</dpl>
```

where `table` lists the table's CSS style and headings (separated by commas), and `tablerow` describes the format of one row (two values separated by commas, representing the second and third columns; the first column contains the article link and is implied). The syntax `%%` means "the next template parameter, in the order listed," so the first `%%` means `habitat` and the second means `description`.

Whew! As mentioned previously, DPL syntax really does get complex and you'll need the manual in front of you most of the time. We hope you'll find that the results are worth the effort, however. Once you set up a DPL tag, it just keeps working, and you can forget about it.

Recipes for Refactoring

Now that you've seen templates, parser functions, and DPL, let's put them to work to combat redundant content. Have you found some articles that contain exactly the same text? Do you need to avoid repeating yourself in multiple articles? Are you tired of maintaining lists of similar links manually? Here are several common patterns for addressing these issues.

Recipe 1: Promote and Link

This simple recipe moves redundant content to a single location and links to it from its former locations.

For example, if the articles `Collie`, `Beagle`, and `Chihuahua` all discuss the same dog diseases and treatments, move that content into a new article, `dog diseases`, and link to it from all three. This recipe is best when the redundant information is large or stands on its own.

Recipe 2: Transclude

This recipe moves redundant content to a template and transcludes it into its former locations.

For instance, if all dog articles contain the same telephone number:

```
During a dog emergency, call 555-1234.
```

move the number to `Template:Dog emergency telephone number` and transclude it into the articles:

```
During a dog emergency, call {{dog emergency telephone number}}.
```

This is preferable to linking because the phone number alone would not be a useful article.

Recipe 3: Share Structure with Parameters

This recipe addresses redundant structure or layout, rather than content. It creates a template to hold the structure, and represents the content by template parameters. Use the template in all articles that need the common structure.

An example is `Template:Notable` from "Nesting Templates" on page 115:

```
<div class="notable">
<span>{{{heading}}}:</span> {{{message}}}
</div>
```

The `heading` and `message` parameters make the template reusable in many situations.

Recipe 4: Share Structure with Subpages

This recipe, like the previous one, addresses redundant structure or layout, but instead of using parameters, it places the content into transcluded subpages. Use the template in all articles that need the common structure.[‡] Wikipedia's `Template:Documentation`, discussed in "Transcluding Subpages" on page 120, uses this recipe.

As another example, suppose you're creating a corporate intranet where each department has a wiki article with a standard layout. Define a template (say, `Template:Department page`) to hold the layout, and assume test subpages will hold the content:

```
<div id="header">{{global header}}</div>
<div id="welcome">{{/welcome}}</div>
```

[‡] Articles that use this method must be in namespaces that permit subpages.

```
<div id="content">{{/content}}</div>
<div id="footer">{{global footer}}</div>
```

Now, each departmental wiki article becomes simply:

```
{{department page}}
```

If the article `Sales Department` transcludes this template, it will render four `div` regions containing the contents of:

```
Template:Global header
Template:Sales Department/welcome
Template:Sales Department/content
Template:Global footer
```

All articles containing `{{department page}}` will have the same header and footer, with overall layout controllable via CSS thanks to the `<div>` IDs.

 To ensure that a table of contents does not appear and disturb the layout, add `__NOTOC__` to the template. (See "Table of Contents" on page 53.)

To prevent unauthorized changes to the structure of these articles, protect `Template:Department page`, `Template:Global header`, and `Template:Global footer` from modification (see "Protecting Articles" on page 242), while still permitting edits to the subpages `welcome` and `content`.

This is a subtle recipe, so try it out. If your wiki doesn't permit subpages in the main namespace, experiment by transcluding your templates within the `Talk` namespace or others that traditionally support subpages.

Recipe 5: Generate Lists of Links

This recipe is for multiple articles that contain the same list of wiki links, manually maintained. It collects the linked articles into a category and generates the list automatically within each article, using DPL. Optionally, place the DPL code into a template and transclude it.

An example is a "See Also" template for a series of related articles. Suppose you're writing a set of articles on the best pets for hackers. At the end of each article, you'd like to include a "See Also" section that lists all the other pets. This is easily done with DPL:

1. Put all your articles in a category, `Hacker pets`.
2. Create `Template:Hacker pet list` containing:

   ```
   == Other pets for hackers ==
   <dpl>
   ```

```
category = Hacker pets
</dpl>
```

3. At the end of each article, add:

```
{{hacker pet list}}
```

which will list all other hacker pets (not including the pet that is the subject of the current article because DPL automatically omits the transcluding article from the list).

Another example is creating a navigation bar across the tops of a series of articles. Place all the "navigation" articles into a category (say, `Navigation`), and put the following DPL tag into a template transcluded into all the articles:

```
<dpl>
category = Navigation
mode = inline
inlinetext =  &bull; 
shownamespace = false
skipthispage = false
</dpl>
```

This produces the list of navigation titles in a single row, separated by bullet symbols.

A crucial parameter is `skipthispage=false`, which forces the current article into the navigation bar as well. When an article links to itself, no link is rendered, just bolded text. So, the current article title will always be bolded in the list, providing that familiar "navigation" feel as you move from article to article.

Recipe 6: Split and Generate

This recipe is for an article that is a collection of related topics, instead of a single topic. It splits the topics into separate articles and generates the original collection automatically with DPL.

A classic example is a glossary of terms. You might be tempted to create a wiki article called `Glossary` and define lots of terms within it, but this is a consistency maintenance problem waiting to happen, as the glossary definitions likely repeat information from the linked articles. Instead, use a separate article (new or existing) named for each term, put all these articles into a category called `Glossary terms`, and replace your old `Glossary` article content with:

```
<dpl>
category = Glossary terms
</dpl>
```

Or, create a fancier DPL tag that transcludes the first 60 characters of each definition into the list:

```
<dpl>
category = Glossary terms
format = ,;[[%PAGE%|%TITLE%]]:,\n\n
includepage = %0[60]
notnamespace = Category
</dpl>
```

which produces:

> *Aardvark*
> A mammal with a long snout that eats...
>
> *Bear*
> A grizzly mammal that lives in the woods...

It might seem wasteful to have separate articles for each term, particularly if the definitions are short, but this method is superior to a plain glossary page for several reasons:

- Because all terms are actually articles, other articles can link to them easily.

- When someone wants to look up an unfamiliar term, he's going to search for the term itself, not for "glossary". With this recipe, you get a page for each term (simplifying the search), plus a glossary list for free.

- If the term is defined in a glossary page, chances are it's defined elsewhere, too (say, in the most important article that uses the term), which will be redundant. The two definitions will get out of sync as one changes and the other doesn't.

To end this chapter with a grand finale, let's grab the introductory text from each article (up to its first heading, `include=%0`) and display it in sections (`format`) that link back to each article. We'll also put this code into a template so the author can pass in a category name parameter, `category`, with `Glossary terms` as the default. (In order to do this, we must switch to parser function syntax, `#dpl`.) This code also sorts case insensitively (`ordercollation`), trims whitespace (`includetrim`), avoids articles in the `Category` and `Template` namespaces (`notnamespace`) so we don't get unwanted transclusions, but includes redirects (`redirects`), and prevents category tags from being transcluded into the glossary (`reset`). Finally, we'll provide text to display if no articles are found (`noresultsheader`), and here we have `Template:Glossary builder`:

```
{{#dpl:
|category = {{{category|Glossary terms}}}
|format = ,\n==[[%PAGE%|%TITLE%]]==\n\n,,
|notnamespace = Category
|notnamespace = Template
|include = %0
|includetrim = true
|noresultsheader = No glossary entries
|redirects = include
|ordercollation = latin1_general_ci
|reset = categories
}}
```

Now, go read that DPL manual and have fun!

## CHAPTER 8

Special Pages

Most MediaWiki pages are articles, but some are web applications called *special pages*. We've encountered several of them:

- The search results page ("Searching for Articles" on page 12)
- A list of all articles in the wiki ("Namespaces" on page 16)
- The login page ("Logging In and Out" on page 30)
- Your preferences page ("Preferences" on page 35)
- The file upload page ("Uploading a File" on page 57)
- A list of all categories ("Adding an Article to a Category" on page 90)

and there are dozens of others with diverse purposes.

Special pages live in the `Special` namespace, and have names such as `Special:AllPages` and `Special:Categories`. You can jump to a special page by entering its name in the search box, browse special pages by clicking the Toolbox link "Special pages", or link to them by name (e.g., `[[Special:Upload]]`). You'll also find their links sprinkled around the wiki, such as the Move tab for renaming articles (leading to `Special:Move`) and many links in the user options and toolbox menus.

In this chapter, we'll cover the special pages included with MediaWiki and a few others found on Wikipedia. Some special pages will be immediately useful, while others might seem obscure to all but wiki administrators. Because there are so many special pages, this book presents them in three different ways:

- The following sections cover the special pages in the default order in which they appear on `Special:SpecialPages`, where they are grouped by purpose.[*]
- "Special Pages Grouped by Task" on page 165 presents the special pages in terms of tasks you may be trying to accomplish.
- Finally, the special pages are listed alphabetically in the index (see the entries of the form "Special:..").

> Some special pages are extensions (see Chapter 14) and not found on all MediaWiki sites. You will surely find special pages on Wikipedia that are not documented here.

Spend 15 minutes trying out all the special pages: you'll be glad you did. They make life with MediaWiki more convenient and illustrate its power for organizing information. And, if you can't find a special page that does what you want, you'll see how to locate and install them in Chapter 14, and even how to program your own in Chapter 15.

> Some special pages require permissions to view because they perform system administration tasks, like granting privileges to users (`Special:UserRights`) and blocking wiki access (`Special:BlockIP`). These appear in the special pages list, bolded, if you're logged in as a wiki sysop or bureaucrat (see "Administrative Roles" on page 216).

Maintenance Reports

Beginning at the top of the list, maintenance reports are special pages to monitor problems and inconsistencies to be fixed. When articles are changed by many people over a long time, they can become sloppy, inconsistent, disorganized, or full of "cruft"—content that seemed like a good idea at the time, but is now unused. These special pages help keep a wiki neat and tidy.

Broken Redirects

`Special:BrokenRedirects`: *List redirects that point to nonexistent pages*

---

[*] Your wiki's `Special:SpecialPages` might group them differently or present them as one alphabetical list, depending on the version of MediaWiki and the whims of the wiki administrator (see "Special Page List" on page 252).

Redirects (see "Redirects" on page 101) are a handy feature of MediaWiki, providing an alternate name for an article. For example, `Canines` could be a redirect to `Dogs`. Occasionally, the target of a redirect (in this case, `Dogs`) gets deleted, leaving the redirect (`Canines`) pointing to a nonexistent article. This situation is called a *broken redirect*.

This special page lists all broken redirects so they can be fixed, either by re-pointing the redirect somewhere legitimate, or deleting the redirect. In our example, `Special:BrokenRedirects` displays:

> 1. <u>Canines</u> (<u>edit</u>) --> <u>Dogs</u>

Click `Canines` to change the redirect.

 Tired of fixing redirects manually? Check out the Pywikipedia bot (*http://pywikipediabot.sourceforge.net/*), which includes an automatic repair tool for broken and double redirects, *redirect.py*.

Dead-End Pages

`Special:DeadendPages`: *List articles with no links*

A dead-end article contains no links, so it's not fully participating in the wiki experience. It is the opposite of an orphaned article (see "Orphaned Pages" on page 142). This special page lists all dead-end articles in the wiki.

Double Redirects

`Special:DoubleRedirects`: *List redirects that point to other redirects*

You cannot redirect twice in a row, from one article to another to a third. If article `Canine` redirects to `Man's Best Friend` which redirects to `Dog`, and you click a `Canine` link, you'll get only as far as `Man's Best Friend` and see:

```
Man's Best Friend
  (Redirected from Canine)
    --> Dog
```

which stops short of displaying the `Dog` article.

This situation, called a *double redirect*, arises most commonly when an article is renamed twice with the Move tab (`Special:MovePage`). The first move produces a single redirect that works fine, but the second creates an unhelpful double redirect.

This special page detects and lists all double redirects in the wiki, like this:

> 1. <u>Canine</u> (<u>Edit</u>) -> <u>Man's Best Friend</u> -> <u>Dog</u>

In each entry, it provides an Edit link to fix the problem manually. In this case you'd change the first redirect (`Canines`) to point directly to `Dog`, so both it and `Man's Best Friend` redirect properly.

> Why are double redirects not supported? To prevent loops, where a sequence of redirects leads back to the original article (*A* redirects to *B*, which redirects to *C*, which redirects to *A*).

Long Pages

`Special:LongPages`: *List articles from longest to shortest*

The longest articles in the wiki are candidates for breaking up into multiple articles, if the information is too varied or does not flow well. This special page lists articles sorted by their length, with the longest first, so you can examine the articles and decide whether to split them.

Oldest Pages

`Special:AncientPages`: *List articles from oldest to newest*

Sometimes articles get neglected for a long time and end up on this special page. It lists the articles that have not been changed for the longest time, sorted by the date and time of their last edit.

Orphaned Pages

`Special:LonelyPages`: *List articles not linked from anywhere else*

When an article is not linked from any others, it's called an *orphaned* article. For example, if your wiki has an article `Beagle` but no other articles link to it, `Beagle` is orphaned. This is bad because it makes `Beagle` harder to find by browsing. This special page lists all orphaned articles in a simple, alphabetical list.

> Placing an article into a category does *not* prevent it from being orphaned. It must be linked from a different article.

Pages with the Fewest Revisions

`Special:FewestRevisions`: *List articles from least-edited to most-edited*

This special page lists articles that haven't been edited much. Unless these pages are very new, they are likely candidates for further editing.

 Sometimes the entries on this special page are redirects, which is unhelpful when looking for articles to update. The only way to recognize redirects is to visit the articles.

Contrast this with "Pages with the Most Revisions" on page 161.

Pages Without Language Links

`Special:WithoutInterwiki`: *List articles with no interlanguage links*

Articles that have no interlanguage links are candidates for translation. This special page identifies these articles. See "Interlanguage Links" on page 84 for more information on interlanguage links.

Protected Pages

`Special:ProtectedPages`: *List all protected pages (sysops only)*

As a sysop, you can protect individual articles so only members of particular user groups can edit them (see "User Groups" on page 230). This special page lists all protected articles. Each entry includes the article name and size, any expiration date for the protection, and the protection level. "Full protected" means that only sysops can change the article, and "semi-protected" means the article is protected from anonymous users.[†]

Protected Titles

`Special:ProtectedTitles`: *Pages that can't be created except by privileged users*

Articles with protected titles (see "Protecting titles" on page 243) are listed on this special page. These are nonexistent articles that have been protected, effectively preventing them from being created by any user without the appropriate permissions.

Short Pages

`Special:ShortPages`: *List articles from shortest to longest*

[†] If your wiki has custom user groups ("Creating a user group" on page 233), other protection levels may appear here.

Another helpful task is to find short articles and expand them. This special page lists the wiki pages containing the least text, beginning with the smallest.

Uncategorized Categories

`Special:UncategorizedCategories`: *List category pages that are not categorized*

Category pages can have categories, too (or more precisely, subcategories). Each entry on this special page is a category that has no parent. This usually represents a disconnect in the category structure. In an ideal wiki, every category should have a parent, unless it is intentionally a "topmost" or "highest level" category for a good reason.

To fix this problem, edit each category page in question, and insert one or more category tags. For example, if the category `Lizards` has no parent, you might insert tags for categories `Reptiles` and `Pets` as parents on its category page.

Uncategorized Files

`Special:UncategorizedImages`: *List uploaded files whose Image pages are not categorized*

Images, like articles, can have categories. This fact is forgotten rather often: uploaders are sometimes in a hurry to get back to whatever article they're editing. To fix this problem, edit the file's `Image` page and insert category tags.

Uncategorized Pages

`Special:UncategorizedPages`: *List articles not in any category*

This special page lists articles that don't appear in any category, and therefore cannot be found by browsing categories. To fix this, edit an article and insert one or more category tags. For example, the article `Dog` might be placed into the categories `Mammals` and `Pets`.

Uncategorized Templates

`Special:UncategorizedTemplates`: *List templates not in any category*

This special page is virtually identical to "Uncategorized pages", except that it applies to templates.

When categorizing a template, remember to enclose the category tag within `<noinclude>` tags so that you're tagging the template, not the articles that transclude it.

Unused Categories

`Special:UnusedCategories`: *List categories that contain no articles*

A category is unused if no articles belong to it. This situation arises as articles get moved from category to category, eventually producing an empty category. (It's also possible that someone created an empty category from scratch, but this is less common.)

This special page lists all empty categories. Don't confuse it with "Wanted Categories" on page 147 (`Special:WantedCategories`), which displays categories that do have members, but lack a category page.

Unused Files

`Special:UnusedImages`: *List uploaded files not referenced by any article*

Suppose user Bilbo is working on a large, fancy article with many illustrations. He uploads 36 images, but by the time he's done, only 34 of them have been used in the article. What happens to the other two? They sit unused, needlessly taking up space.

This special page lists all uploaded files in this situation: no articles refer to them via `Image` or `Media` links. For each file, it displays the name, a thumbnail image, a link to the `Image` page, and the file size. Using the links, you can quickly jump to each file and delete it if you're sure it's unused.

Unused Files...or Are They?

In a few cases, files can show up in `Special:UnusedImages` even if they are "used" on the wiki. For example, if your wiki logo (see "Logos and Icons" on page 258) is an uploaded image referenced by its file path, `Special:UnusedImages` is unaware of this use. Likewise, some wiki extensions (Chapter 14) could reference an uploaded file. To work around these cases, consider creating a wiki article whose sole purpose is to link to these indirectly, used images (say, `Administrative images on this wiki`), just to keep them out of the unused file list. It's a hack, but it works. (Alternatively, don't use uploaded images for these purposes.)

Unused Templates

`Special:UnusedTemplates`: *List templates not used in any article or other template*

If a template is unused by any article or template, it shows up on this special page. Each entry includes the template name (linked to the template page) and a link to `Special:WhatLinksHere` to identify any articles that link to the template.

Wait a minute...if the template is unused, why is `Special:WhatLinksHere` relevant? It's because of the difference between transcluding a template (see "Templates and Transclusion" on page 112) and merely linking to it. Consider a template called `Template:Moon phases` that displays the phases of the moon in a convenient table. If no articles transclude the template, i.e., nobody does this:

```
{{Moon phases}}
```

then the template is considered unused. Even so, a template can still be linked from another page:

```
[[Template:Moon phases]]
```

In this case, the template is still considered "unused," but if you delete it, you'll break these links. So this special page includes links to `Special:WhatLinksHere` so you can conveniently check for this case.

Unwatched Pages

`Special:UnwatchedPages`: *List articles not on any watchlist (sysops only)*

Sysops can list all wiki pages that are not present in anybody's watchlist. Each entry in the list includes the article name and a "Watch" link for conveniently watching the article.

In theory, this special page provides a broad picture of which wiki articles are not being monitored by anyone, and might therefore need attention. In practice, however, this list gets so long that it's not clear what purpose it serves.

Wanted Pages

`Special:WantedPages`: *List titles of articles that have been linked to, but not yet created*

Want to be helpful? Write a highly desired article. This special page lists non-existent articles that other wiki users would like to see.

This page obtains its information by relying on lazy linking as MediaWiki authors link to nonexistent articles. Recall how these work (from "Links to Nonexistent Articles" on page 76): if you're editing the Dog article and want to link to Cat, you needn't worry whether Cat exists. Just create the link. If Cat exists, it'll work just fine, but if not, the link will show up in red and encourage other users to create the article.

When people create links to nonexistent articles, they show up on this special page, sorted by the number of links. An entry such as:

> 14. Cat (55 links)

indicates that the #14 wanted page is Cat, and 55 other articles link to it. Click "Cat" and you'll be taken to its edit page.

 At press time, this special page is disabled on Wikipedia, though it works fine in MediaWiki software. As an alternative, visit Wikipedia:Most wanted articles.

Wanted Categories

Special:WantedCategories: *List categories that have no category page*

Similar to Special:WantedPages, this special page lists category tags that have been used in articles, but whose category pages have not been created yet. Each time someone tags an article with a nonexistent category (see "Creating a Category" on page 91), that category shows up here. To create it, simply click the category name and edit and save its category page.

List of Pages

These special pages contain lists of articles, redirects, and more.

All Pages

Special:AllPages: *List all pages in a namespace*

This special page displays the titles of every article in the wiki in alphabetical order, organized by namespace. On a large wiki such as Wikipedia, this page might seem overwhelming, but with a little understanding, it can become very useful.

In the box "Display pages starting at", enter some text and click Go. The results list all articles in the wiki, page by page, in alphabetical order, starting from whatever text you entered. So, if you enter "Bag", you might see Bag,

Bagheria, and Bat. Also, navigation links allow you to jump to the previous or next page of results.

Results are restricted to one namespace, the default being the main namespace of articles. To search another namespace, simply select it.

Tips:

- Authors can locate templates by setting Namespace to "Template".
- Administrators can see which system messages in the `MediaWiki` namespace have been overridden by setting Namespace to "MediaWiki".
- You can set the namespace to "Category" to list categories, but try `Special:Categories` or `Special:MostLinkedCategories` instead for more useful results.

Categories

`Special:Categories`: *List all categories alphabetically*

You'll find a list of all wiki categories on this special page, along with a count of articles in each category. The list is alphabetical, which is not always what you need, so check out `Special:MostLinkedCategories` as well.

Disambiguation Pages

`Special:Disambiguations`: *List all articles that link to disambiguation pages*

Sometimes, articles link to a disambiguation page (see "Disambiguation Pages" on page 103) instead of to a more specific article that would arguably be more correct. This special page points out these articles to be examined and potentially fixed.

For example, suppose article `Bone` is a disambiguation page that distinguishes skeleton bones, funny bones, trombones, and other meanings of the word. If article `Dog` links to `Bone`, then `Dog` would be listed in `Special:Disambiguations`:

1. Dog (Edit) → Bone

From there, you can edit `Dog` to point correctly to `Chewing Bone`.

MediaWiki detects disambiguation pages because they contain a certain template, `{{disambig}}`. You can change this choice of template: see "Disambiguation" on page 237.

List Redirects

`Special:ListRedirects`: *List all redirects alphabetically*

This special page lists all the redirects on the wiki: remember, these are articles that redirect your web browser to a different article (see "Redirects" on page 101). For example, the article `Dogs` on Wikipedia is a redirect, sending your browser to the article `Dog`.

Redirects are listed as two links separated by an arrow:

```
Redirect name -> Target article
```

For example, our `Dogs` redirect would show up in this list as:

```
Dogs -> Dog
```

`Dogs` is the redirect, and if you click the link, you'll visit the redirect article itself (say, for modifying where it points). `Dog` is the destination, and its link leads to the real article.

Prefix Index

`Special:PrefixIndex`: *List all pages beginning with a prefix*

(Called "All pages with prefix" on Wikipedia)

This special page is very similar to "All pages" but with one difference: it lists only the article titles that begin with the prefix you enter. So, if you enter "Bag", you might see `Bag` and `Bagheria`, but never `Bat`. A common application is locating subpages; for example, to list the subpages of article `Dog`, enter `Dog/` in the search box.

Login/Sign Up

These special pages are for logging in and out and creating accounts.

Log In/Create Account

`Special:UserLogin`: *Log into the wiki*

This is the MediaWiki login page. If you're not logged in, a link to this page is found on every wiki page. If you're already logged in, but want to log in as a different wiki user, you can find this link on `Special:SpecialPages`.

Log Out

`Special:UserLogout`: *Log out of the wiki (not listed)*

This is the MediaWiki logout page. If you're logged in, it can be reached from the "log out" link found on each wiki page.

Users and Rights

These special pages collect and display information about wiki users and their privileges. See also "User Options Menu" on page 25 for other user-related special pages.

Block User

`Special:BlockIP`: *Ban a wiki user (sysops only)*

Not all wiki participants are productive, responsible citizens. This administrative page bans people from the wiki, either by username (if they have one) or by IP address (if they don't).

List of Blocked IP Addresses and Usernames

`Special:IPBlockList`: *List wiki users who have been banned*

An entry appears in this list when a wiki user has been banned using `Special:BlockIP`. Anyone can view `Special:IPBlockList`: it is not restricted to sysops.

Preferences

`Special:Preferences`: *Change your personal wiki settings*

See "Preferences" on page 35.

User Contributions

`Special:Contributions`: *List the edits that a given user has made to wiki articles*

This special page, accessed via the "my contributions" link on each wiki page (assuming you're logged in), leads to your personal contributions page (see "Tracking Your Contributions" on page 35).

Special Page Parameters

Many special pages, when accessed by name (`Special:Whatever`), accept parameters in the URL. Unlike traditional query parameters that follow a question mark, these parameters follow a slash as if they were a subpage name. For example, the page to view user contributions is `Special:Contributions`, but to see the contributions of user Jones, it's `Special:Contributions/Jones`.

These parameters are conveniently available to programmers who create special pages. We'll see this in "A More Interesting Special Page" on page 304.

User Group Rights

`Special:ListGroupRights`: *Describe the user rights of all rights groups*‡

Different wiki users have different permissions and privileges, as explained in "User Rights and Permissions" on page 229. This special page is a reference that describes all the rights available on the wiki.

To see the rights a given user has, click the link "list of members" on this page, or visit `Special:ListUsers`. Only privileged users, such as bureaucrats, can change these rights.

User List

`Special:ListUsers`: *List all wiki users alphabetically by username*

(Called "Users" on Wikipedia)

This special page displays a simple list of all users on the wiki, sorted by username. Each entry links to a user page. Additionally, if a user belongs to a user group (see "User Groups" on page 230), the entry is followed by a list of groups that the user belongs to.

For a list of users who are administrators on the wiki, visit `Special:ListUsers/Sysop`, which is also accessible as `Special:ListAdmins`.

User Rights Management

`Special:UserRights`: *Assign wiki users to groups (bureaucrats only)*

If you're a wiki bureaucrat, you can bestow special privileges on other users by assigning them to user groups. We'll discuss this in detail in "User Rights and Permissions" on page 229.

Your User Page

`Special:MyPage`: *A designated wiki page about you (not listed)*

Your user page, normally accessed as `User:Your_username`, is also available as `Special:MyPage`.

‡ New in MediaWiki 1.13.

Your User Talk Page

`Special:MyTalk`: *A designated wiki page for others to communicate with you (not listed)*

Your user talk page, normally accessed as `User_talk:`*Your_username*, is also available as `Special:MyTalk`.

Email This User

`Special:EmailUser`: *Send email to a wiki user (not listed)*

Whenever you view a user page, the Toolbox displays the link "Email this user", leading to this special page. Here you can compose and send an email to that user, but only if you and the user have email addresses in your preferences, as shown in "User Profile Preferences" on page 35.

 You can also contact users by leaving messages on their user talk pages. (See "User Talk Pages" on page 31.)

Recent Changes and Logs

These special pages help monitor the activity on the wiki, such as edits, uploads, renames, and deletions.

Gallery of New Files

`Special:NewImages`: *List uploaded files from newest to oldest*

Want to see the latest uploads on the wiki? This special page displays a thumbnail for each upload, beginning with the most recent file, as well as the uploader's username, the upload date, and the file size. To see which articles contain the image, click the thumbnail to visit the associated image page, then "What links here" in the Toolbox.

Logs

`Special:Log`: *List significant events on the wiki*

This special page displays the many logs of system activity provided by MediaWiki, including:

Block log
    When users are banned from the wiki

Deletion log
> When articles are removed

Import log
> When articles are imported via `Special:Import`

Move log
> When articles are renamed

Patrol log
> When articles are marked as "acceptable"

Protection log
> When article access is restricted

Upload log
> When files are uploaded

User rights log
> When users have privileges bestowed or removed

Some third-party extensions create and write to additional logs, such as `Extension:Newuserlog`, which displays new accounts in reverse chronological order (see *http://www.mediawiki.org/wiki/Extension:Newuserlog*).

My Watchlist

`Special:Watchlist`: *Work with your watchlist*

This special page, accessed via the "my watchlist" link on each wiki page (assuming you're logged in), displays and manipulates your watchlist, i.e., articles you have elected to "watch." See "Watchlists" on page 33 for more information.

New Pages

`Special:NewPages`: *List articles from newest to oldest*

Here, you'll see the most recently created articles, an obviously useful list for readers and administrators. Each line on this special page is quite busy-looking, and includes:

- Time and date of creation
- Link to the article
- Link to the article's history
- Article size
- Links to the creator's user page, talk page, and contributions page
- An excerpt from the beginning of the article

Administrators will also see a link for quickly blocking the user from accessing the wiki any further. This is to stop abuse by people and bots who create new pages wastefully or maliciously.

Recent Changes

`Special:RecentChanges`: *List recent edits from newest to oldest*

For an up-to-the-second view of edits on the wiki, visit this special page. For most changes, the layout is similar to that of history pages (see "History" on page 18):

- A "diff" link to display the change
- A "hist" link to display the article's full history
- "m" if the edit was minor
- Link to the article
- The time of the edit
- Links to the creator's user page, talk page, and contributions page
- The change comment, if the user entered one

Other events, such as file uploads, article deletions, and user creations, are listed here as well, with slightly different formats.

Related Changes

`Special:RecentChangesLinked`: *List changes made to articles linked within the current article*

Most wiki articles are not complete in themselves, but rely on other linked articles. The article Dog, for example, might link to the articles Carnivore and Cat rather than defining these words itself. So, a natural question for readers and authors is, "Have any of my linked articles changed?" This is the purpose of the "Related changes" link found in the Toolbox. It displays a listing much like "Recent changes" (`Special:RecentChanges`), but only for articles that are linked from the current one. So, if you click "Recent changes" on the Dog article, you'll see the most recent changes to Carnivore and Cat.

 For category pages, `Special:RecentChangesLinked` lists changes to articles in the category.

Media Reports and Uploads

These special pages deal with uploaded files.

File List

Special:ImageList: *List all uploaded files*

(Called "Files" on Wikipedia)

This special page displays a table of all files that have been uploaded to the wiki, including:

Date
> The date the file was uploaded. If this file has been uploaded several times, this is the date of the most recent upload.

Name
> Two links. The first is the name of the file as used in wiki articles, linked to the file's image page (see "Image Pages" on page 60). The second is a link to the file itself, labeled "File".

User
> The wiki user who uploaded the file, linked to his or her user page.

Size
> The size of the file.

Description
> Any text entered by the uploading user.

The table is sortable. Click any heading to sort the entries by upload date, filename, or file size.

File Path

Special:FilePath: *Display the filesystem path to an uploaded file*

Uploaded files are accessible in two ways: via the Image namespace and via the Media namespace, (explained in "Image Pages" on page 60). For example, the uploaded file *Schnauser.jpg*, referenced as [[Image:Schnauser.jpg]], is accessed directly as a file by [[Media:Schnauser.jpg]]. This file might be located in the filesystem as */wiki/images/e/e5/Schnauser.jpg*, or perhaps be available by URL, such as *http://wiki.example.com/wiki/images/e/e5/Schnauser.jpg*.

This special page translates from the Image name (Schnauser.jpg) to the file path (*/wiki/images/e/e5/Schnauser.jpg*) by hitting the URL (*http://wiki.example.com/wiki/images/e/e5/Schnauser.jpg*) directly. Simply enter the image name and click the Path button, and the image file is loaded into the browser.

MIME Search

Special:MIMEsearch: *List all files of a given MIME type*

MIME (Multipurpose Internet Mail Extensions) is a standard format for describing and distinguishing different types of files on the Internet, such as JPEG images, Excel spreadsheets, Adobe PDFs, and plain text files. The MIME type of a file is written as two words separated by a slash. The four examples here would be image/jpeg, application/vnd.ms-excel, application/pdf, and text/plain.

This special page lists all uploaded files that match a particular MIME type. Simply enter the type (e.g., image/jpeg) and click the Search button to display the list. A typical entry like this:

> (download) chipmunk.jpg . . 160×160 . . 6,615 bytes . . Jsmith . .
>   04:10, 21 February 2008

can be broken down like this:

(download)
> A link to the file itself

chipmunk.jpg
> Filename, linked to its image page

160×160
> Image width and height in pixels

6,615 bytes
> File size

Jsmith
> User who uploaded the file, linked to his user page

04:10, 21 February 2008
> Time and date of the upload

Search for Duplicate Files

Special:FileDuplicateSearch: *Detect identical uploaded files**

If you're working with an uploaded file (say, Image:Myfile.jpg) and want to check if another wiki file is identical, use this special page. Enter the filename Myfile.jpg, click Submit, and you'll get a report:

---

* New in MediaWiki 1.13.

1. <u>Myfile.jpg</u> . . <u>Dan</u> . . 00:52, 27 March 2008
2. <u>Otherfile.jpg</u> . . <u>WikiSysop</u> . . 04:54, 26 February 2008

The file "Myfile.jpg" has 1 identical duplication.

Upload File

`Special:Upload`: *Copy a file into the Image namespace*

This page is for adding images and other files so they can be included in articles, as discussed in "Working with Uploads" on page 56. A link to this page is found in the Toolbox, labeled "Upload file".

Some MediaWiki sites prohibit uploads. In this case, the Toolbox link will be absent, and the special page will simply say that file uploads are disabled. See "Enabling File Uploads" on page 188 for details.

Wiki Data and Tools

These special pages provide views of the wiki infrastructure.

Statistics

`Special:Statistics`: *Display statistics about the articles within the wiki*

This page gives a high-level overview of the size of the wiki, including counts of:

* Pages
* Uploaded files
* Page views
* Page edits
* Registered wiki users

and more. Some values are estimates, such as the number of "legitimate content" articles, ignoring redirects and other pages not worth counting.

System Messages

`Special:AllMessages`: *List all system messages in the MediaWiki namespace*

Consider all the text you see in MediaWiki that is not part of an article, such as:

* Menus
* Labels on tabs, such as "edit", "history", and "watch"

- The names of special pages
- Error messages

These "infrastructural" words and phrases are known as *system messages*. These messages are not hardcoded into the MediaWiki program, but stored within the wiki. They can be accessed and modified via a special namespace called `MediaWiki` (see "System Messages" on page 218). The special page title "Recent changes", for example, is found in `MediaWiki:Recentchanges`.

The "System messages" special page displays all system messages by name (e.g., `Recentchanges`) and value ("Recent changes").

 To see which system messages have been modified on your wiki, visit the "All pages" special page (`Special:AllPages`), set the namespace to `MediaWiki`, and click the Submit button. Only modified system messages show up as pages in this list.

Version

`Special:Version`: *List the software installed on the wiki*

Want to know what software is installed on a MediaWiki site? Visit this special page, which displays the versions of:

- MediaWiki
- PHP (and type of web server)
- Database software (usually MySQL)

It also displays a list of installed extensions—additional, nonstandard features —available on the wiki. If you've enjoyed a feature on Wikipedia, for example, but it doesn't work or appear on another MediaWiki site, check this page on both wikis and compare software versions and extensions.

Redirects and Random Pages

These special pages transport you to other articles.

Random Page

`Special:Random`: *Jump to a randomly selected article*

Don't know what to read? Feeling random? Click the "Random page" link in the Navigation box or the list of special pages, and your browser will be directed to a randomly selected article. Add a namespace as a parameter, e.g., `Special:Random/Help`, to visit a random article in that namespace.

Random Redirect

`Special:RandomRedirect`: *Jump to a randomly selected redirect*

Much like "Random page", this special page displays a randomly selected redirect from the wiki. Frankly, it's hard to see the use for this special page, but it's there if you need it!

Search

`Special:Search`: *Search all articles by keyword*

We've already encountered the search page in "Searching for Articles" on page 12. Most of the time, you'll view it as the result of a search, but if desired, you can navigate to it directly.

High-Use Pages

High-use wiki pages can point out trends on the wiki, or indicate trouble spots such as inconsistencies or ongoing user battles.

Most Linked-To Categories

`Special:MostLinkedCategories`: *List categories from largest to smallest*

Want to know which categories contain the most articles? This special page displays categories from largest to smallest. This can give a high-level view of the coverage of various topics on the wiki.

Note that this is different from "Pages with the most categories" (`Special:MostCategories`), which displays a list of articles, whereas "Most linked-to categories" displays a list of categories.

Most Linked-To Files

`Special:MostImages`: *List uploaded files from most-used to least-used*

Find the most-used images or other uploaded files on the wiki using this special page. Each entry includes a thumbnail of the image, a link to the image page, the number of links, and the file size.

Most Linked-To Pages

`Special:MostLinked`: *List articles from most-linked to least-linked*

This special page reveals the articles that are most often referenced by other articles. This is useful for determining the most informative, reliable, and trusted articles on the wiki. It's also a measure of the importance of an article: if many other articles depend on it, you'd better keep it up to date! Each entry on this special page includes links to the article and `Special:WhatLinksHere` (see "What Links Here" on page 162), so you can quickly see the other articles that link to it.

Most Linked-To Templates

`Special:MostLinkedTemplates`: *List templates from most-used to least-used*

Here you'll find a list of the most-used templates on the wiki. If you're new to a MediaWiki site, this special page can guide you to the most important local templates to learn. And as an administrator, you might consider protecting some of these templates (see "Protecting Articles" on page 242): they are clearly critical to the operation of your wiki, as so many other articles depend on them. As with `Special:MostLinked`, each entry on this special page includes a link to the template and a link to `Special:WhatLinksHere`.

Pages with the Most Categories

`Special:MostCategories`: *List articles by number of category tags, in descending order*

When the categories on a wiki are poorly maintained, articles may end up belonging to too many categories. For example, if your wiki has overly general categories like `Information` or `Data`, 99% of the articles could legitimately be part of them. As another example, consider an article about dogs that belongs to the categories `Mammals`, `Animals with Hair`, and `Warm-Blooded Creatures`. These categories are redundant, as every mammal article could belong to all of them.

This special page helps to diagnose problems with poor category structure. It lists articles that appear in the most categories, which may point to categories that are too general or that are problematic in some other way.

Pages with the Most Revisions

`Special:MostRevisions`: *List articles edited the most times, in descending order*

This special page locates "hot" articles that have been modified many times. Readers may find this useful to locate popular topics, and administrators may want to track these articles to keep them orderly and prevent abuse. Each line on this page includes links to the article and its history page.

You can contrast this page with "Pages with the fewest revisions" (`Special:FewestRevisions`), which helps to locate articles of lesser interest that may need to be cleaned up or deleted.

Page Tools

These special pages are used for bringing data into and out of the wiki, plus a few other miscellaneous operations.

Export Pages

`Special:Export`: *Convert articles to XML*

Any MediaWiki article can be converted to XML using `Special:Export`. Once it's in this format, you can easily hand-edit the article, then ask a wiki sysop to import the article back into the wiki using `Special:Import` (see "Import Pages" on page 162).

The export-edit-import sequence might seem like a lot of trouble for one article, but if you're modifying a large set of articles (say, everything in a category) and have a great XML editing program, this method might be faster than using the MediaWiki edit page.

To export one or more articles:

1. Enter the names of the articles in the space provided. To list all the articles in a category, enter the category name where you're prompted and click Add.
2. Decide whether you want to export only the current revision or all revisions of the articles, and click the appropriate checkbox.
3. Decide whether you want to save the results as a file or display them in the web browser, and click the appropriate checkbox.
4. Click Export.

Exporting is also one method of backing up wiki articles for safekeeping, as described in "Database Backups" on page 321.

Import Pages

`Special:Import`: *Convert an exported XML file to articles (sysops only)*

This special page reads an XML file produced by `Special:Export` and creates or modifies the wiki articles it specifies. Importing is restricted to sysops: if misused, this feature can damage large numbers of articles in one shot. See "Database Backups" on page 321 for more details on importing large numbers of articles.

View Deleted Pages

`Special:Undelete`: *Restore a deleted wiki article (sysops only)*

When an article is deleted, it doesn't really go away. It remains in MediaWiki's revision control system. Sysops can view and restore these deleted articles through this special page.

Suppose the article `Movies starring dogs` was deleted and you want to restore it. Visit `Special:Undelete` and enter the article name, or a prefix such as "Movie". After clicking the Submit button, you'll see a list of all deleted pages matching that name or prefix. Click `Movies starring dogs` and you'll be offered a choice:

- Restore the entire article, including all revisions
- Restore only selected revisions, using checkboxes

Then, follow the directions to do one or the other.

What Links Here

`Special:WhatLinksHere`: *List articles that link to the current one*

Most articles contain links you can follow to other related articles, but what if you want to travel these paths in reverse? This special page answers the question, "Given an article, what other articles link to it?" From any article, look in the Toolbox and click "What links here". Alternatively, visit the special page list, click "What links here", and enter the name of your desired article, or, hit `Special:WhatLinksHere/`*NameOfArticle* directly. Either way, you'll be presented with a list of articles that link to your desired article.

This special page helps you understand the impact of deleting an article (say, `Dog`). Click "What links here" in the Toolbox to see which other articles link to `Dog`, as those links will be affected if `Dog` is deleted.

Other Special Pages

The remaining special pages cover a variety of topics. Third-party special pages often wind up here. For more specific groupings of these and other pages, see "Special Pages Grouped by Task" on page 165.

Book Sources

`Special:BookSources`: *Generate links to books by ISBN*

Need to reference a book in your wiki article? This special page produces links to a given book on *amazon.com*, *barnesandnoble.com*, and other relevant websites, ready to be copied and pasted into your article. Enter an ISBN number such as 9780596519797, and the page generates and displays links to the associated book.

CategoryTree

`Special:CategoryTree`: *Display a single category and its subcategories and articles interactively (nonstandard)*

The CategoryTree special page displays any category and all its subcategories in a convenient outline (or "tree") format. Similar to the "folders" view in Windows Explorer, the category tree is interactive. Click the "+" symbol next to any category name to expand and display its subcategories, and the "–" symbol to collapse the category.

 This page uses a special web technology called AJAX to refresh itself rapidly when you click the "+" and "–" signs.

Expand Templates

`Special:ExpandTemplates`: *Develop wiki templates interactively (nonstandard)*

See "ExpandTemplates" on page 279.

External Links

`Special:LinkSearch`: *Search for links to external websites (nonstandard)*

MediaWiki articles have two kinds of links, internal and external. Internal links point to other pages on the same wiki,[†] and external links point to other websites. This special page locates external links that match a pattern, such as "yahoo.com" or "*.yahoo.com", and lists the articles that contain them. So for example, if you'd like to find articles that link to *www.google.com*, enter "www.google.com" and click the Search button. You may include the wildcard "*" at the beginning to match any character except a dot.

Only full words are matched. So, "yahoo.com" will match URLs beginning with http://yahoo.com, but "yaho", "ahoo", "yahoo.co" and "*ahoo.com" will not.

Move

`Special:MovePage`: *Rename an article (not listed)*

This special page, available from the Move tab on any article, renames an article.[‡] The old article sticks around, becoming a redirect to the new article, so any links to the old name remain valid.

 If an article already has redirects pointing to it, then moving it will create double redirects (see "Double Redirects" on page 141). To prevent this, visit `Special:WhatLinksHere` ("What links here" in the Toolbox) to check for redirects and after moving it, visit `Special:DoubleRedirects` to detect and fix any double redirects.

Popular Pages

`Special:PopularPages`: *List the most often viewed articles in descending order*

This special page displays articles with the most hits, which is helpful for gauging their popularity. (At press time, this page is disabled on Wikipedia and other Wikimedia sites, but it's a standard part of MediaWiki.)

Each entry includes the article name and the number of page views. They are sorted by number of page views, from most to least.

[†] Except for interwiki links, which masquerade as internal links but point to other websites.

[‡] This can be disabled by the wiki administrator.

This page appears only if page statistics are enabled in *LocalSettings.php*, with the configuration setting `$wgDisableCounters` set to `false`.

Special Pages Grouped by Task

If you have a particular task in mind, you may find this grouping of special pages helpful.[*]

Finding Content of Interest

Browsing articles:

- All pages (`Special:AllPages`)
- Categories (`Special:Categories`)
- CategoryTree (`Special:CategoryTree`)
- Prefix index (`Special:PrefixIndex`)
- View deleted pages (`Special:Undelete`)
- What links here (`Special:WhatLinksHere`)

Searching:

- Book sources (`Special:BookSources`)
- External links (`Special:LinkSearch`)
- MIME search (`Special:MIMESearch`)
- Search (`Special:Search`)
- Search for duplicate files (`Special:FileDuplicateSearch`)

Uploaded files:

- File list (`Special:ImageList`)
- File path (`Special:FilePath`)
- Gallery of new files (`Special:NewImages`)
- MIME search (`Special:MIMESearch`)
- Search for duplicate files (`Special:FileDuplicateSearch`)
- Unused files (`Special:UnusedImages`)
- Upload file (`Special:Upload`)

---

[*] Wiki administrators can change the grouping: see "Special Page List" on page 252.

Redirects:

- Broken redirects (`Special:BrokenRedirects`)
- Double redirects (`Special:DoubleRedirects`)
- List redirects (`Special:ListRedirects`)
- Random redirect (`Special:RandomRedirect`)

Popular content:

- Most linked-to categories (`Special:MostLinkedCategories`)
- Most linked-to files (`Special:MostImages`)
- Most linked-to pages (`Special:MostLinked`)
- Most linked-to templates (`Special:MostLinkedTemplates`)
- Pages with the most revisions (`Special:MostRevisions`)
- Popular pages (`Special:PopularPages`)

Writing

Finding topics to write about:

- Dead-end pages (`Special:DeadendPages`)
- Oldest pages (`Special:AncientPages`)
- Pages with the fewest revisions (`Special:FewestRevisions`)
- Short pages (`Special:ShortPages`)
- Wanted categories (`Special:WantedCategories`)
- Wanted pages (`Special:WantedPages`)

Adding content:

- Export pages (`Special:Export`)
- Import pages (`Special:Import`)
- Upload file (`Special:Upload`)

Categories:

- Categories (`Special:Categories`)
- CategoryTree (`Special:CategoryTree`)
- Most linked-to categories (`Special:MostLinkedCategories`)
- Pages with the most categories (`Special:MostCategories`)
- Uncategorized categories (`Special:UncategorizedCategories`)
- Uncategorized files (`Special:UncategorizedImages`)

- Uncategorized pages (`Special:UncategorizedPages`)
- Uncategorized templates (`Special:UncategorizedTemplates`)
- Unused categories (`Special:UnusedCategories`)
- Wanted categories (`Special:WantedCategories`)

Templates:

- Expand templates (`Special:ExpandTemplates`)
- Most linked-to templates (`Special:MostLinkedTemplates`)
- Uncategorized templates (`Special:UncategorizedTemplates`)
- Unused templates (`Special:UnusedTemplates`)

People

Pages about you:

- Log in / create account (`Special:UserLogin`)
- Log out (`Special:UserLogout`)
- My watchlist (`Special:Watchlist`)
- User contributions (`Special:Contributions`)
- Your user page (`Special:MyPage`)
- Your user talk page (`Special:MyTalk`)

Pages about the community:

- Block user (`Special:BlockIP`)
- Email this user (`Special:EmailUser`)
- List of blocked IP addresses and usernames (`Special:IPBlockList`)
- User contributions (`Special:Contributions`)
- User list (`Special:ListUsers`)
- User group rights (`Special:ListGroupRights`)
- User rights management (`Special:UserRights`)

Watchlists:

- My watchlist (`Special:Watchlist`)
- Unwatched pages (`Special:UnwatchedPages`)

Getting the Big Picture

The wiki as a whole:

- Logs (`Special:Log`)
- Statistics (`Special:Statistics`)
- Version (`Special:Version`)

Recent activity:

- Gallery of new files (`Special:NewImages`)
- Logs (`Special:Log`)
- My watchlist (`Special:Watchlist`)
- New pages (`Special:NewPages`)
- Recent changes (`Special:RecentChanges`)
- Related changes (`Special:RecentChangesLinked`)

Administration

Keeping things organized:

- Pages with the most categories (`Special:MostCategories`)
- Dead-end pages (`Special:DeadendPages`)
- Disambiguation pages (`Special:Disambiguations`)
- Long pages (`Special:LongPages`)
- Move (`Special:Move`)
- Orphaned pages (`Special:LonelyPages`)
- Pages without language links (`Special:WithoutInterwiki`)
- Uncategorized categories (`Special:UncategorizedCategories`)
- Uncategorized files (`Special:UncategorizedImages`)
- Uncategorized pages (`Special:UncategorizedPages`)
- Uncategorized templates (`Special:UncategorizedTemplates`)

Fixing problems:

- Broken redirects (`Special:BrokenRedirects`)
- Double redirects (`Special:DoubleRedirects`)
- Search for duplicate files (`Special:FileDuplicateSearch`)
- View deleted pages (`Special:Undelete`)

Pruning unused information:

- Unused categories (`Special:UnusedCategories`)
- Unused files (`Special:UnusedImages`)
- Unused templates (`Special:UnusedTemplates`)

Users and access control:

- Block user (`Special:BlockIP`)
- User rights management (`Special:UserRights`)
- Protected pages (`Special:ProtectedPages`)

Infrastructure:

- System messages (`Special:AllMessages`)

## PART III

Running and Administering MediaWiki

## CHAPTER 9

Installing MediaWiki

Want to create your own wiki? MediaWiki runs great on Linux, Microsoft Windows, Apple Macintosh, and other systems. The software is very stable (just look at Wikipedia), and its web-based installation program is straightforward and reliable, as long as your system has the right prerequisites. It's best if you have direct (shell) access to the server on which MediaWiki runs, but if not, you can still do quite a bit.

In this chapter, we'll discuss:

- Installing MediaWiki on Linux, Windows, and Macintosh systems
- Some optional features
- The structure of the MediaWiki file tree
- Maintaining a MediaWiki site with version control and a reasonable release process

Read this entire chapter before installing MediaWiki seriously. We discuss the pros and cons of various approaches and recommend some advance setup to ease maintenance. If you're just playing around with MediaWiki, you can install it however you like, but come back later and read the whole chapter before installing it in a production environment.

This chapter assumes that you have enough technical background to install system-level software packages on your platform of choice, edit configuration files, set permissions on directories, and similar system tasks. It also assumes you're aware of the security issues of running a server—such as MediaWiki—that allows outside users to access the computer on which it runs.

Additional installation help can be found at *http://www.mediawiki.org/wiki/ Manual:Installation_guide*.

Before You Begin

Before installing MediaWiki on a server machine, there are various things you'll need to install and consider.

Software Prerequisites

MediaWiki requires the following software in order to run (instructions and URLs will be provided shortly):

A *web server*
> The most popular and well tested web server for MediaWiki is Apache. On Windows you can also use IIS, but in this author's experience, you'll regret the decision.

A *database server*
> The choices are MySQL and PostgreSQL, but MediaWiki is primarily developed and optimized to run on MySQL, as that's what Wikipedia uses in production. PostgreSQL support is well maintained, but it is a "second-class citizen": certain functionality occasionally requires extra effort. (There is no support to speak of for Oracle, Microsoft SQL Server, or other similar systems at press time, though rumors circulate every once in a while.) You will also need a login for the database server with permission to create databases and tables.

PHP
> PHP is the programming language interpreter that runs MediaWiki. It's recommend to use version 5; if you are forced to use version 4 (e.g., if your web provider has only version 4 and won't upgrade), you cannot install the latest MediaWiki, only the version 1.6 branch. This is stable, but it lacks many features and doesn't support many extensions.

> If your environment lacks all of these applications, consider XAMPP (*http://www.apachefriends.org*), an Apache distribution that also installs MySQL, PHP, and Perl in one shot.
>
> If installing these applications manually, install Apache before PHP. Some installation programs for PHP helpfully configure Apache for you if it's already installed.

Hosting Prerequisites

What sort of web hosting provider can handle a MediaWiki site? If you have your own hardware or work in a corporation, this might not be an issue, but for general Internet sites, here are some tips.

The easiest approach to use is a provider that specializes in hosting MediaWiki sites, such as Wikia (*http://www.wikia.com*). Barring that, if you'll be installing the software yourself, make sure the provider meets the prerequisites listed at *http://www.mediawiki.org/wiki/Installation*: an appropriate web server, SQL database server, and PHP. For PHP in particular, make sure it's executable not only via their web server, but also on the command line if you have shell access. (There are some providers where PHP 5+ is available in Apache but not via shell.)

Speaking of shell access to your account, it's optional, but it makes installation and maintenance easier. Some tasks that become more difficult without shell access include:

- Downloading and installing packaged software
- Running MediaWiki's maintenance scripts (see "Maintenance Scripts" on page 320), including backups and MediaWiki upgrades
- Running scheduled jobs, particularly those that require superuser privileges

If a provider does not have shell access, see if they support a self-service, web-based maintenance interface such as the powerful cPanel (*http://www.cpanel .net*). If they do have shell access, see if they support secure logins and file transfers via SSH and SFTP (*http://www.openssh.org*) to keep your account password safe.

Another important consideration is whether you plan to run a multilingual wiki (see "Interlanguage Links" on page 84, and "Enabling Interlanguage Link Support" on page 333). A setup like Wikipedia's with a website per language (*en.wikipedia.org*, *fr.wikipedia.org*, *de.wikipedia.org*, etc.) requires a subdomain per language, so ideally, your hosting provider should permit you to create subdomains yourself without cost. (It's possible to go multilingual without subdomains, however.)

Early Decisions

Sometime after you install MediaWiki but before you allow other users in, you have several important decisions to make. These will be summarized here so you know they're coming up, and then cover them in more detail after installation.

Authentication
> MediaWiki has its own authentication system for user logins, and it works fine. But if you're in a corporate environment with Kerberos, Active Directory, LDAP, or other authentication service, you might want to use that

service for MediaWiki authentication. Settle this before your users set up MediaWiki accounts with passwords. See "LDAP Authentication" on page 280 for more details.

Short URLs

By default, MediaWiki URLs are long and not memorable. You can configure your web server to shorten and beautify them, but make this decision early before people start bookmarking wiki pages, sending wiki URLs in email messages, and linking to your wiki from external sites. See "Enabling Short URLs" on page 191 for instructions.

Version control of code

If you plan to write or install third-party extensions or modify MediaWiki's code in any way, it's strongly recommended you place your MediaWiki source tree under version control so you can track and control all changes. We'll discuss this further in "Maintaining the Code" on page 196.

Release process

If you are using MediaWiki in a corporate or other serious environment, come up with a proper release process for making changes and performing upgrades. Have at least two wiki servers: one (or two) for development and testing, and one for your real production system. Use scripts or other automation to copy changes between your development, test, and production environments. If you run just one wiki server and make changes directly on disk, you will surely introduce bugs and typos and bring down the system without warning, making your users unhappy. We'll talk more about this in "A Simple Release Process" on page 199.

Installing the Prerequisites

So, you're ready to take the plunge and install MediaWiki! This can be done on a shared server (assuming it already has the prerequisite software) or your own server. Here's how to prepare Linux, Windows, and Macintosh systems for installation.

Linux Prerequisites

Most modern Linux systems have all the prerequisites for a basic MediaWiki system: PHP 5, MySQL, and Apache. If your distribution makes these components available as installable packages, use them. If not, download them from their official sites and follow their installation instructions, which should be straightforward:

- Apache: *http://www.apache.org/*

- MySQL: *http://www.mysql.com/*
- PHP: *http://www.php.net/*

Now you're ready to install MediaWiki.

Microsoft Windows Prerequisites

MediaWiki was written for Linux and similar systems, but runs fine on Windows, with one caveat: don't use Microsoft's IIS as the web server. It is possible to run MediaWiki with IIS, but in this author's experience, the combination is not reliable, leading to all sorts of mysterious intermittent crashes and other problems, particularly on 64-bit Windows. Yes, there are people out there who have made IIS work, but it's so much more difficult and problematic than Apache, which "just works" with MediaWiki.

In this book, it's assumed that you'll be installing Apache. If your system already has IIS installed, you might need to disable it in the Services control panel or run it on a different TCP/IP port for Apache to work.

If you simply must use IIS, there are several sites to help you get started:

> *http://www.mediawiki.org/wiki/Manual:Installing_MediaWiki_on_Windows_Server_2003*
> *http://www.ehartwell.com/TechNotes/MediaWikiOnASPnix.htm*
> *http://www.scottdstrader.com/blog/ether_archives/000329.html*

Install Apache on Windows

Install Apache first, before the other prerequisites (MySQL and PHP). The easiest method is to download a binary Windows distribution. This is available on Apache's official site (*http://www.apache.org*), but it does not include SSL (HTTPS) support. MediaWiki does not require SSL, but if you want it for more general use, you can download SSL-enabled binaries from *http://www.apachelounge.com*. Detailed installation documents are at:

> *http://httpd.apache.org/docs/2.2/platform/windows.html*

Assuming you've installed Apache in *C:\Apache2*, set it up as a Windows service with:

```
C:\Apache2\bin\httpd -k install
```

Hit http://*hostname* and you should see a success message like "It works!" This is displayed by the *index.html* file found in Apache's root web folder, in this case *C:\Apache2\htdocs\index.html*.

Install MySQL on Windows

Once Apache is running, install MySQL using a binary installer from *http://www.mysql.com*. At press time, the free community version of MySQL is at *http://dev.mysql.com/downloads*, and the installer you want is called "Windows Essentials."

When the installer runs, choose options appropriate for your system, but make sure to include InnoDB table support, and to include the *bin* directory in the Windows search path when asked. You'll also need to choose a root password for the database: be sure to remember it, as you'll need it to complete the MediaWiki installation!

Install PHP

Finally, install PHP with a binary installer from *http://www.php.net*. When run after Apache is installed, the PHP installer will modify Apache's configuration file so the web server can execute PHP web pages. The PHP installer offers a long list of optional components to install. Here are the most important ones:

- Apache 2.2 or higher
- mysql
- mysqli
- PDO/MySQL
- SMTP
- PEAR Install

It's also a good idea to install:

- GD2: image file manipulation used for thumbnails (alternatively, you can use ImageMagick, which supports more image formats and may produce better thumbnails: see *http://www.mediawiki.org/wiki/ImageMagick*
- LDAP: authentication with LDAP services such as Active Directory
- mssql and PDO/Microsoft SQL Server: Microsoft SQL Server integration

After PHP installation, if your Windows server is 64-bit, you might need to inform Windows that the PHP DLL isn't a 64-bit application. This is done with the following command (all on one line):

```
cscript %SYSTEMDRIVE%\inetpub\adminscripts\adsutil.vbs
    SET W3SVC/AppPools/Enable32bitAppOnWin64 1
```

Test your PHP installation by placing the following script into a file *test.php* in the root of your web server so that it's reachable as http://*hostname*/test.php:

```
<?php
phpinfo();
?>
```

If all is well, you'll see a detailed display of your PHP configuration when you hit this page. Now, you're ready to install MediaWiki.

Apple Macintosh OS X Prerequisites

The installation procedure for MediaWiki on Mac OS X varies greatly with the version of OS X, as some versions have PHP and/or MySQL preinstalled. This author followed the instructions at *http://www.mediawiki.org/wiki/Manual: Running_MediaWiki_on_Mac_OS_X* and installed MediaWiki 1.13 on OS X 10.5 (Leopard), and MediaWiki 1.12 on OS X 10.4 (Tiger). The following instructions assume you're running Leopard.

Enable Apache on Macintosh

Apache is already installed on Leopard. To make your web server run, visit System Preferences, select Sharing, and in the Services tab, enable Personal Web Sharing. Now hit http://*hostname* to confirm that the server is running. It should be that simple.

Enable PHP on Macintosh

PHP 5 is already installed on Leopard.[*] To enable it within Apache, edit the Apache configuration file */etc/apache2/httpd.conf* and locate the line containing LoadModule php5_module. If it begins with a hash mark (#), remove the hash mark to uncomment the line, so it looks like this:

```
LoadModule php5_module libexec/apache2/libphp5.so
```

Now, restart Apache with the command:

```
$ sudo apachectl restart
```

Test your PHP installation by placing the following script into a file *test.php* in the root of your web server (*/Library/WebServer/Documents* by default) so that it's reachable as http://*hostname*/test.php:

```
<?php
phpinfo();
?>
```

If all is well, you'll see a detailed display of your PHP 5 configuration when you hit this page.

---

[*] Older versions of OS X (such as 10.4 Tiger) come with the older PHP 4, so you'll need to install PHP 5.

Install MySQL on Macintosh

For a detailed treatment of this subject, go to *http://www.mediawiki.org/wiki/Manual:Running_MediaWiki_on_Mac_OS_X*. This author installed MySQL 5.0.51b from *http://dev.mysql.com/downloads*. At press time, the instructions are as follows:

- Double-click the main MySQL "pkg" file (e.g., *mysql-5.0.51b-osx10.4-powerpc.pkg*) to install MySQL.
- Double-click *MySQLStartupItem.pkg* to install the MySQL startup script.
- Double-click *MySQL.prefPane* to install a MySQL system preferences application, and start the MySQL server.
- Immediately secure the initial MySQL accounts as described at *http://dev.mysql.com/doc/refman/5.0/en/default-privileges.html*. The following commands are examples:[†]

```
$ export PATH=$PATH:/usr/local/mysql/bin
$ mysqladmin -u root password "password here"
$ mysqladmin -u root -h hostname password "password here"
$ history -c
$ mysql -u root
mysql> DROP USER '';
mysql> exit
$
```

One last thing: MySQL and MediaWiki disagree on the location of a socket file. This can cause MediaWiki's installation to fail later, so run:

```
$ sudo mkdir /var/mysql
$ sudo ln -s /tmp/mysql.sock /var/mysql/
```

Now, you're ready to install MediaWiki.

Installing MediaWiki

Once your prerequisites are in place, you're ready to download the latest version of MediaWiki from *http://www.mediawiki.org*. It comes in a compressed tar file with a name like *mediawiki-x.y.z.tar.gz*, where *x.y.z* is the version number. Uncompress and untar the files in an appropriate location:[‡]

```
cd wherever
tar xvzf mediawiki-x.y.z.tar.gz .
```

[†] If you're concerned about security, run these commands with your network cable disconnected and nobody else logged in, and clear your shell history afterward.

[‡] Some downloading programs will automatically uncompress the tar file, so you won't see a *.gz* extension on the filename. In this case, you can omit the "z" option of *tar*, i.e., *tar xvf* instead of *tar xvzf*.

This creates a directory *mediawiki-x.y.z*.

> Microsoft Windows programs to extract these files include
> WinZip (*http://www.winzip.com*), 7-Zip (*http://www.7-zip
> .org*), and many others. Windows command-line versions of
> *tar* and *gzip* are also available at *http://gnuwin32.sourceforge
> .net* and *http://unxutils.sourceforge.net*.

If You Have Administrative Access

Move this directory into your web server's root directory as a subdirectory
named *w*. So, on a Linux system, if your web server's root is */var/www/
htdocs*, run:

```
mv mediawiki.x.y.z /var/www/htdocs/w
```

or, for convenience on Linux or Macintosh (which support symbolic links):

```
mv mediawiki.x.y.z /var/www/htdocs/mediawiki.x.y.z
cd /var/www/htdocs/
ln -s mediawiki.x.y.z w
```

> Make sure that the installation directory is readable by the web
> server (i.e., the user running the Apache process) and that the
> *config* and *images* subdirectories are writable by the web
> server.

A convenient installation location on a Windows system is *C:\Apache\htdocs
\w*, and on a Macintosh, */Library/WebServer/Documents/w*. At this point, you
can hit this *w* directory by URL (e.g., `http://hostname/w`) and run the installer
program.

If you choose a different location for MediaWiki, edit Apache's configuration
file (e.g., *httpd.conf*) to point to the software. On Windows machines, use
slashes (*C:/Apache2/htdocs*) instead of DOS backslashes in all Apache configuration files:

```
<IfModule alias_module>
    Alias /wiki "/var/www/htdocs/w"    /* Change path for Windows or Mac */
</IfModule>

<Directory "/var/www/htdocs/w">    /* Change path for Windows or Mac */
    Options Indexes FollowSymLinks ExecCGI
    AllowOverride None
    Order allow,deny
    Allow from all
</Directory>
```

Restart Apache and hit `http://`*`hostname`*`/wiki`. If everything is set up correctly, you'll be directed to MediaWiki's web installer. If you see an error about the *config* subdirectory not being writable by the web server, set up appropriate permissions on that subdirectory.

If `http://`*`hostname`*`/wiki` doesn't work, your Apache configuration might be wrong. Try `http://`*`hostname`*`/w` instead, and if it works, Apache is likely misconfigured. (Perhaps the Alias module isn't enabled.)

Shared Server or No Administrative Access

Move the *mediawiki-x.y.z* directory into the root of your personal web directory as a subdirectory named *w*, for example:

```
mv mediawiki.x.y.z /your/personal/web/dir/w
```

Now, hit the *w* folder with a web browser (e.g., `http://`*`path_to_your_web site`*`/w`) to invoke MediaWiki's web installer.

The Web Installer

MediaWiki 1.12.0

Please <u>set up the wiki</u> first.

Figure 9-1. Initial web installer display

MediaWiki's web-based installer (Figure 9-1) first checks that your computer has all the prerequisites. For example:

```
Checking environment...

Please include all of the lines below when reporting installation problems.

    * PHP 5.2.3-1ubuntu6.3 installed
    * Found database drivers for: MySQL
    * PHP server API is apache2handler; ok, using pretty URLs...
    * Have XML / Latin1-UTF-8 conversion support.
    ...
```

Next, you must answer a series of questions about your desired MediaWiki environment. Most of them you can change later by editing the MediaWiki configuration file, *LocalSettings.php*.

Site configuration

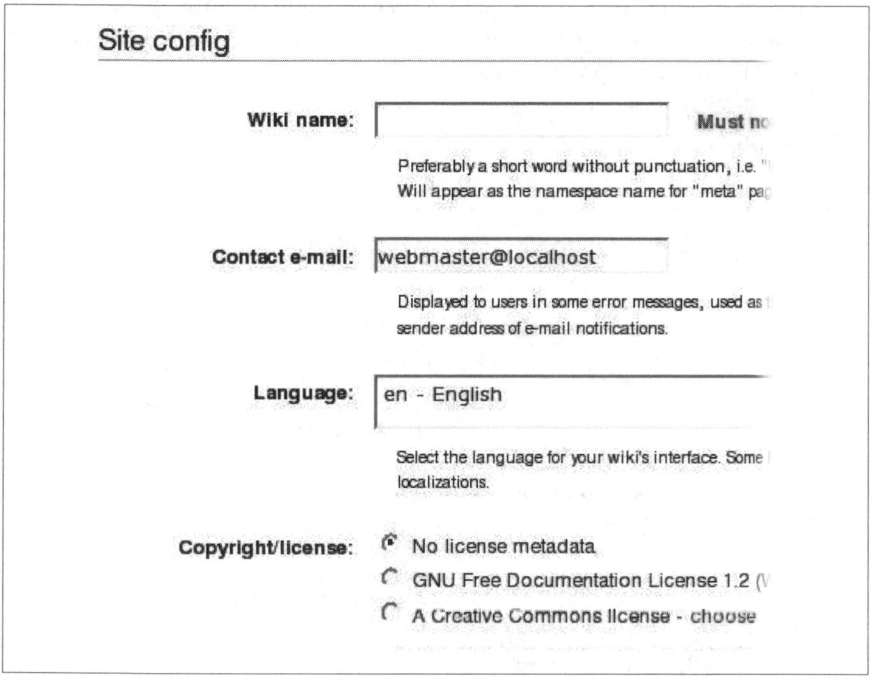

Figure 9-2. MediaWiki installer: site configuration

Figure 9-2 shows the first section of the installation page. Here is a description of the fields:

Wiki name
> The name of your wiki as it will appear to users.

Contact email
> A valid email address for the wiki administrator.

Language
> The preferred spoken language for the wiki.

Copyright/license
> A license for the content your users will create.

Admin username and password

The username and password for the wiki sysop who has permission to do any operations within the wiki. The default name is WikiSysop and can be changed. Later you can create as many sysop accounts as you like.

Caching

Leave blank for now. Caching can greatly improve the performance of your wiki, but it needs to be set up. We strongly recommend it. You can read more about it at *http://www.mediawiki.org/wiki/Manual:Cache* and in "PHP Acceleration" on page 324.

Email setup

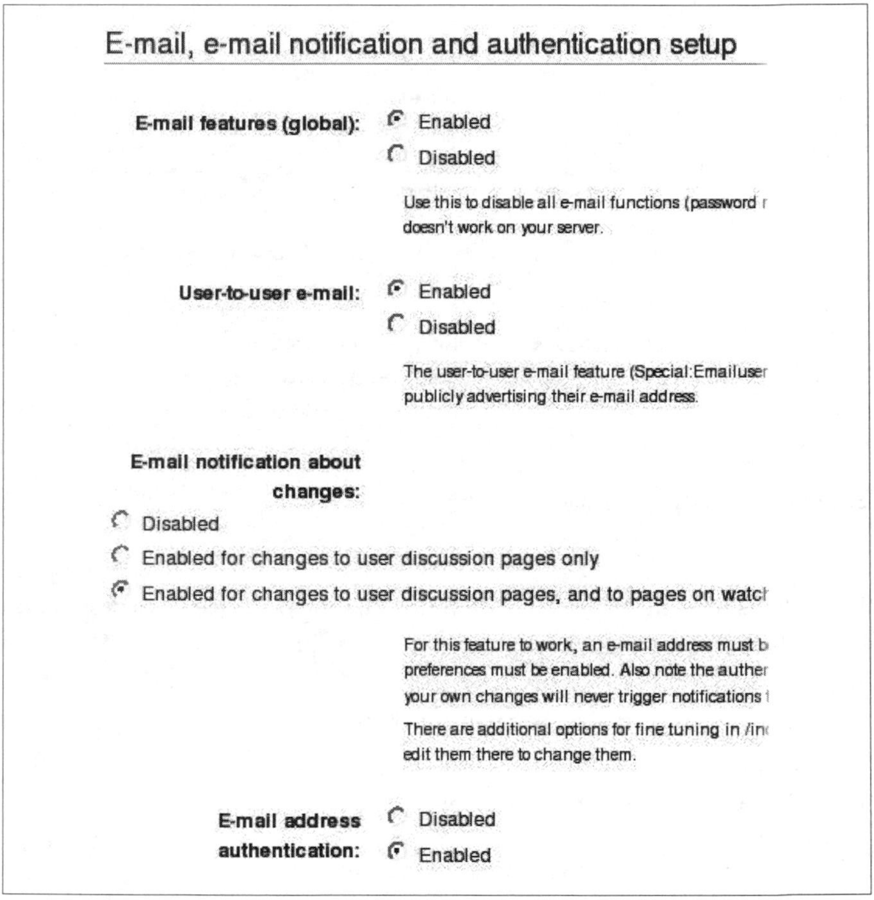

E-mail, e-mail notification and authentication setup

E-mail features (global): ⦿ Enabled
    ◯ Disabled

Use this to disable all e-mail functions (password doesn't work on your server.

User-to-user e-mail: ⦿ Enabled
    ◯ Disabled

The user-to-user e-mail feature (Special:Emailuser publicly advertising their e-mail address.

E-mail notification about changes:
◯ Disabled
◯ Enabled for changes to user discussion pages only
⦿ Enabled for changes to user discussion pages, and to pages on watch

For this feature to work, an e-mail address must b preferences must be enabled. Also note the auther your own changes will never trigger notifications

There are additional options for fine tuning in /in edit them there to change them.

E-mail address authentication: ◯ Disabled
    ⦿ Enabled

Figure 9-3. MediaWiki installer: email configuration

Figure 9-3 shows the next section of the installation page. Here is a description of the fields:

Email features
> Globally enable or disable email within the wiki.

User-to-user email
> Permit wiki users to email each other from within the wiki.

Email notification about changes
> Permit automatic emails to be sent when articles are changed.

Email address authentication
> Require users to confirm their supplied email address is valid.

Database setup

Database config

Database type:	⦿ MySQL
Database host:	localhost
	If your database server isn't on your wel
Database name:	wikidb
DB username:	wikiuser
DB password:	
DB password confirm:	
	If you only have a single user account below) you can specify new accounts/d case, ensure that it has SELECT, INSE
Superuser account:	☐ Use superuser account
Superuser name:	root
Superuser password:	
	If the database user specified above do within it, please check the box and pro

Figure 9-4. MediaWiki installer: database configuration

The next section of the installation page (Figure 9-4) concerns the MediaWiki database. Here is a description of the fields:

Database type
> Choose the database platform. If you've been following the instructions in this chapter, choose MySQL.

Database host
>If your MySQL database will live on the wiki server, choose `localhost`; otherwise, enter the name of your MySQL server machine.

Database name
>A new database to hold MediaWiki's data. It is traditionally named `wikidb`, but you can enter any unique name you like.

Database username and password
>A database user for accessing the MediaWiki database, traditionally `wikiuser`. This can be an existing user as long as it has the permissions mentioned on the installer page (select, insert, update, delete). Otherwise, enter a new user to be created.

Superuser account
>You can skip this if your MediaWiki database user (e.g., `wikiuser`) already exists and has sufficient permissions to create the MediaWiki database. Otherwise, check "Use superuser account" and enter your database's administrative username and password.

Finally, you'll see specific options for the database type you selected. For MySQL, you'll see:

Database table prefix
>Invent a short prefix to be attached to every table name, such as `mw_`. This lets you run multiple wikis (each with a different prefix) in the same database.

Storage engine
>Choose the default unless you have a reason otherwise.

Database character set
>Choose the default unless you have a reason otherwise.

For PostgreSQL, you'll see:

Database port
>TCP/IP port for accessing the database.

Schema for mediawiki
>Choose the default unless you have a reason otherwise.

Schema for tsearch2
>Choose the default unless you have a reason otherwise.

Final installation steps

Click the Submit button and watch the messages that appear, (Figure 9-5). If the installation is successful, move the file *config/LocalSettings.php* to the parent directory (i.e., the root of your MediaWiki install tree). Now, hit the wiki at `http://`*`hostname`*`/wiki` and you should see your very own MediaWiki home page.

```
Generating configuration file...
■ Database type: MySQL
■ Loading class: DatabaseMysql
■ Attempting to connect to database server as root...success.
■ Connected to 5.0.45-Debian_1ubuntu3.1-log
■ Attempting to create database...
■ Created database wikidb
■ Creating tables... done.
■ Initializing data...
■ Granting user permissions to wikiuser on wikidb...success.
■ Created sysop account wikisysop.
  Creating LocalSettings.php...
```
Installation successful! Move the `config/LocalSettings.php` file to

Figure 9-5. MediaWiki installation complete

 LocalSettings.php is the most important file for the wiki administrator. It is the master file for configuring MediaWiki for your site.

Once you've verified the wiki is working, delete the *config* directory that contains the installation script. It is not needed for the wiki to function, and represents a security risk if other users can access it.

Important Optional Features

MediaWiki has hundreds of configuration parameters and optional features. We'll cover a few that are good to set up before users arrive:

- File uploads
- Email
- Help page installation
- Math mode
- Short URLs

Some features require you to edit the *LocalSettings.php* file created at installation time (see "The Web Installer" on page 182), which is written in the PHP programming language. To perform these modifications:

1. Locate *LocalSettings.php* in the root of the MediaWiki source tree.
2. Search the file for the name of the setting. Setting names usually begin with `$wg`.
3. Set the value:
   - If the setting is already present, change it to match the instructions in the following sections.
   - Otherwise, add it to the *end* of the file exactly as written in the instructions.

If MediaWiki pages no longer operate correctly after changing *LocalSettings.php*, examine the Apache error log file (e.g., */var/log/apache2*, */var/log/httpd*, *C:\Apache2\logs*) for likely error messages.

Enabling File Uploads

File uploads are optional and disabled by default. Here are the steps to enable this common feature.

Make the images directory writable

First, make sure that the *images* subdirectory in your MediaWiki install directory is writable by MediaWiki. That is, it must be writable by the account under which your web server is running (e.g., daemon, www, your local system account, etc.).

Set $wgEnableUploads

In *LocalSettings.php*, make sure the `$wgEnableUploads` is set to true:

```
$wgEnableUploads = true;
```

This makes the "Upload file" link appear in the Toolbox menu. Test the uploads feature by clicking this link and uploading a JPEG file, then embedding it in a wiki article with an `[[Image:...]]` tag. Other upload configuration options are explained in "File Uploads" on page 248.

Enabling Email

Email within MediaWiki is used for automatic notifications (e.g., changes to articles on your watchlist) and user-to-user communication. To configure it, you'll need to add or change several settings in *LocalSettings.php*.

Mail software

On Linux and Macintosh systems, MediaWiki uses the standard *mail* program supplied by mail agents like Sendmail or Postfix. If *mail* is not available or installable, or if you're using Windows, obtain PHP's PEAR SMTP software. Run from the PHP installation folder on the wiki server:

```
go-pear
  ...follow the prompts...
pear install Mail
pear install Net_SMTP
```

LocalSettings.php mail settings

Once your mail software is available, configure the following settings in *LocalSettings.php* as needed:

$wgEnableEmail = true;
> The global setting for enabling MediaWiki's email features.

$wgEnableUserEmail = true;
> Permit users to send mail to one another from their user pages.

$wgEmergencyContact = 'administrator@example.com';
> The email address of the wiki administrator.

$wgPasswordSender = "$wgSitename Mail <reply@not.possible>";
> The return email address for password reminders, watchlist notifications, and other automatic emails. Set it to something fake unless you want people to reply to it. Here we used the $wgSitename setting, which is the wiki name, to form part of the address.

$wgSMTP *values*
> This array variable specifies your SMTP server:
>
> ```
> $wgSMTP['host'] = 'mailserver.example.com';
> $wgSMTP['IDHost'] = 'mailserver.example.com';
> $wgSMTP['port'] = "25";
> ```
>
> If your mail server requires authentication to accept mail for delivery, also set:
>
> ```
> $wgSMTP['auth'] = true;
> $wgSMTP['username'] = 'the username';
> $wgSMTP['password'] = 'the password';
> ```
>
> otherwise, set:
>
> ```
> $wgSMTP['auth'] = false;
> ```
>
> For more information, see *http://www.mediawiki.org/wiki/Manual: $wgSMTP*.

```
$wgEmailConfirmToEdit
```
Determines whether users must supply and confirm their email address before they're allowed to edit articles. Set to true (a valid email address is required) or false (not required, which is the default).

Installing Help Pages

MediaWiki comes with *no* online help—that is, the `Help` namespace is empty. The "Help" link in the navigation menu points to `Help:Contents`, but the article does not exist.

If you want to write your own help pages, feel free, but a simple alternative is to copy the public domain help pages from *http://www.mediawiki.org/wiki/Help:Contents* into your wiki's `Help` namespace. To accomplish this, visit *http://www.mediawiki.org/wiki/Help:Copying* and follow the instructions:

1. Back up the wiki if it already contains important content, since this procedure will overwrite existing help pages with the same names (see "Backups" on page 320).
2. Visit `Special:Export` on MediaWiki.org.
3. Copy the list of help pages from *http://www.mediawiki.org/wiki/Help:Copying* into the text box.
4. Check the checkboxes as shown in Figure 9-6.
5. Click Export and save the resulting export file to your local disk.
6. On your wiki, visit `Special:Import`, browse to the export file, and upload it (you must be logged in as a sysop to do this).
7. The help pages should now be available on your wiki.

This method isn't perfect (at least at press time), as not all help pages are in the `Help` namespace, and some images are missing. But by browsing the imported pages, you'll see what else to export and import.

Alternatively, you could create a `Help:Contents` article that links to help pages at Wikipedia or elsewhere. However, this might be confusing to new users, who might not realize they've left your wiki by clicking the help links. ("Strange, I could swear I was logged in a minute ago....")

Enabling Math Mode

MediaWiki has an optional component to display complex mathematical formulas using the `<math>` tag (discussed in "Mathematical Formulas" on page 70). To install the math software on Linux and similar systems, follow the

---

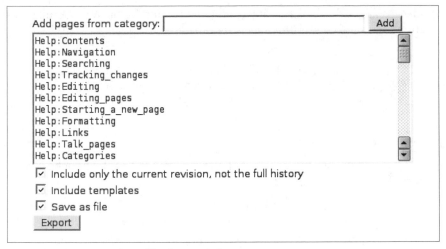

Figure 9-6. Exporting the public domain help pages

instructions in the *README* file in the *math* subdirectory. On a modern Linux system, this usually entails the following:

1. Install *tetex*, *dvipng*, and *ocaml* (as explained in the *README* file).
2. In MediaWiki's *math* directory, run *make*.
3. Enable in *LocalSettings.php*:

   ```
   $wgUseTeX = true;
   ```
4. Test with a formula such as:

   ```
   <math>z = \sqrt{x^2 + y^2}</math>
   ```

On Windows, things are more complicated, so it's recommended you read *http://www.mediawiki.org/wiki/Manual:Running_MediaWiki_on_Windows* for advice. There are several different implementations, and you might need to experiment to find one that works for you. This author has used Benjamin Zeiss's approach (documented on that page) successfully for more than a year.

Enabling Short URLs

Depending on your platform and web server configuration, MediaWiki URLs have one of the following forms by default:

```
http://hostname/.../index.php/ArticleName
http://hostname/.../index.php?title=ArticleName
```

Wikipedia's URLs, however, have a cleaner and more memorable look that many wiki administrators find desirable:

```
http://www.wikipedia.org/wiki/ArticleName
```

You can achieve this look by configuring Apache and MediaWiki. A full treatment of this subject is at *http://www.mediawiki.org/wiki/Short_URL*.

 You can also make prettier URLs for the pages that perform edits, moves, deletions, page history, and more. See *http://www.mediawiki.org/wiki/Manual:$wgActionPaths* for details.

If you have administrative access

If you have administrative access to the wiki server to edit the Apache configuration files, use this method:

1. Make sure your MediaWiki tree is stored in a folder that is *not* called *wiki*. Assuming you've named it *w* as described so far in this chapter, the physical path to the tree is */var/www/htdocs/w* (or *C:/Apache2/htdocs/w* on Windows, or */Library/WebServer/Documents/w* on the Mac).

2. In your *LocalSettings.php* file, set:

   ```
   $wgScriptPath = '/w';
   $wgArticlePath = '/wiki/$1';
   ```

3. In your Apache configuration file, remove any `Alias` line you created in "If You Have Administrative Access" on page 181, and add:

   ```
   <IfModule alias_module>
   Alias /wiki "/var/www/htdocs/w/index.php"
   </IfModule>
   ```

4. Restart Apache and hit your wiki home page. Your URLs should now look like *http://hostname/wiki/ArticleName*.

Shared server or no administrative access

If you don't have administrative access to the wiki server, try this method:

1. In the root directory of your website, create a file named *.htaccess* containing these lines:[*]

   ```
   RewriteEngine On
   RewriteRule ^wiki/(.*)$ w/index.php?title=$1 [PT,L,QSA]
   RewriteRule ^wiki/*$ wiki/ [L,QSA]
   RewriteRule ^/*$ wiki/ [L,QSA]
   ```

2. In *LocalSettings.php*, set:

   ```
   $wgScriptPath = '/w';
   $wgArticlePath = '/wiki/$1';
   ```

---

[*] Credit to *http://www.mediawiki.org/wiki/Manual:Short_URL/wiki/Page_title_--_no_root_access*.

3. Hit your wiki home page. Your URLs should now look like *http://host-name/wiki/ArticleName*.

For this method to work, your site's Apache must be configured:

- with the optional module `mod_rewrite`
- without the directive `AllowOverride None`

If you run into problems, confirm with your system administrator that these configuration options are set up.

A Tour of MediaWiki's Files

Here is a quick tour of the files and directories included in the MediaWiki distribution. They are divided into three categories—important, less important, and ignorable—based on their interest to the typical wiki administrator.

Important Files

Here are the most important files and directories for most wiki administrators:

INSTALL, README, RELEASE-NOTES, UPGRADE
> Basic documentation on the MediaWiki distribution. Always read these files before installing or upgrading the software. The related *HISTORY* file contains old release notes.

COPYING, FAQ
> More documentation. Read these files at least once to understand Media-Wiki's licensing agreement and the location of its Frequently Asked Questions.

AdminSettings.sample
> An example of setting up a (very important) *AdminSettings.php* file, required for running scripts in the *maintenance* directory. (See "Maintenance Scripts" on page 320.)

docs/
> Programmer documentation discussing MediaWiki's code and database setup. Helpful for extension writers.

extensions/
> Third-party and custom extensions for MediaWiki, initially empty. We'll populate the directory in Chapters 14 and 15.

images/
> Uploaded and generated files are placed here automatically, so you can ignore this directory most of the time. There are a few situations where

you need to pay attention to it, however. During initial setup, confirm that the wiki has write permission here. When determining your backup strategy, this is a directory you'll need to back up. Finally, you might view the files in this directory for debugging purposes when something's not working right.

includes/
> MediaWiki's PHP source code, loaded by the top-level *index.php* file. If you write extensions (Chapter 15), you'll refer to these files often to see how MediaWiki works. Some important files are *DefaultSettings.php* (all MediaWiki's of settings, which you override in *LocalSettings.php*), *Defines.php* (useful constants), and *GlobalFunctions.php* (useful functions). Try not to modify the files in this directory, or future MediaWiki upgrades will be harder to install without losing your changes.

index.php, index.php5, wiki.phtml
> The main entry point for MediaWiki. All these files are identical; your system will determine which one is used.

LocalSettings.php
> The most important file, but it doesn't exist until after you've installed MediaWiki. It contains all your local customizations.

maintenance/
> Scripts for the wiki administrator, run manually to accomplish maintenance tasks: uploading batches of images, deleting batches of articles, etc. You'll need an *AdminSettings.php* file to use most of them. We'll discuss some of these in "Maintenance Scripts" on page 320.

skins/
> Files that determine the look and feel of a MediaWiki page. It's common to modify or extend these files, as shown in "Creating a Skin" on page 313.

The following files and directories are intended to be modified by a wiki administrator:

- *LocalSettings.php* (created at installation time)
- *AdminSettings.php* (created from *AdminSettings.example*)
- *extensions/* (you put extensions here)
- *skins/* (you modify the look and feel here)

Less Important Files

These files and directories are necessary to the functioning of the wiki, but you'll rarely need to work with them directly:

---

config/
> Contains the MediaWiki installer. You'll hit the script once at installation time and might never use it again. Delete this directory after you've installed MediaWiki, for security reasons.

languages/
> Translated text and associated infrastructure for MediaWiki's system messages. Don't modify these files; use the system messages system within the wiki instead (see "System Messages" on page 218).

math/
> The software for MediaWiki's <math> tag, which you might need to install; see "Enabling Math Mode" on page 190.

serialized/
> Infrastructure for an optional performance optimization. Refer to the *README* file if you're interested.

Files You Can Ignore

The rest of the files and directories, while critical to the correct functioning of the wiki, are mainly for the MediaWiki development team and gurus. Most wiki administrators can ignore them.

api.php, api.php5
> The main entry point for MediaWiki's API, a way of controlling the wiki without viewing its web pages (see "The MediaWiki API" on page 317).

bin/
> A few miscellaneous scripts.

img_auth.php, img_auth.php5, install-utils.inc, redirect.php, redirect.php5, redirect.phtml, thumb.php, thumb.php5, trackback.php
> Infrastructural pages for the correct functioning of the wiki.

locale/
> Contains generated files from a maintenance script.

Makefile, t/, tests/, profileinfo.php, StartProfiler.php
> Internal tests to check MediaWiki's behavior.

opensearch_desc.php, opensearch_desc.php5
> Software that places a MediaWiki search engine option automatically in your browser: see "Searching for Articles" on page 12.

Maintaining the Code

So, you've installed MediaWiki and are having a grand old time with it. At some point in the future, however, you're likely to change the software: configuring a setting in *LocalSettings.php*, installing an extension, updating to the latest MediaWiki version, or even modifying the core MediaWiki code.

 Don't modify MediaWiki core code unless you have *no other alternative*. Write extensions instead (Chapter 15). And, if you believe an extension cannot do what you need, think twice, ask in the `mediawiki-l` mailing list, and think a third time. Beginning MediaWiki developers don't always realize the surprising power and flexibility of extensions, even after writing a few.

If you absolutely must modify core code, do so by introducing a single, custom hook in the necessary spot in the source code —usually just one line—and writing an extension to use it. See "Hooks and Callbacks" on page 286 for details.

```
wfRunHooks('YourCustomHookName',
          array(&$whatever, &$inputs, &$you, &$need));
```

If you're running MediaWiki for a "serious" application—a corporate intranet, a popular website—these kinds of changes can trip you up if you're not careful. If, for example, you make changes by editing live code files directly on your web server, you'll make syntax errors from time to time and break the wiki. Worse, you could make an incorrect change, forget what the working code used to look like, and be unable to roll back to a working wiki. Or, you could make a perfect change to the code, but when you upgrade MediaWiki to the next version, you could accidentally overwrite your changes or the changes could be incompatible.

These kinds of scenarios would not be acceptable for a critical site. In this section, we'll discuss ways to avoid such problems.

A Minimal Solution

At the very least, keep backup copies of locally modified MediaWiki files, and never change any core MediaWiki code. Here are the critical files:

- *LocalSettings.php*, which definitely has local modifications
- *AdminSettings.php*, if it exists
- The *extensions* directory, if you've installed extensions
- The *skins* directory, if you've made skin changes

Maintenance with Version Control

The next step is to maintain your changes under version control. Subversion (*http://subversion.tigris.org*) is a good choice, and is available free for all popular platforms. (The rest of this chapter assumes familiarity with Subversion.) At the very least, you should version all changes made to the locally modified, critical files listed earlier.

A more robust solution is to version the entire MediaWiki code base using a *vendor branch* setup, an advanced but highly recommended solution that will allow your changes—even those to core MediaWiki code—to survive updates. (See *http://svnbook.red-bean.com/nightly/en/svn.advanced.vendorbr.html* for details.)

In this technique, you create Subversion diffs between vendor releases and apply them to your locally modified release, thereby preserving your changes. When conflicts occur, resolve them manually.

Here is the initial setup:

1. Create your main Subversion folder for the code, called *MediaWiki*.
2. Within *MediaWiki*, create a subfolder called *Vendor*.
3. Within *Vendor*, create a subfolder for the first MediaWiki release you're installing. Assume it is *mediawiki-1.2.3*. (As new releases come out, you'll create a new folder for each one here.) Commit.
4. Also in the *Vendor* folder, create a subfolder called *LatestVendorBranch* that is an exact copy (*svn copy*) of the first vendor folder, *mediawiki-1.2.3*.
5. As a sibling to the *Vendor* folder (in *MediaWiki*), create a folder *Local* that is also a copy (*svn copy*) of *mediawiki-1.2.3*. Commit.

At this point, you should have three folders. For now, they all contain exactly the same code, but in the future they will diverge as follows:

MediaWiki/Vendor/mediawiki-1.2.3
> This is an untouched vendor release. You'll create a separate folder like this for every vendor release.

MediaWiki/Vendor/LatestVendorBranch
> This will always contain the latest official release from MediaWiki.org, constructed in such a way that you can obtain diffs (deltas) between official releases.

MediaWiki/Local
> This will always contain your locally modified version of MediaWiki. We'll be applying the deltas from *LatestVendorBranch* into here. See Figure 9-7 for details.

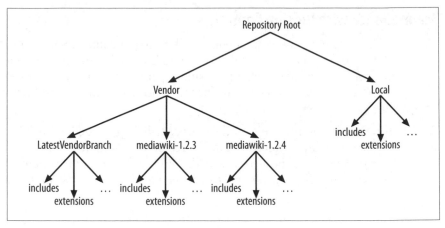

Figure 9-7. Vendor branch setup

Your daily work should always be done within *MediaWiki/Local*. Make any changes you like here, and then deploy them to your live MediaWiki site. When an official MediaWiki upgrade occurs, do the following:

1. Extract the new version of MediaWiki to a new folder in (e.g., *MediaWiki/Vendor*, *MediaWiki/Vendor/mediawiki-1.2.4*), but do not add or commit it to Subversion yet. (This avoids dealing with the *.svn* subdirectories that Subversion creates.)

2. Copy the contents of the new folder on top of *MediaWiki/Vendor/Latest VendorBranch*.

3. Using your favorite "diff" tool,[†] compare the folders *LatestVendor Branch* and *mediawiki-1.2.4*. Using *svn add* and *svn delete*, make *Latest VendorBranch* look exactly like *mediawiki-1.2.4*.

 Any difference, no matter how small, is a bug in your files and must be resolved.

4. Commit *LatestVendorBranch* and *mediawiki-1.2.4* to Subversion, and take note of the Subversion revision number: this revision is *precisely a delta* (or "diff") between official MediaWiki versions 1.2.3 and 1.2.4!

5. Merge (*svn merge*) the delta you just created from *LatestVendorBranch* into *MediaWiki/Local*. This applies the official changes to your local branch. Resolve any conflicts and commit *Local*.

† Linux and Macintosh have the standard *diff* command. On Windows, you can try Beyond Compare, *http://www.scootersoftware.com*.

Your *Local* branch now has all the official changes from the new release. As future MediaWiki releases appear, repeat this process to create a new diff and apply it to *Local*.

Upgrading MediaWiki

Subscribe to the MediaWiki announce mailing list to hear about upgrades and security patches:

> *https://lists.wikimedia.org/mailman/listinfo/mediawiki-announce*

If your MediaWiki site code is 100% unmodified (other than *LocalSettings.php* and *extensions*), upgrades are easy and generally reliable. New MediaWiki releases are run on large, popular sites such as Wikipedia for months before the software is released for others, so they tend to be quite stable.

Once you've read the *UPGRADE* and *RELEASE-NOTES* files found in the new version, upgrades generally follow these steps:

1. Back up your wiki, including the database, code, and images (see "Backups" on page 320).
2. Deploy the new MediaWiki files on top of the old.
3. Run the *maintenance/update.php* script and watch for error messages.

That's usually it. Hit `Special:Version` to confirm the new version number is present, and edit a few articles to make sure the basics are working. In a serious environment, you should create and run a suite of regression tests to verify that the wiki is fully operational.

If you've been modifying MediaWiki using a vendor branch (discussed in "Maintenance with Version Control" on page 197), you're also in good shape. Follow the same upgrade procedure, but instead of copying the new, official MediaWiki files on top of the old, copy your *MediaWiki/Local* files.

A Simple Release Process

A *release* copies MediaWiki files from one server to another (say, a development server to a production server). You could use ordinary copy commands, but it's preferable to use *rsync* (*http://samba.anu.edu.au/rsync/*), which efficiently copies only the differences between the file trees. It is supplied with Linux and Macintosh and available for Windows.

If your production wiki server is called prodserver, where MediaWiki's *w* directory is located in */var/www/htdocs*, and your development code is in *Local*, then the command:

```
cd Local
rsync -av --cvs-exclude . prodserver:/var/www/htdocs/w
```

copies all the changes to prodserver, skipping Subversion's special subdirectories.

 On Windows servers, to copy files to a share with *rsync*, use:

```
cd Local
rsync -rtv --cvs-exclude . \\prodserver\c$\Apache2\htdocs\w
```

It's also a good idea to preserve a copy of every release to your production server, as in Figure 9-8, so you can roll back if an error occurs. This is easily done with Subversion's *svn copy* command:

1. Create a sibling folder to *Vendor* and *Local*, called *Releases*.

2. Before each release, run:

```
svn copy Local Releases/Release-N
commit
```

to save a copy of the release, which you've now labeled as release *N* (or whatever you like).‡

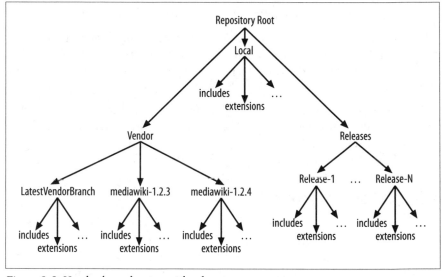

Figure 9-8. Vendor branch setup with releases

---

‡ More efficiently, run the *svn copy* directly against the repository (by URL) to avoid copying a whole branch to disk and back:

```
svn copy -m"release N" http://svnserver/.../Local http://svnserver/.../Releases/Release-N
```

When you create or modify an extension for your wiki, consider appending an ID to the MediaWiki version number, $wgVersion, in *LocalSettings.php* for your records. For example:

```
// Create MediaWiki 1.13.0-local.6.c
$wgVersion .= '-local.6.c';
```

Caveat: some third-party extensions might check the MediaWiki version number and balk at this nonstandard format, especially if they use the PHP function version_compare (*http://www.php.net/version_compare*), but there have been no problems in over a year.

Protecting the Database Password in Subversion

After a MediaWiki installation, your database password is stored in *LocalSettings.php*. This is not great if other people have access to the file. To give it a bit more protection, do the following:

1. Create a branch *B* in Subversion that is protected by access control.
2. Store the database password definition in a PHP file *Passwords.php* in branch *B*:

   ```
   <?php
   $wgDBpassword      = 'dbpass';
   $wgDBadminpassword = 'adminpass';
   ```

3. Make branch *B* available within *MediaWiki/Local* using Subversion's *externals* feature (*http://svnbook.red-bean.com/nightly/en/svn.advanced.externals.html*), an advanced capability that references another branch seamlessly. Set it up by running:

   ```
   cd Local
   svn propset svn:externals "Secure http://svnserver/path/to/B"
   commit
   ```

4. Now, update the *Local* directory on disk with *svn update* and you'll get a subdirectory *Secure* that maps to *B*.
5. In *LocalSettings.php* and *AdminSettings.php*, remove the database passwords and replace them with:

   ```
   require_once("Secure/Passwords.php")
   ```

Now, *LocalSettings.php* pulls the passwords from *Secure/Passwords.php*, which you see on disk, but is protected by access control in the Subversion repository. This is not high security, but it's better than the default setup, given that MediaWiki needs the database password in plain text.

## CHAPTER 10

Practical Wiki Design

So, you've installed the wiki software (Chapter 9), but what happens next? Just invite people and see what happens? How do you make your wiki *succeed*?

The answer depends on your goals. Is your wiki just for fun? Or does it need to become a serious information resource? Can anybody write articles, or is membership restricted? Can anybody read it, or only authorized users? Do you care about a consistent look and feel for articles? How much time do you want to spend on maintenance? Consider these questions in advance, and you'll save a lot of work down the road.

In this chapter, we'll discuss:

Using MediaWiki (or not)
> The challenges of adopting MediaWiki.

Planning the wiki
> How much structure should you set up in advance?

Standards
> Setting standards for articles, categories, templates, and more.

Governance
> Who should be in charge?

 This chapter, unlike most others in this book, is largely opinion. The ideas are based on successful wiki deployments in corporate, university, and fun/informal environments, as well as general experience in organizing information.

Adopting MediaWiki

MediaWiki is a fantastic system, but not appropriate for every application. It's easy to use but not necessarily easy to learn, particularly for nontechnical users.

Some of the issues that can cause difficulty for new users are discussed below. These things aren't bad; they just take some getting used to.

Ownership and access control

On a typical wiki, articles have no set "owner," and anyone can edit any article (for the most part). To set up a stricter or more flexible model than this, you have to jump through hoops. MediaWiki has an access control system (see "User Rights and Permissions" on page 229), but it's not intended for complex, large-scale control with dozens (or hundreds) of security groups.

Non-WYSIWYG editing

If your users grew up on Microsoft Office, they'll find the MediaWiki edit page a challenge. You'd think MediaWiki's button bar would help, but it also causes confusion. Sure, you can make a word bold by highlighting it and clicking the "bold" button—which surrounds the word with triple quotes—but there's no similar feature to *unbold* the word. (Click the "bold" button again and you get *six* quotes instead of three.) This behavior makes sense to a techie, but not necessarily to other humans.*

Case-sensitivity

While beneficial for authors, MediaWiki's case-sensitivity rule (see the sidebar "Article Titles and Case-Sensitivity" within) is wildly different from other systems and therefore not immediately intuitive. Try explaining to your nontechnical CEO that article titles are "case-sensitive, except for the first letter of the first word, but we sometimes create redirects to work around this, though MediaWiki does automatically capitalize that first letter when you view a page, and oh yes, search is case-insensitive, except the Go button gives special treatment to capitals in the middle of words."

File handling

MediaWiki is absolutely *not* a document management system (and never claims to be), but it does support uploads, so its shortcomings are worth pointing out. It's easy to upload a file, but maintaining that file takes more effort within the wiki than on disk, and this added work may discourage nontechnical people from using MediaWiki. Consider the steps necessary to revise a file:

---

* At press time, a promising WYSIWYG extension called MediaWiki+FCKeditor (*http://mediawiki .fckeditor.net/*) offers a glimmer of hope, but it's still in the prototype stage. WYSIWYG is not a trivial undertaking for MediaWiki developers. How should an editor handle the advanced features from Chapter 7: templates, parser functions, DPL tags, or locally written extensions?

1. Locate and download the file from the wiki to your local disk. (You can't just keep a working copy on disk, as someone might change it in the wiki without notifying you, rendering your copy obsolete.)

2. Edit it and save to disk.

3. Locate the file's name in the wiki, `Image:whatever`, which might differ from the name on disk.

4. Visit the image page, `Image:whatever`.

5. Check the revision history to make sure nobody uploaded another version while you were working. (Unlike articles, uploads have no conflict detection; your revision would silently wipe out their changes.) If necessary, redownload the file and merge your changes. Repeat this step as often as necessary.

6. Upload your new version.

Compare this to (say) Microsoft SharePoint 2007: click the file's icon, edit it, and save, creating a new revision. If your users are accustomed to this level of ease, MediaWiki might be a tough sell (and might be an inappropriate system for them).[†]

Tables

A generation raised on Microsoft Office is not accustomed to creating tables using a markup language. When editing large tables, you have to keep a lot in your head. Think about the wikitext necessary to create Table 10-1.

Table 10-1. A wikitext nightmare

	A	B	C	D	E
One		x	x	x	
Two		x		x	
Three	x	x	x		x
Four	x	x	x	x	x
Five		x			x
Six		x		x	x

Hint: the wikitext can be up to 50 lines long. Imagine a nontechnical person staring at that wikitext, trying to find the one "x" he needs to change.

[†] On the other hand, SharePoint's wiki has maybe 5% of the power of MediaWiki. Neither system is "better" than the other—they just serve different purposes.

Numbered lists
> The numbering is easy to break—just insert a blank line between entries—and is limited to integer labels beginning with 1, even when nesting lists.

When adopting MediaWiki as a platform, think about these common difficulties. Will they present a barrier to your intended users? What training will be necessary to make people productive and enthusiastic?

Planning

Assuming you've determined that MediaWiki is a good choice for your community, let's talk about planning your wiki's structure. Here are some important dimensions:

- Initial structure: the first articles and categories
- Ownership of the articles
- Users and access control

The approaches we discuss in this section are not the only ones, but they're representative of common setups.

Initial Structure

What should your wiki contain before the first visitors arrive? Here are some approaches to setting up the initial structure:

Blank slate
> Start with nothing. Stick a welcome message on the home page, sit back, and let the wiki grow. This is the easiest way to begin because there's literally nothing to do. This approach might be fine for an informal, fun wiki, where nobody cares if 12 different articles cover roughly the same material.

Infrastructure
> Create infrastructural articles and templates before visitors arrive, so your wiki will have consistency from article to article. Examples abound on Wikipedia: disambiguation pages when the same word has multiple meanings, templates to point out unreferenced material or conflicts of interest, the `documentation` template from "Transcluding Subpages" on page 120, and much more. If you use this approach, you'll need to encourage/teach people to use your infrastructure.

Preplanned categories and articles
> Instead of allowing categories to be created ad hoc, pre-create a *taxonomy* of categories and subcategories that arise naturally for your wiki's

topic. You could even create blank articles within those categories, perhaps in a standard format with particular headings and subheadings, on common subjects within your wiki's topic.‡ For example, when starting a wiki about automobiles, you could create categories for all manufacturers and makes, and blank articles for all models and auto parts. This encourages people to edit existing articles rather than create redundant ones, reducing their work (see the sidebar "Corporate Settings"). It also predetermines the names, spelling, and capitalization of these topics, so people don't accidentally create duplicate ones with slightly different titles.

No matter how much planning you do, in an active wiki, the structure will certainly change. Be ready to create new categories, change category/subcategory relationships, rename articles, move material between articles, introduce new infrastructural templates, and perform other tasks to make the content findable and maintainable.

Corporate Settings

If you're thinking of introducing a wiki at work, don't just install one and let it run itself (the "blank slate" approach). Corporate history is littered with failed attempts to roll out new intranet technologies, so think before acting. A year from now, will your wiki be maintainable, and by whom? Can it integrate with your other corporate intranet sites? Will other departments follow your daring lead, roll out their own wikis, and create chaos where nobody knows which wiki has the information they need?

A successful corporate wiki is not just about the technology, but also about *people* and *process*. The best technology is a waste of time if people don't use it. Take time to gather requirements, find out what people need, and consider MediaWiki as one possible technology for your setting.

When you create a general-purpose wiki on the Internet, you'll attract users who are inherently motivated: they *want* to contribute. Corporate wikis are different: your users might be disinterested (ho hum, yet another intranet system) or even unmotivated, seeing the wiki as "thrust upon them" and an unwanted addition to their workload. People are busy and may believe they don't have time to document their knowledge and processes. In these cases, try to reduce the amount of work for writers by pre-structuring the wiki (see "Initial Structure" on page 206), making it more of a "fill in the blanks" experience rather than writing from scratch. Eventually, as the wiki fills with useful information, people will come to see it as a vital resource, and motivation will come from within.

---

‡ This suggestion contrasts with Wikipedia's "no blank articles" policy (*http://en.wikipedia.org/wiki/Wikipedia:No_blank_pages*), but it can be an excellent way to jump-start a corporate wiki.

People may also be distrustful of the MediaWiki model of access control: "You mean anybody in the company can edit my articles? That's not acceptable!" In some situations they're right: a wiki might not be the ideal solution. But if you believe a wiki is appropriate, explain how MediaWiki's automatic version control means that no information is ever lost, and watchlists mean that changes can be easily monitored.

Don't underestimate the work needed to maintain the content in a corporate wiki. If left to their own devices, users will create wildly inconsistent articles, some relevant to the business, and others that might be completely inappropriate: "for sale" ads, timely information that's obsolete tomorrow ("Anybody want two tickets to tonight's baseball game? Email me!"), photos of their kids, misplaced requests for help that nobody will read ("Hey, anybody know how to use this wiki thing?")...and quicker than you'd think, the wiki is 50% garbage.

Pilot the wiki with a small group of users before expanding it to your department, organization, or entire company. Better to shake out the problems before inflicting them on a large audience.

Finally, if your wiki will be accessible via the Internet, make sure you get buy-in from your IT department. Server technology such as MediaWiki has inherent security risks.

Ownership

It's funny to talk about "ownership" of wiki articles when everyone and their grandmother can edit them. But ownership in this sense is not about executive control: it's about motivated people overseeing the content so it's readable, well organized, and consistent. Here are some approaches:

Informal
> Articles do not have assigned owners: you trust that the community will produce good material. This is fine for informal sites, but probably not for (say) a critical medical guide.

Semi-formal
> Articles have owners, perhaps by category or namespace. Owners might be assigned by someone with authority, or might just be interested parties. Owners ensure that articles follow the wiki's standards. They might also refactor articles (see "Recipes for Refactoring" on page 132) to avoid consistency maintenance problems (see "Maintaining a Consistent Wiki" on page 108). They do not, however, change the meaning of the content in articles.

Formal
> Articles have strong ownership by experts in their domain, formally as-
> signed. Owners not only uphold standards but also modify the content to
> correct, clarify, or otherwise change its meaning. This kind of ownership
> is good for wikis containing critical information.

The stronger the ownership, the more likely it is that your wiki will be correct
and consistent (assuming the owners are competent!). If the ownership model
is too strong for your intended audience, however, it can lead to demotivation
or battles.

Users and Access Control

Who can visit your wiki? Who can edit its articles? Make these decisions early
so you don't annoy your early members with constantly changing rules.

Access to the wiki

There are several approaches to controlling access to your wiki with regard to
anonymous and registered users:

No restrictions
> Anonymous users have full access

Logins required to write
> Anonymous users cannot edit articles; they must create an account first

Logins required to read
> Nobody can see wiki content unless they create an account

Invitation only
> Users cannot create their own accounts; a sysop creates them and invites
> people to the wiki

"User Rights and Permissions" on page 229 explains how to set up these different types of access control.

Access control lists

Controlling access to particular pages by particular users is possible in
MediaWiki, but is not scalable to large groups. (MediaWiki is not a content
management system.) To learn your options, see "Creating a user group" on
page 233 and "Protecting Articles" on page 242. There are also third-party
extensions that offer access control, but read *http://www.mediawiki.org/wiki/
Security_issues_with_authorization_extension* to learn their security
limitations.

Motivation

Do people *want* to participate in your wiki, or do they need encouragement, as in busy corporate environments (see the sidebar "Corporate Settings" within "Initial Structure" on page 206)? If you're lucky enough to have motivated users, that's great—but if it's your job to roll out a wiki and get people to adopt it, here are some things to try:

Create structure
  Pre-create categories, help pages, and other infrastructure before the users arrive, as in ("Initial Structure" on page 206).

Pre-announce
  Let people know what's coming with a series of announcements. Remember the old saying, "Tell 'em what you're going to tell 'em; then tell 'em; then tell 'em what you told 'em."

Motivate by example
  If other wikis have succeeded in your company, point skeptics to `Special:AllPages` and say, "Don't you wish you had all this documentation in *your* area? And it takes only minutes per day!" If there are no other examples in your company, point them to a public wiki.

Provide training
  A fully populated `Help` namespace might not be enough for some users, particularly nontechnical ones. Consider holding training classes with plenty of realistic examples from people's work lives. And create a printable cheatsheet of wiki syntax appropriate to the environment.

Establishing Standards

If you want your wiki content to be maintainable, establish standards. These standards can be simple (such as "article titles should be capitalized") or more complex (such as "all articles about dogs must include the following six templates, filled out").

 When you need inspiration, look to Wikipedia. Its guidelines, standards, and processes might work for your wiki, too, and they're documented in detail. Why reinvent the wheel?

Helpful Templates

Make your wiki more consistent and maintainable with custom templates. On Wikipedia, for example, when an author creates an article without references, a sysop might add this template:

```
{{unreferenced|date=November 2007}}
```

which produces a box at the top of the article, saying:

> This article does not cite any references or sources. (November 2007) Please help improve this article by adding citations to reliable sources. Unverifiable material may be challenged and removed.

with links to relevant Wikipedia policies. This template is just one of many for articles that violate Wikipedia's guidelines or policies. See them all at:

> *http://en.wikipedia.org/wiki/Wikipedia:Template_messages*

Another example is Wikipedia's disambiguation pages: these are articles that distinguish multiple meanings of the same word or phrase, as discussed in "Disambiguation Pages" on page 103. By thinking about your intended community of users, you can come up with other helpful templates to set and enforce standards. For more information, see:

> *http://en.wikipedia.org/wiki/Category:Wikipedia_guidelines*

Content Standards

For consistency on your wiki, consider some simple content standards to help your readers and authors. Here are some examples:

Plurals in titles
> Make all article titles singular, or make them all plural. This way your authors don't have to recall, as they type an internal link on the edit page, whether the target article is singular or plural. There will always be exceptions, but if 98% of articles adhere to this standard, it helps.

Effective titles
> Begin titles with a relevant word so they alphabetize well on category pages. The title "How to walk a dog" alphabetizes under "H", which is not where most people would look for it. It's better to alphabetize under "D" for "Dog walking" or "W" for "Walking a dog".

Article introductions
> Insist that every article contain an introduction (at least a sentence or two), so that first-time readers can quickly get an idea of what the article is about.

Choose content owners on the wiki to enforce these standards. For more examples, see:

> *http://en.wikipedia.org/wiki/Help:Contents/Policies_and_guidelines*

Governance

Who will be in charge of your wiki? If it's small (say, 200 users or fewer), a single, motivated sysop can set and enforce standards without too much trouble. As the community and content grow, however, you might need multiple sysops, and those sysops might need rules to live by so they can reach consensus on nontrivial issues.

Choosing Sysops

Sysops (see "Administrative Roles" on page 216) are users with the right to modify any content on the wiki, so choose them wisely. Sysops should be:

- Responsible
- Good organizers
- Knowledgeable about wikitext
- Ideally, good writers

Wikipedia has helpful guidelines at:

> *http://en.wikipedia.org/wiki/Wikipedia:Administrators*

Establishing Processes

If your wiki has multiple sysops, establish processes to help them work consistently. Wikipedia has detailed documentation on its processes, which you can use as a model:

Deleting articles
http://en.wikipedia.org/wiki/Wikipedia:Deletion_process

Protecting articles
http://en.wikipedia.org/wiki/Wikipedia:Protected_page

Blocking users
http://en.wikipedia.org/wiki/Wikipedia:Blocking_policy

Forming and discussing policies
http://en.wikipedia.org/wiki/Wikipedia:Policies_and_guidelines

Spend a few happy hours poring over Wikipedia policies and guidelines at:

> *http://en.wikipedia.org/wiki/Wikipedia:List_of_policies*
> *http://en.wikipedia.org/wiki/Category:Wikipedia_guidelines*

Other User Groups

If your wiki will need finer-grained permissions than just "registered users" and "sysops," plan to create other user groups. See "User Rights and Permissions" on page 229 for guidance.

Integrating with Other Websites

Is your wiki independent? Or will it frequently link to and share data with other sites? If the latter, some planning may aid your users in this linking and sharing. For example, in a corporate intranet, you might want your wiki integrated with your file servers, share drives, bug-tracking system, content management system, or other web-based tools. Two simple forms of integration are interwiki links and RSS.

Interwiki Links

Interwiki links (see "Interwiki Links" on page 84) point to other websites, but conveniently look like internal links. On many MediaWiki sites, for example, links that begin [[wp:...]] point to Wikipedia. You can create new kinds of interwiki links pointing to systems of your own choosing (see "Creating Interwiki Links" on page 332). Plan and evangelize your site's interwiki links as early as possible so that authors learn to use them instead of external URLs.

Interwiki links work for any external website that has a flat, predictable link structure. "Flat" means that all the desired URLs have the same format, varying only in one place. For example, the bug-tracking website for PHP (the programming language of MediaWiki) has URLs of the form:

```
http://bugs.php.net/bug.php?id=XYZ
```

where *XYZ* is a bug ID. This is a perfect candidate for an interwiki link. Any external MediaWiki site also works well, as its article URLs are all the same except for the title.

RSS and Atom Feeds

Out of the box, a few MediaWiki articles provide data feeds in RSS and Atom formats, notably history pages, the recent changes page (`Special:RecentChanges`), and the new articles page (`Special:NewPages`). When visiting each page, you can access these feeds from the RSS and Atom links in the Toolbox menu.

For additional syndication capabilities, try these extensions available from *www.mediawiki.org*:

Extension:RSS
> Pull RSS content easily into any wiki page. Learn more at *http://www.me diawiki.org/wiki/Extension:RSS*.

Extension:WikiArticleFeeds
> Turn any wiki article into an RSS feed by inserting a few custom tags. Learn more at *http://www.mediawiki.org/wiki/Extension:WikiArticleFeeds*.

Other Integration

For more powerful integration with other systems, check out the large selection of third-party MediaWiki extensions (Chapter 14). If none exists for your purposes, write your own extensions (Chapter 15).

## CHAPTER 11

Configuring MediaWiki: An Overview

Once you've installed MediaWiki, planned your wiki's mission, and invited users, it's time for the wiki to begin its life. And you're in charge! This means you set the wiki's appearance, choose its features, and generally keep things running smoothly for your user community.

As a wiki sysop or administrator (we'll define the difference shortly), you have many tools at your disposal. In this chapter, we'll survey the various kinds, including:

Advanced page constructs
> Templates and Dynamic Page List, described in Chapter 7, now applied to running the wiki

Special pages
> The built-in web applications we saw in Chapter 8, now applied to running the wiki

System messages
> All the hard wired text in MediaWiki, found in menus, buttons, error messages, and other "system-supplied" areas

System-wide CSS
> Changing cascading stylesheets for wiki pages

System-wide JavaScript
> Changing client-side behavior for wiki pages

Configuration settings
> Hundreds of global PHP variables for you to tweak via the file *LocalSettings.php* in the root of the MediaWiki source tree

Extensions
> Custom programming to change MediaWiki's behavior, available from third parties or created by you

Skinning
Changing the overall look and feel of MediaWiki

SQL programming
Directly accessing MediaWiki's database

Maintenance scripts
A collection of PHP scripts supplied with MediaWiki for diverse purposes

As you can see, there are a lot of ways to configure and maintain a MediaWiki site. (Perhaps too many!) Sometimes similar-looking tasks have wildly different methods to accomplish them. A classic example is changing the system menus on each page. The Navigation menu is controlled within the wiki by a system message, the Toolbox menu is controlled by programming an extension, and the footer menu is modified by editing a skin file. So much for consistency! Moreover, the latter two operations may require a wiki administrator to deploy the changed files.

So, for complete maintenance of a MediaWiki site, you'll need a broad, diverse set of knowledge, including programming and system administration. If you don't have some of these technical skills yet, don't be discouraged: you can do a tremendous amount of configuration entirely within the wiki, without programming, just by editing articles. Here are some good starting points for reference material:

> *http://www.mediawiki.org/wiki/Manual:Contents*
> *http://www.mediawiki.org/wiki/Category:Manual*
> *http://en.wikipedia.org/wiki/Help:Moderator*

Administrative Roles

Different MediaWiki capabilities require different levels of access:

Users
Some features available to every wiki user can also be applied to running the wiki.

Sysops
Designated users who can edit "protected" articles and access restricted special pages. Related to sysops are *bureaucrats*, who can bestow rights and privileges on other users.

Wiki administrators
People with access to the infrastructure outside the wiki, such as the server machine, operating system, web server, and database.

Table 11-1 lists the tools at your disposal and the level of expertise required to use them. The following sections discuss each type of tool.

Table 11-1. Tools for running a MediaWiki site

Tool	Access Level	Programming?	Database Access?
Templates	User	No, but it helps	No
DPL	User[a]	No, but it helps	No
Special pages	User	No	No
System messages	Sysop	No	No
JavaScript	Sysop	Yes, JavaScript	No
CSS	Sysop	Yes, CSS	No
Configuration settings	Administrator	Yes, PHP (minimal)	No
Extensions	Administrator	Yes, PHP (minimal to install, more to create)	No
Skinning	Administrator	Yes, PHP	No
SQL programming	Administrator	Yes, SQL	Yes
Maintenance scripts	Administrator	No	Yes

[a] An administrator is required to install this third-party extension.

Advanced Page Constructs

We saw templates and Dynamic Page List (DPL) back in Chapter 7 in the context of writing wiki articles. These powerful tools are also helpful for running the wiki. For example, DPL is great for writing quick reports of wiki activity. Suppose you'd like to monitor the status of all articles in a category Animal habitats. This DPL tag displays all articles in the category, sorted by their last modification time (most recent first), and the name of the last person to edit them, excluding minor edits:

```
<dpl>
category = Animal habitats
ordermethod = lastedit
order = descending
addlasteditor = true
addeditdate = true
minoredits = exclude
</dpl>
```

Likewise, templates and transclusion are excellent for setting and enforcing wiki standards. The documentation template from "Transcluding Subpages" on page 120 is one example.

Special Pages for Sysops and Bureaucrats

Most special pages (Chapter 8) are available to all users, and they're terrific for monitoring wiki activity. `Special:NewPages` shows you pages that have recently been created, `Special:AncientPages` lists old articles that might need revision, and so on.

Additionally, some special pages are accessible only to sysops or bureaucrats. Examples are `Special:Import`, where sysops can load wiki content in batches, and `Special:UserRights`, where bureaucrats bestow privileges on users.

As usual, special pages are listed in your wiki at `Special:SpecialPages`. If you're logged in as a sysop or bureaucrat, additional special pages will be listed.

System Messages

Throughout a MediaWiki site, you'll see a lot of text that seems built into the MediaWiki software, such as:

- Menu items, button labels, and top tabs
- Menu names, such as "navigation" and "toolbox"
- Preferences page text
- Error and warning messages
- Instructions for uploading a file or using your watchlist
- The names of special pages

These pieces of "infrastructural" text are called *system messages*. Each system message has a name and a value. Table 11-2 has a few examples.

Table 11-2. Sample system messages

Message Name	Default Value	Purpose
mypreferences	My preferences	The text of the "my preferences" link in the user options menu.
move	Move	The title of the "move" tab for renaming an article.
copyrightwarning2	Please note that all contributions to `{{SITENAME}}` may be edited, altered, or removed by other contributors. If you do not want your `height="1in"` writing to be edited mercilessly, then do not submit it here...	A warning on the edit page. (Excerpt.)

Message Name	Default Value	Purpose
namespaceprotected	You do not have permission to edit pages in the '''$1''' namespace.	A "permission denied" message. The $1 symbol indicates a parameter to be passed in.

Though supplied with MediaWiki, system messages can be conveniently modified (overridden) by any wiki sysop in three steps:

1. Locate the name of the desired system message, e.g., `funky-message`.
2. Edit the article `MediaWiki:Funky-message`, i.e., the article `Funky-message` in the `MediaWiki` namespace.
3. Save your changes.

That's it! If you prefer (say) the "move" tab to read "rename", "zap", or even "grapefruit", simply locate its system message (which happens to be `move`), edit `MediaWiki:Move` like any other wiki article, enter a change comment, and save. Because system messages live within the wiki, they are easily changed without programming, though you must be a sysop to do it.

Locating System Messages

Before changing a system message (there are thousands), you need to know its name. For example, the text "my preferences" is found in `mypreferences`, the Navigation menu text is found in `sidebar`, and the instructions on creating a new article are found in `newarticletext`. If you don't know the name of your message of interest, here are a few ways to find it.

Viewing all system messages via the wiki

To see all system messages and their values, visit the "System Messages" special page (`Special:AllMessages`). Be patient, as it is large and might take a few moments to display. The messages are presented alphabetically by name.

Using your browser's search function, look through the table for the message text you want to change and note its name. Beware that the same text might appear in several messages with different purposes, so experiment to make sure you're modifying the right one.

Viewing all system messages via source code

System messages appear in wiki pages, but are actually defined within MediaWiki's source code in the *languages/messages* subfolder, one file per language. The files are named *MessageXX.php*, where *XX* is a two-letter language code, so the English file is *MessagesEn.php*. Once you have your file, use your favorite search tool (text editor, *grep*, *less*, etc.) to locate messages of interest.

Do not modify these files! Instead, override their messages by creating articles in the `MediaWiki` namespace.

Viewing only changed system messages

To see only the system messages that have been modified on your wiki, visit the "All pages" special page (`Special:AllPages`), set the namespace to `MediaWiki`, and click the Submit button. Only modified system messages show up as articles in the `MediaWiki` namespace.

Changing a System Message

To change a system message (say, `my-message`), simply visit `MediaWiki:My-message` and edit the contents. If `MediaWiki:My-message` has been edited, this action will be straightforward, just like editing any other article. If `my-message` has never been changed before, however, your experience will vary based on the version of MediaWiki:

MediaWiki 1.12.0 and later
> Simply visit `MediaWiki:My-message`, where you'll see the default text. Click the edit link, modify the message, and save.

Prior to MediaWiki 1.12.0
> On visiting `MediaWiki:My-message`, you'll be told the article does not exist. If you edit it, however, the default message text will be loaded into the edit box, where you can change and save it.

The article `MediaWiki:My-message`, in fact, does not exist until you override the default value. MediaWiki 1.12.0 and later produce the illusion that the article always exists, but you can see through it by visiting `Special:AllPages`. Select the `MediaWiki` namespace, click Submit, and you'll see that the only articles in the namespace are those overriding the default values.

To restore the default value of a system message, set it to no value (erase its content and save) or delete its article in the `MediaWiki` namespace.

System Messages with Parameters

In some system messages, you'll see values such as `$1` and `$2`. These stand for parameters that MediaWiki substitutes into the message. For example, system message `rcnote` has the value:

```
Below are the last '''$1''' changes in the last '''$2''' days, as of $3.
```

In this message, which appears on the recent changes page (`Special:RecentChanges`), MediaWiki replaces `$1` by a count of changes, `$2` by a count of days, and `$3` by a date. How can you know this? Often, a guess or a little trial-and-error is enough to figure things out. For a definitive answer, search the MediaWiki source code to locate the message and see how it's used.

You can't control what substitutions are made, but you can reorder or remove `$` parameters from the message. For instance, if you changed the `rcnote` message to:

```
Wow, you've got $1 changes as of $3!!
```

the missing parameter `$2` (counting days) is simply not used or displayed. You could even replace the message with an empty value to suppress the display altogether.

Displaying a System Message Within Another Wiki Article

Suppose you're documenting a feature of your wiki: how to view a list of recent changes. You might write something like this:

```
To see recent changes, click the "recent changes" link
in the navigation menu.
```

While this looks correct today, it'll become wrong tomorrow when the wiki sysop modifies the "recent changes" system message to read, "What's New?" What's worse, your article will become wrong *silently*, still claiming the link is "recent changes".

To make your article obsolescence-proof, reference and *transclude* the system message directly instead of hardcoding the phrase "recent changes". Remember "Templates and Transclusion" on page 112, where we pulled the contents of one wiki article into another? Since system messages appear as articles in the `MediaWiki` namespace, you can transclude the desired message (`MediaWiki:Recentchanges`) into your documentation:

```
To see recent changes, click the "{{MediaWiki:Recentchanges}}" link
in the navigation menu.
```

Or, even better, as the menu title "navigation" also comes from a system message, `MediaWiki:Navigation`, write:

```
To see recent changes, click the "{{MediaWiki:Recentchanges}}" link
in the {{MediaWiki:Navigation}} menu.
```

Creating Custom System Messages

Extension authors can create their own system messages using the method call `$wgMessageCache->addMessages` (see "Multilanguage Tag Extension" on page

298). Messages added in this manner work just like the system-supplied ones, and can be overridden in the MediaWiki namespace.

You might be tempted to create an arbitrary article in the MediaWiki namespace—say, MediaWiki:*Whatever*—and treat it like a system message, including it on other wiki pages as {{MediaWiki:*Whatever*}}. This is not recommended. It might seem to work fine, but it's not a "real" system message unless it has a default value that displays if MediaWiki:*Whatever* doesn't exist. Use a template instead. The MediaWiki namespace is for overrides only, while the Template namespace is designed for transcluding any custom content.

Accessing System Messages

System messages are pervasive in MediaWiki for sysops and programmers. Depending where and when you need a message, there are different ways to obtain its value. (Some of them apply only to PHP programmers modifying MediaWiki.)

Viewing and editing in the wiki
MediaWiki:*Name-of-message*

This simply displays the message on its own wiki page. Click the edit link to change it.

Within a wiki page
{{MediaWiki:*Name-of-message*}}

This inserts the text of the message into a wiki article by transclusion, without any need for PHP programming.

Within PHP source code
wfMsg('*name-of-message*', optional parameters...)

The wfMsg function, which is defined in the MediaWiki source file *in cludes/GlobalFunctions.php*, displays a system message in a MediaWiki extension such as a custom special page (see "Creating a Special Page" on page 301), when the message may vary by language or other user preferences. This function takes a variable argument list to match the parameters $1, $2, etc., in the message text.

If the system message text does not change based on the user's preferences (e.g., selected language), use wfMsgForContent instead. Examples are link targets (not titles!) and log messages. *GlobalFunctions.php* defines other message-related functions as well, and is recommended reading for programmers.

In a skin class
$this->msg('*name-of-message*')

Skins such as MonoBook and Modern use this function defined in the QuickTemplate class in *includes/SkinTemplate.php*. Other message-related

---

> functions are defined in the same class, so it's recommended reading for skin programmers.

Cascading Stylesheets

Want to change the look and layout of wiki pages? The system message `MediaWiki:Common.css` can contain cascading stylesheet (CSS) directives that are inserted into every wiki page as it renders[*] and override the default styles. There is also a system message `MediaWiki:Monobook.css` for any CSS specific to the MonoBook skin. Modifying these messages is the simplest way to alter the look and feel of your MediaWiki site in small ways. For major changes, see "Creating a Skin" on page 313.

For example, to turn all article titles green, edit `MediaWiki:Common.css` and insert:

```
h1.firstHeading { color: green; }
```

After saving the article, force-refresh your browser to ensure the change is picked up (as old CSS may be cached in the browser). To learn CSS style names, display a wiki page and view its HTML source. As with user-supplied CSS (see "User CSS and JavaScript" on page 43), the more familiar you are with the CSS classes and IDs used on a MediaWiki page, the more effective your CSS can be.

JavaScript

The system message `MediaWiki:Common.js` can contain JavaScript code that is inserted into every wiki page as it renders.[†] There's also a corresponding `MediaWiki:Monobook.js` that renders its JavaScript only for the MonoBook skin. Changing these messages is the simplest way to inject custom JavaScript onto pages. For more complex or dynamic JavaScript tasks, consider writing an extension that emits JavaScript via `$wgOut->addInlineScript` (see "Running JavaScript" on page 311).

 To use custom JavaScript effectively—particularly to add on-load hooks—get familiar with the JavaScript functions in the MediaWiki directory *skins/common*, such as *wikibits.js* and *edit.js*.

---

[*] MediaWiki emits an HTML `style` tag pointing to `MediaWiki:Common.css`.

[†] MediaWiki emits an HTML `script` tag referencing `MediaWiki:Common.js`.

Configuration Settings

MediaWiki is designed to be tweaked. Its PHP source code defines hundreds of global variables, called *configuration settings*, that enable, disable, and modify all kinds of features. These PHP variables all have names beginning with $wg ("wiki global"). Here are a few examples:

- $wgLogo, the path to the graphical logo for your wiki
- $wgEnableEmail, which toggles the use of email on and off
- $wgDBtype, which defines the type of database in use (e.g., MySQL)
- $wgAllowUserCss, which permits individual users to define cascading stylesheets

We don't cover every single configuration setting here, just those that are most useful to the average wiki administrator. It's not likely you'll need to change the number of characters permitted in a username, for example:

```
$wgMaxNameChars = 36;  // was 255
```

but it's quite likely you'll permit a new type of uploaded file:

```
$wgFileExtensions[] = 'pdf';  // Adobe PDF files
```

To modify a configuration setting:

1. *Locate* the setting you want. Settings are defined in the source file *includes/DefaultSettings.php*, but *do not modify them there*. You can also look up settings on *www.mediawiki.org* at *http://www.mediawiki.org/wiki/Manual:Configuration_settings*.

2. *Read* the setting's documentation at *www.mediawiki.org* (which is itself a wiki) by navigating to the article Manual:$nameOfSetting. For example, the setting $wgLogo is documented at Manual:$wgLogo (or as a URL, *http://www.mediawiki.org/wiki/Manual:$wgLogo*).

3. *Override* the setting's value in your wiki's *LocalSettings.php* file, located in the root of your MediaWiki source tree, by assignment:

   ```
   $wgLogo = 'your value here';
   ```

Never modify the *includes/DefaultSettings.php* file, only *LocalSettings.php*. During MediaWiki upgrades, your modified *LocalSettings.php* is preserved, while *includes/DefaultSettings.php* is overwritten with the latest official version, deleting any local changes.

Add configuration settings at the *end* of *LocalSettings.php*, so they override default values as desired. If *LocalSettings.php* ends with an "end of PHP" symbol, ?>, add your configuration settings *just above* this line. (Or, better yet, delete the "end of PHP" line: you don't need it.)

Extensions

Extensions are plug-in software, written in PHP, that provide features to MediaWiki or change its core behavior *without modifying its source code*. They get installed in the *extensions* directory of the MediaWiki software on your server, then loaded in *LocalSettings.php* with:

```
require_once( "$IP/extensions/path-to-extension-file" );
```

Hundreds of extensions are available. Chapter 14 covers installing third-party extensions, and Chapter 15 explains how to create your own.

Skinning

MediaWiki skins are PHP files that control the overall look and feel of wiki pages. They are located in the *skins* directory. We'll cover them in "Creating a Skin" on page 313.

SQL Programming

On rare occasions, you might want to modify the MediaWiki database directly using SQL, a database programming language. We'll look at a few examples as they come up. One of the most common applications is seen in "Creating Interwiki Links" on page 332.

 Dynamic Page List can accomplish many database-query tasks without resorting to SQL.

MediaWiki uses two database logins: one for general wiki operation (traditionally called **wikiuser**, defined in *LocalSettings.php*), and one with more access (e.g., the administrative or "root" database account) for backups, schema changes, and wiki maintenance scripts.

The MediaWiki database schema is documented at *http://www.mediawiki.org/wiki/Manual:Database_layout*. The PHP database programming layer for

MediaWiki extensions is documented at *http://www.mediawiki.org/wiki/Manual:Database_access*. Generally, you can visit *http://www.mediawiki.org/wiki/Category:Database* for links to all database-related material. There's also a little information in the file *docs/database.txt* in the MediaWiki distribution.

Maintenance Scripts

The MediaWiki distribution includes a *maintenance* directory full of useful scripts for the wiki administrator. The purposes of these scripts include changing passwords, deleting uploaded files, running administrative SQL queries, dumping and restoring all wiki content, and more.

To run a script, log into your MediaWiki server, enter the *maintenance* directory, and run:

```
php nameOfScript.php [options]
```

Make sure *php* is in your search path. We'll cover common scripts in "Maintenance Scripts" on page 320.

 Most maintenance scripts require a file *AdminSettings.php* to be set up first, providing login credentials to access your MediaWiki database. See "AdminSettings.php" on page 320.

## CHAPTER 12

Controlling Wiki Features

MediaWiki's feature set is *extremely* configurable through the methods we saw in Chapter 11. In this chapter, we'll configure users, rights, articles, the edit page, namespaces, file uploads, the search engine, and more. There's no way we can cover every feature, but we'll explore a good selection of common and useful settings and techniques. (Read Chapter 11 first to learn about configuration in general.)

Remember that all configuration settings, which are set in *LocalSettings.php*, are documented on *www.mediawiki.org* in the `Manual` namespace. Just search for `Manual:$wgName OfSettingHere` (e.g., `Manual:$wgLogo`). The full set is documented here: *http://www.mediawiki.org/wiki/Manual:Configuration_setting*.

Users

As a wiki sysop or administrator, you may want to create, rename, and delete users. We'll talk about those operations here.

Creating Users

To create a single user, simply create an account at `Special:UserLogin`. To create users in batches, try a script such as the one in Example 12-1. To use it, create a file of usernames and passwords, where each line consists of one username, a tab character, and the user's password. Then, run:

```
php CreateUsersInBatch.php name-of-file
```

All users (which must not already exist) will be created in the MediaWiki database with the given passwords. Your *AdminSettings.php* file (see "Admin-Settings.php" on page 320) must be set up for this script to work.

Example 12-1. CreateUsersInBatch.php

```php
<?php
# Run from MediaWiki's "maintenance" folder.
# Usage:
#   php CreateUsersInBatch.php infile
#
# where each line of "infile" contains a username, a tab, and a password.

# Include the standard command line functions for maintenance scripts
require_once('commandLine.inc');

# Read the file of 'username \t password' lines
$data = file_get_contents($args[0]);
foreach (split("\n", $data) as $line) {
  // Skip blank lines
  $line = trim($line);
  if (! $line) continue;

  // Get the username and password
  $userInfo = split("\t", $line);   // Or any other separator characters you prefer
  $username = ucfirst($userInfo[0]);
  $password = $userInfo[1];

  // Create the user in the database; must not exist already
  $u = User::createNew($username);
  if ($u) {
    // Set and save password
    $u->setPassword($password);
    $u->saveSettings();
    echo "Created $username\n";
  } else {
    echo "Error creating $username\n";
  }
}
```

Renaming Users

MediaWiki has no feature to rename a user, and doing it manually (via SQL) is not recommended. Instead, get the third-party extension RenameUser (*http://www.mediawiki.org/wiki/Extension:Renameuser*), which works like a charm. It installs in the standard manner covered in "Installing an Extension" on page 272 and creates a special page for renaming a user easily.

Deleting and Blocking Users

Don't delete users: you'll mess up the revision history of any articles the user modified. Instead, deactivate the account by blocking the username at Special:BlockIP, as described in "Block User" on page 150. Merely changing

---

the account password is not sufficient, as the user might already be logged in and cookied.

User Rights and Permissions

You might wish to bestow special rights or privileges on certain users in your wiki community. Sysops and bureaucrats are two examples of users with special capabilities. MediaWiki has an infrastructure for user rights, including:

Rights
> Actions that are permitted, or not, in the wiki. Examples are reading pages, creating articles, and deleting articles.

User groups
> Named collections of rights. For example, the user group user represents logged-in users and includes many rights by default: editing articles, renaming articles, etc. It does not include the right to delete articles, however. Wiki administrators can create user groups containing custom sets of rights.

Assigning users to groups
> Users are given membership in user groups on the special page Special:UserRights.

Assignment permissions
> Who is allowed to bestow rights on other users, and which rights? Bureaucrats (i.e., members of the user group bureaucrat) may bestow any rights on any users, but you can give this permission to other user groups according to your taste.

Rights

The available rights are listed at:

> *http://www.mediawiki.org/wiki/Manual:User_rights*

Common rights are shown in Table 12-1.

Table 12-1. Common user rights

Right	Description
read	Read wiki pages
createpage	Create wiki articles
edit	Modify wiki articles, except protected articles
move	Rename articles
delete	Delete articles

Right	Description
undelete	Undelete articles
protect	Protect articles from edits
patrol	Mark revisions as patrolled (approved)
createaccount	Register users with a username and password
editinterface	Modify system messages in the MediaWiki namespace
userrights	Assign rights to users

User Groups

A *user group* is a collection of rights (say, read, edit, and move) that is given a name for convenient reuse. For example, the group user has the rights read, edit, move, and many others, but not delete. The standard user groups are listed at:

http://www.mediawiki.org/wiki/Manual:User_rights

and you can view them on the special page Special:ListGroupRights. The most common groups are shown in Table 12-2.

Table 12-2. Common user groups

User group	Description
*	All wiki visitors, including anonymous visitors
user	All logged-in users
emailconfirmed	All logged-in users whose email addresses have been autoconfirmed
bot	Bots: programs that simulate wiki users
sysop	Sysops: users who can administer the wiki
bureaucrat	Bureaucrats: users who can assign rights

Notice that some of these groups overlap. Any right assigned to the user group, for example, also applies to the more restricted groups emailconfirmed, sysop, bot, and bureaucrat—unless these groups override the user group. We'll see examples in "Assigning rights to groups" on page 231.

You can also create custom user groups, as we'll see in "Creating a user group" on page 233.

Sysops and Bureaucrats

When editing user rights, you'll come across two groups called sysop and bureaucrat. Sysops are the superusers of the wiki, able to edit articles in the MediaWiki namespace, delete and undelete articles, protect articles, access

---

some restricted special pages, and more. Bureaucrats are the rights administrators, able to add and remove users from groups. A user can be a sysop, a bureaucrat, both, or neither. The default sysop, usually named `WikiSysop`, is both.

Trivia: on Wikipedia and other wikis run by the Wikimedia Foundation, there's a user group called `steward` with all the privileges of `sysop` and `bureaucrat`. Stewards have global rights across *all* the wikis run by the Wikimedia Foundation. This user group is not present in MediaWiki by default.

Assigning rights to groups

`$wgGroupPermissions` is the most important configuration setting for user rights. Each entry in this two-dimensional array looks like:

```
$wgGroupPermissions[name of group][name of right] = true or false
```

For example, to allow all logged-in users to delete articles, you'd specify in *LocalSettings.php*:

```
$wgGroupPermissions['user']['delete'] = true;
```

and to allow all users except bureaucrats to delete articles, you'd write:

```
$wgGroupPermissions['user']['delete'] = true;
$wgGroupPermissions['bureaucrat']['delete'] = false;
```

Rights are *additive*: each assignment to `$wgGroupPermissions` adds to, or overrides, previous assignments. So, to prevent all users except sysops from creating accounts, you'd set:

```
$wgGroupPermissions['*']['createaccount'] = false;
```

but you also must ensure that no other groups (e.g., `user`) have the right set to true. You could also explicitly set sysops to have the right, but it's not necessary:

```
$wgGroupPermissions['sysop']['createaccount'] = true;   // Redundant
```

This is because sysops already have it by default (assigned in *includes/Default Settings.php*). This setup—forbidding the creation of accounts except by sysops—is typical for wikis that use other authentication methods such as LDAP (see "LDAP Authentication" on page 280), where user accounts are created by a central authority.

 Remember that rights are additive. So, this means that each `$wgGroupPermissions` assignment adds to, or overrides, previous assignments.

Requiring logins

Some wikis require users to log in before they can edit—or even view—wiki pages. This is easily set up by assigning the appropriate user rights.

To permit only registered, logged-in users to edit wiki articles, set:

```
$wgGroupPermissions['*']['edit'] = false;
```

To require users to log in to read the wiki at all, you might be tempted to specify:

```
// Not sufficient
$wgGroupPermissions['*']['read'] = false;
```

but this might be too restrictive, as it excludes the wiki's main page. Use the configuration setting $wgWhitelistRead in *LocalSettings.php* to specify the articles (by title) that everyone can read, regardless of other permissions settings:

```
$wgGroupPermissions['*']['read'] = false;
$wgWhitelistRead = array(
 'Main Page',
 'MediaWiki:Common.css',
 'MediaWiki:Monobook.css',
 'MediaWiki:Modern.css',
 '-',
);
```

Now, even anonymous users can view the home page and necessary stylesheets. (The '-' dash is also stylesheet-related.) You needn't specify the login and logout pages (Special:UserLogin and Special:UserLogout), which are automatically whitelisted.

 These restrictions do not prevent access to the wiki's uploaded files directly by their URLs. For more information on protecting these files from view, see *http://www.mediawiki.org/wiki/ Manual:Image_Authorization*.

Requiring logins except for talk pages

A common situation is to require logins to edit articles, but permit anonymous users to edit talk pages. This is accomplished by setting $wgNamespaceProtec tion in *LocalSettings.php* for non-talk namespaces:

```
$myProtectedNamespaces = array(NS_MAIN, NS_CATEGORY, NS_PROJECT);  // etc.
foreach ($myProtectedNamespaces as $ns) {
  $wgNamespaceProtection[$ns] = array('user');  // Registered users only
}
```

Namespace constants such as NS_MAIN are found in the source file *includes/Defines.php*.

Creating a user group

If existing user groups like sysop and bureaucrat are not sufficient for your wiki, define your own. First, invent a string name for your user group, such as superheroes. Then set the rights bestowed upon members of this group, using the $wgGroupPermissions array; here, read, edit, and delete:

```
$wgGroupPermissions['superheroes']['read'] = true;
$wgGroupPermissions['superheroes']['edit'] = true;
$wgGroupPermissions['superheroes']['delete'] = true;
```

Now you have a user group, superheroes, with the three given rights, and users can be assigned to it on Special:UserRights.

Let's now define a namespace, Headquarters, in which superheroes members can create and edit articles, but ordinary users cannot. (See "Creating Namespaces" on page 246 for more details.)

```
// Define namespace IDs.
// The prefix NS_ is traditional for namespace constants.
define('NS_HEADQUARTERS', 102);
define('NS_HEADQUARTERS_TALK', 103);

// Create namespaces
$wgExtraNamespaces[NS_HEADQUARTERS]= 'Headquarters';
$wgExtraNamespaces[NS_HEADQUARTERS_TALK]= 'Headquarters_talk';

// Make namespace read-only except to those with the editinterface
// right, such as sysops
$wgNamespaceProtection[NS_HEADQUARTERS] = array('editinterface');

// Give superheroes the editinterface right
$wgGroupPermissions['superheroes']['editinterface'] = true;
```

If users outside the superheroes group try to create or edit an article in the Headquarters namespace, they will be unable to do so.

Individual articles also can be protected (see "Protecting Articles" on page 242) so that only superheroes members can edit them. First, add superheroes to the configuration array $wgRestrictionLevels in *LocalSettings.php*:

```
$wgRestrictionLevels[] = 'superheroes';
```

Now a sysop (or other user with sufficient rights) can protect a page by clicking its Protect tab and selecting "Require superheroes permission" among the listed user groups. Only superheroes members will be able to edit it.

Creating Rights

"Creating a user group" shows how to create a user group, but how do you create a right? (For instance, the right to edit articles whose titles begin with "R".) This cannot be done simply with configuration settings in *LocalSettings.php*, say, to permit only sysops to edit these articles:

```
// Not sufficient
$wgGroupPermissions['*']['edit-pages-beginning-with-R'] = false;
$wgGroupPermissions['sysop']['edit-pages-beginning-with-R'] = true;
```

This is enough to get your new right listed on `Special:ListGroupRights`, but not enough to have any effect, as the MediaWiki code was not written to *respect* and *enforce* your new right. That requires a wiki extension, or possibly a modification of MediaWiki's core code, where rights are checked via the `isAllowed` method of the `User` class:

```
// MediaWiki core code
if ($wgUser->isAllowed('createpage')) {
 // do something
}
```

For our silly example of "R" articles, you could write an extension that uses the hook `AlternateEdit` (see the file *docs/hooks.txt*) to check the article title and the right, and take appropriate action. See "Hooks and Callbacks" on page 286 to learn about hooks.

Assigning Users to User Groups

Users are assigned to user groups within the wiki on the "User rights management" special page, `Special:UserRights`:

1. Log in as a user in the `bureaucrat` user group, such as `WikiSysop` (or whatever user you created at installation time).
2. Visit `Special:UserRights`.
3. Enter the target user's name and click "Edit User Groups".
4. Assign the user to groups following the instructions on the page.

Assignment permission

The preceding section instructed you to log in as a bureaucrat to assign users to user groups. By default, members of the `bureaucrat` user group are the only users who can bestow rights like this, but you can change that behavior.

Suppose your wiki has three custom user groups: `carnivores`, `herbivores`, and `zookeepers`. Let's assign `zookeepers` the ability to control membership in the herbivores and carnivores rights groups. This is accomplished with the $wgAddGroups configuration setting in *LocalSettings.php*:[*]

```
$wgAddGroups['zookeepers'] = array('carnivores', 'herbivores');
```

Now, any zookeeper, by visiting Special:UserRights, can add members to the carnivores and herbivores groups, but no other groups. To allow zookeepers as well to create other zookeepers, you'd instead specify:

```
$wgAddGroups['zookeepers'] = array('carnivores', 'herbivores', 'zookeepers');
```

The $wgAddGroups setting does not control removal from user groups, however. That is specified separately with $wgRemoveGroups:

```
$wgRemoveGroups['zookeepers'] = array('carnivores');
```

Now zookeepers can remove users from the carnivores group only. To allow zookeepers to add and remove users for *all* user groups, making them as powerful as bureaucrats, specify:

```
$wgAddGroups['zookeepers'] = true;
$wgRemoveGroups['zookeepers'] = true;
```

Assignment permissions for everyone

If your wiki has some user groups that you want anyone to be able to join or leave as they please without the assistance of a bureaucrat, use the configuration setting $wgGroupsAddToSelf in *LocalSettings.php*:

```
$wgGroupsAddToSelf = array('carnivores', 'herbivores');
```

Now all users can add themselves to these groups via Special:UserRights. The complementary setting $wgGroupsRemoveFromSelf determines the groups from which users can remove themselves.

 Special:UserRights might not show up in the list of special pages for ordinary users, but they can visit it directly by name via the search box.

User Rights Extensions

Various third-party extensions claim to control user rights, but this is very difficult to do correctly and securely. For more information, see:

http://www.mediawiki.org/wiki/Security_issues_with_authorization_extensions

---

[*] In older versions of MediaWiki, you might need to add $wgGroupPermissions['zookeepers'] ['userrights'] = false, or else zookeepers could assign to all rights groups.

Article Content

In this section, we'll discuss how you can control the content of articles, such as their size, links, and images.

Size Limits

If you're concerned about disk space or for any reason want to enforce a size limit on articles, use the configuration setting `$wgMaxArticleSize` in *LocalSettings.php*:

```
$wgMaxArticleSize = 50;
```

The size is given in kilobytes. If an article is edited to be longer than this limit, it cannot be saved, and the author will see the following message:

> ERROR: The text you have submitted is 52 kilobytes long, which is longer than the maximum of 50 kilobytes. It cannot be saved.

This error text is found in the system message `MediaWiki:Longpageerror`, so you can tailor it to fit your needs.

URL Protocols for External Links

External URLs can have various protocols: `http`, `https`, `ftp`, `mailto`, and more. The full set is defined in the configuration array `$wgUrlProtocols`, which you can change in *LocalSettings.php*. To add support for another protocol, just append it to the array:

```
$wgUrlProtocols[] = 'file://';     # Support for file links
$wgUrlProtocols[] = 'code://';     # Support for .NET Reflector
```

 If you enable `file` links, but they don't seem to work, be aware that Firefox disables them by default for security reasons. They work in Internet Explorer on Windows, however. For Firefox workarounds, see *http://kb.mozillazine.org/Firefox_:_Issues_:_Links_to_Local_Pages_Don't_Work*.

External Images

MediaWiki does not display external images by default. You can change this behavior with the configuration setting `$wgAllowExternalImages` in *LocalSettings.php*:

```
$wgAllowExternalImages = true;
```

Now, if you enter the URL of an image in wikitext:

```
Here is an image:
http://www.example.com/pictures/face.jpg
```

the image itself will be displayed, rather than a link. To permit external images from just one external site—say, a local image server—and forbid them from all other sites, use the configuration setting $wgAllowExternalImagesFrom:

```
$wgAllowExternalImages = false;
$wgAllowExternalImagesFrom = 'http://images.example.com/';
```

Math Mode

Math mode (see "Enabling Math Mode" on page 190) can be turned on and off with the configuration setting $wgUseTeX in *LocalSettings.php*:

```
$wgUseTeX = false;
```

Images for math mode are created by default in the same directory as uploads (see "File Location" on page 249), in a subdirectory *math*. You can change this location with two configuration settings:

```
// URL path
$wgMathPath = "$wgScriptPath/data/tex/math/images";
// Physical file path
$wgMathDirectory = "$wgUploadDirectory/data/tex/math/images";
```

Disambiguation

Disambiguation pages distinguish articles with similar titles (see "Disambiguation Pages" on page 103). By default, the template {{disambig}} tags an article as a disambiguation page, but you can choose a different template by modifying the system message MediaWiki:Disambiguationspage. Its default content is Template:Disambig, but you can change it to any other article (presumably still a template[†]). You can use articles other than templates, but there isn't much point to doing so. The special page Special:Disambiguations, which lists all disambiguation pages, will adjust itself to use whatever template you select.

HTML Header

When MediaWiki serves a wiki page, it begins with the usual tags:

[†] You can use articles other than templates, but there's not much point to doing so.

```
<!DOCTYPE html PUBLIC "-//W3C//DTD XHTML 1.0 Transitional//EN"
 "http://www.w3.org/TR/xhtml1/DTD/xhtml1-transitional.dtd">
<html xmlns="http://www.w3.org/1999/xhtml"
 xml:lang="en" lang="en" dir="ltr">
<head>
<meta http-equiv="Content-Type"
      content="text/html; charset=utf-8" />
...
<script type="text/javascript" src="...">
...
```

You can control this header information in *LocalSettings.php* with the configuration settings in Table 12-3.

Table 12-3. HTTP header control

Setting	Default Value
$wgDocType	-//W3C//DTD XHTML 1.0 Transitional//EN
$wgDTD	http://www.w3.org/TR/xhtml1/DTD/xhtml1-transitional.dtd
$wgXhtmlDefaultNamespace	http://www.w3.org/1999/xhtml
$wgLanguageCode	en
$wgMimeType	text/html
$wgOutputEncoding	UTF-8
$wgJsMimeType	text/javascript

Configuring the Editing of Articles

The entirety of MediaWiki's editing experience can be configured: the edit page itself, article creation, edit links, conflicts, and more.

The Edit Page

Let's scan the edit page from top to bottom and see what we can change.

New article message

We begin with MediaWiki:Newarticletext, the system message that appears when creating a new article: "You've followed a link to a page that doesn't exist yet. To create the page, start typing in the box below..." You could customize this, say, to give instructions to new users or to describe your wiki's standards.

Adding buttons to the edit page

Next we come to the edit toolbar[‡] with its buttons for bold, italics, links, and so on. You can append buttons to the toolbar via JavaScript, by modifying the predefined JavaScript array `mwCustomEditButtons` within `MediaWiki:Common.js`. To append one or more buttons onto the array, write:

```
mwCustomEditButtons[mwCustomEditButtons.length] = {
    "imageFile": PATH TO A 16x16 IMAGE,
    "tagOpen": FIRST PART TO RENDER,
    "sampleText": SAMPLE TEXT TO RENDER,
    "tagClose": SECOND PART TO RENDER,
    "speedTip": HOVERING TOOLTIP
};
```

`imageFile` is a file path or URL of the button image, which must be 16×16 pixels. This can be an uploaded image in the wiki, but you'll need its file path, which you can get from `Special:FilePath` (see "File Path" on page 155). For example, if the uploaded file is `Image:Myfile.jpg`, enter "Myfile.jpg" and click Submit. The image will be displayed, and the path to its file will appear in the browser's address bar.

The next three elements get inserted into the edit box when you click the button: first the `tagOpen` value (usually an opening tag or wikitext symbol), then `sampleText` (usually instructions like "text goes here"), and finally `tagClose` (usually a closing tag or wikitext symbol). The `sampleText` value will be highlighted, ready to be replaced when the user types. Lastly, the `speedTip` text appears when the mouse hovers over the button.

Here's an example button that inserts a `<code>` tag:

```
mwCustomEditButtons[mwCustomEditButtons.length] = {
    "imageFile": "/w/skins/local/my-code-button.gif',
    "speedTip": "Add a code tag",
    "tagOpen": "<code>",
    "sampleText": "put code here"
    "tagClose": "</code>",
};
```

Remember to force-refresh your browser to ensure the button appears. When clicked, it inserts:

```
<code>put code here</code>
```

with the words "put code here" selected for easy replacement.

[‡] Not to be confused with the Toolbox menu.

Edit box

There's not much to say about the edit box: it is an ordinary HTML textarea. Its CSS ID is `wpTextbox1`, and its size can be set by user preferences (see "Editing Preferences" on page 38).

Copyright notice

After the edit box comes the wiki's copyright notice. This is `MediaWiki:Copyrightwarning` if you've specified a license for the wiki content (see "Changing the Footer Menu" on page 264), or `MediaWiki:Copyrightwarning2` otherwise.

Submit buttons

Finally, we have the submit buttons and related form fields, whose text is found in the system messages in Table 12-4.

Table 12-4. Configuring the edit page submit buttons

Item	System Message	CSS ID
Summary	MediaWiki:Summary	wpSummaryLabel
This is a minor edit	MediaWiki:Minoredit	wpMinoredit
Watch this page	MediaWiki:Watchthis	wpWatchthis
Save page	MediaWiki:Savearticle	wpSave
Show preview	MediaWiki:Showpreviewz	wpPreview
Show changes	MediaWiki:Showdiff	wpDiff

 Want to require authors to preview their work before saving? Check out the ForcePreview extension, *http://www.mediawiki .org/wiki/Extension:ForcePreview*.

Editing a New Article

When you visit a nonexistent article, you're offered an opportunity to create it. This happens in several situations that you can configure:

The Go button in the search box
> The search results page appears, with system message `MediaWiki:Noarticletext` at the top.

Direct access by URL
> System message `MediaWiki:Noexactmatch` is displayed by itself.

In each case, you can modify the system message to customize the text. Additionally, in the "Go" case, you can bypass the search results page entirely and jump to the edit page if you change the configuration setting $wgGoToEdit in *LocalSettings.php*:

```
$wgGoToEdit = true;
```

Now, failed searches with the Go button will skip the search results page and bring the user directly to the edit page.

Edit Links for Sections

Next to each section title in an article, there is an edit link for modifying just that section. You can hide these section-edit links for all articles via CSS:

```
span.editsection {
  display: none;
}
```

To hide the section-edit links for just a single article, insert the magic word __NOEDITSECTION__ anywhere in the article text.

The New Section Tab

Talk pages have an additional top tab, labeled with a "+" sign or the label New Section, that appends a new section onto an article. You can make this tab appear in any article, not just talk pages, by inserting the magic word __NEWSECTIONLINK__ anywhere in the article text.

Edit Conflicts

Conflicts occur when two authors edit the same article simultaneously and both try to save it. (See "Conflicts" on page 72.) In this situation, the second "saver" sees a warning that you can configure in the system message MediaWiki:Explainconflict. The default warning is not very noticeable; here, we'll make it big, bold, and red!

```
<div style="color:red">
<big>'''CONFLICT!! YOUR CHANGE WAS NOT SAVED!'''</big>
Someone else has changed this page.......
</div>
```

Maintaining Articles

As a sysop, you can perform operations on articles that other users cannot, such as deleting and protecting articles.

Deleting Articles

To delete an article, click "delete" in the top tabs. The delete page appears, where you can choose a reason for the deletion from a drop-down list. You can add reasons to this list by editing the system message `MediaWiki:Dele tereason-dropdown`. It is formatted like a bulleted list:

```
* Common delete reasons
** Author request
** Copyright violation
** Vandalism
```

where the first line is the drop-down title and the rest are values to be selected. Add or change values as you see fit.

To delete many articles in a single operation, see "Deleting Multiple Articles" on page 331. To delete all recent articles by the same user (e.g., rapid spam), see "Vandalism" on page 329. Sysops can also undelete articles on the special page `Special:Undelete`:

- To search for deleted articles to restore, visit `Special:Undelete` with no other parameters
- To undelete an article with a known title, visit `Special:Undelete/title-of-article`

Protecting Articles

MediaWiki has a limited form of access control to articles, called *protection*. To protect an article, click its "protect" tab, which shows up only for users permitted to protect articles. You can apply two types of protection (shown in Figure 12-1):

Edit protection
    Only members of a particular group (e.g., sysops) can modify the article
Move protection
    Only members of a particular group can rename the article

Additionally, the protection may have an expiration date, such as 2008-05-23 (May 23, 2008), or the word `infinite` for indefinite protection. You may enter dates and times in a variety of formats, including raw timestamps like `2008-05-23T04:00:00Z`, or more familiar terms like `2 weeks`. Once an article is protected, its "protect" tab becomes "unprotect", which you can use to remove the protection or change the expiration.

By default, only sysops can protect articles, but you can change this behavior via user rights. Create a user group that can protect and unprotect articles, such as `protectors`, in *LocalSettings.php*.

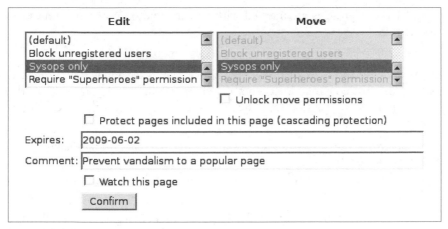

Figure 12-1. Protecting an article

```
$wgGroupPermissions['protectors']['protect'] = true;
$wgGroupPermissions['protectors']['unprotect'] = true;
```

and assign users to it via `Special:UserRights`. Now the "protect" and "unprotect" tabs will show up for these users as well.

To view the list of protected pages, visit `Special:ProtectedPages`. Protection changes are also recorded in the protection log, viewable from `Special:Log`.

Protecting titles

On your wiki, there might be some article titles that should never be created. (Use your imagination and you can surely think of some.) A sysop can protect these articles, even before they exist, by visiting their edit pages and clicking the "protect" tab. (Tricky, no?) This technique effectively prevents the title from being used. If someone tries to create it, they'll see a permission error.

Additionally, some third-party extensions can block certain titles from use. Wikipedia, for example, uses Title Blacklist (*http://www.mediawiki.org/wiki/ Extension:Title_Blacklist*) which forbids titles that match selected patterns (known as regular expressions).

Patrolling Articles

If your wiki content needs to be of high quality, consider *patrolling* it. This means having a team of users who examine recent revisions and, if acceptable, mark them as "patrolled" (OK). MediaWiki keeps track of which articles are patrolled, so your team members don't duplicate each others' work.

You can choose to patrol all recent revisions via `Special:RecentChanges`, or only newly created articles via `Special:NewPages`. Entries on

`Special:RecentChanges` are marked with an exclamation point in front of the article title:

(diff) (hist) .. ! My dog; . . (+8) .. Jsmith (Talk | contribs)

If you click the "diff" link to view the change, you'll see a new link, "Mark as patrolled." If the change is acceptable, click this link and you're done: the exclamation point disappears, indicating to other patrollers that the edit has been approved.

To patrol new articles, start from `Special:NewPages` (or `Special:RecentChanges`), visit a new page, and look for a link near the bottom, "Mark this page as patrolled". Click the link and the page is marked as acceptable.

To disable the patrolling features for `Special:RecentChanges` set the following in *LocalSettings.php*:

```
$wgUseRCPatrol = false;
```

To disable them for `Special:NewPages`, set:

```
$wgUseNPPatrol = false;
```

Who can patrol?

Sysops have two special patrolling powers. First, by default, only sysops can patrol articles. You can change this behavior via user rights (see "Creating a user group" on page 233). A common change is to create a new user group for patrolling and assign a team of users to it. This avoids the need for patrollers to be full-fledged sysops. To create the team, first create a user rights group (say, **approvers**) that has the **patrol** right:

```
$wgGroupPermissions['approvers']['patrol'] = true;
```

and then use `Special:UserRights` to assign users to the **approvers** user group.

Second, edits by sysops are automatically marked as patrolled. (They're considered trustworthy.) To extend this privilege to other users—such as your **approvers** squad—give them the **autopatrol** right as well:

```
$wgGroupPermissions['approvers']['autopatrol'] = true;
```

Patrol log

Patrolling is tracked in the patrol log, available from `Special:Log`. Just select "Patrol log" from the drop-down. You'll notice that edits by sysops (and anyone else with the **autopatrol** right) are marked as "patrolled (automatic)". For more information on patrolling, see *http://meta.wikimedia.org/wiki/Patrol*.

Undo and Rollback

When viewing an article's history, ordinary users see "undo" links next to revisions (as we saw briefly in "History" on page 18). As a sysop, you'll also see "rollback" links. A *rollback* performs an undo of *every consecutive revision by the most recent author*. In other words, if the seven most recent revisions are by user Jsmith, then a rollback will undo all seven of them, returning the article to the state it was in before Jsmith came along.

Search and Replace

MediaWiki does not have a search-and-replace feature for articles, but sysops can approximate it with the export and import features.

 This method is convenient but risky. On a busy wiki, other users could edit an article in the middle of your work, and this procedure will overwrite their changes without warning.

1. List the pages in question. Perhaps you want all pages in a category or namespace, or maybe something more complex. You might find the Dynamic Page List extension helpful for generating such a list (see "Dynamic Page List" on page 124).
2. Export your pages. Visit `Special:Export`, paste the list of titles into the box, and export the articles' text to an XML file.
3. Edit the resulting XML file with your favorite text editor or XML editor.
4. In the XML file, locate all the `<timestamp>` lines:

       <timestamp>2008-05-05T02:03:04Z</timestamp>

   and change them to the current time in the same format (*YYYY-MM-DDThh:mm:ssZ*).
5. Import the file. As a sysop, use `Special:Import`.

Make sure your PHP initialization file (*php.ini*) has long enough timeouts to permit large imports. Or, avoid the timeout issue entirely by performing your XML dump and restore with the maintenance scripts *dumpBackup.php* and *importDump.php*, as described in "Database Backups" on page 321.

Configuring Namespaces

MediaWiki provides many namespaces (see "Namespaces" on page 96), but you can also define your own.

Creating Namespaces

Custom namespaces are created by adding values to the configuration array $wgExtraNamespaces in *LocalSettings.php*. Here's an example that creates a namespace called OReilly and its associated talk namespace, OReilly talk. We'll take a few extra steps to make the result more maintainable.

 If at all possible, plan and create namespaces when setting up the wiki. If creating one later (say, OReilly), first check that no existing article titles begin with "OReilly:" or they will become inaccessible when the OReilly namespace gets created. If any such articles exist, rename them. The script *maintenance/namespaceDupes.php* detects such conflicts: simply run it without arguments to see a report:

```
php namespaceDupes.php
```

1. Pick a name and ID for your namespace. The ID must be an even number greater than or equal to 100, unique among all namespace values in the wiki (see *includes/Defines.php* for the list). Suppose you choose the name "OReilly" and the ID 100, the first available custom namespace ID.

2. Your namespace will have an associated talk namespace. Its ID will be one greater than your namespace's ID, so in this case, 101.

3. Edit *LocalSettings.php*:

   a. Define memorable constants for your namespace and its associated talk namespace. This is optional, but recommended for easier maintenance:

   ```
   define("NS_OREILLY", 100);
   define("NS_OREILLY_TALK", 101);
   ```

   b. Set the configuration array $wgExtraNamespaces to contain your new namespaces. In this array, the indices are the namespace IDs and the values are the namespace names. For example:

   ```
   $wgExtraNamespaces = array(
     NS_OREILLY => 'OReilly',
     NS_OREILLY_TALK => 'OReilly_talk'
   );
   ```

   or, if $wgExtraNamespaces already has values, write:

   ```
   $wgExtraNamespaces[NS_OREILLY] = 'OReilly';
   $wgExtraNamespaces[NS_OREILLY_TALK] = 'OReilly_talk';
   ```

4. Visit Special:AllPages and look in the namespace drop-down. Your new namespaces should appear. You can now create articles in that namespace, e.g., OReilly:Book list and OReilly talk:Publishing.

Namespace Search

Do you want your namespace to be included in searches by default? If so, append values to the configuration array $wgNamespacesToBeSearchedDefault in *LocalSettings.php*:

```
$wgNamespacesToBeSearchedDefault[NS_OREILLY] = true;
$wgNamespacesToBeSearchedDefault[NS_OREILLY_TALK] = true;
```

Users can override this selection in their preferences, as shown in "Search Preferences" on page 41.

Namespace Subpages

Should your namespaces support subpages (see "Subpages" on page 99)? If so, append values to the configuration array $wgNamespacesWithSubpages in *LocalSettings.php*:

```
$wgNamespacesWithSubpages[NS_OREILLY] = true;
$wgNamespacesWithSubpages[NS_OREILLY_TALK] = true;
```

Namespace Security

You can protect a namespace so it's read-only except to particular user groups, usually sysops, by appending in *LocalSettings.php* to the configuration array $wgNamespaceProtection:

```
$wgNamespaceProtection[NS_OREILLY] = array('editinterface');
```

In this case, the OReilly namespace can be edited only by sysops. The value is an array because you can specify multiple rights, all of which will be required for write permission.

You can also prevent all articles in a namespace from being transcluded into other articles via the $wgNonincludableNamespaces configuration array. This is important if you've read-protected a namespace: it prevents unauthorized users from transcluding a read-protected article into another article, where they can then view it.

```
$wgNonincludableNamespaces[] = NS_OREILLY;
$wgNonincludableNamespaces[] = NS_OREILLY_TALK;
```

Various third-party extensions claim to protect the articles in a namespace, but the core MediaWiki software supports only the protections we've listed. For more information, see:

> *http://www.mediawiki.org/wiki/Manual:Preventing_access*
> *http://www.mediawiki.org/wiki/Category:Page_specific_user_rights_exten sions*

File Uploads

In "Enabling File Uploads" on page 188, we enabled file uploads by setting:

```
$wgEnableUploads = true;
```

and making sure the *images* directory was writable by the web server. Let's talk about other configuration options for file uploads.

File Types

By default, MediaWiki accepts PNG, GIF, and JPEG files as uploads by checking their filename extensions (e.g., *.gif*). You can extend this list by modifying the configuration array `$wgFileExtensions` in *LocalSettings.php*:

```
$wgFileExtensions[] = 'doc';    // Microsoft Word documents
$wgFileExtensions[] = 'xls';    // Excel spreadsheets
```

Two other settings control what is done with this list:

`$wgCheckFileExtensions`
Whether file extensions should be checked at all (true/false)

`$wgStrictFileExtensions`
Whether a failure should forbid an upload (true) or merely warn about it (false)

It's a good idea to leave both of these set to true (the default) to prevent malicious or otherwise unexpected file types in your wiki. You can forbid files with certain extensions explicitly with the `$wgFileBlacklist` configuration array:

```
$wgFileBlacklist[] = 'js;      // Disallow JavaScript files
$wgFileBlacklist[] = 'exe';    // Disallow Windows executables
```

and forbid by MIME type using `$wgMimeTypeBlacklist`:

```
$wgMimeTypeBlacklist[] = 'text/javascript';
```

 MediaWiki also checks the MIME type of uploaded files, assuming the configuration setting `$wgVerifyMimeType` is set to true (the default). If a MIME type is not being properly recognized by MediaWiki, you might need to edit the source files *includes/mime.types* or *includes/mime.info*. (These two filenames may be overridden by the configuration settings `$wgMimeTypeFile` and `$wgMimeInfoFile`, respectively.) If all else fails, you can set `$wgVerifyMimeType` to false.

Look for all these settings in *includes/DefaultSettings.php* to see which file extensions and MIME types are already excluded by default.

Maximum File Size

To prevent overly large files from being uploaded, set `upload_max_filesize` to your desired maximum size, such as one megabyte in the PHP initialization file (*php.ini*):

```
upload_max_filesize = 1M
```

This sets the limit for *all* PHP applications on the web server, not just MediaWiki. If this is not acceptable, set it using `php_value` in an appropriate spot in your Apache configuration (see *http://www.php.net/manual/en/config uration.changes.php*) or `ini_set` in *LocalSettings.php* (see *http://www.php.net/ manual/en/function.ini-set.php*).

 In older versions of MediaWiki (prior to 1.13), also set the configuration setting `$wgMaxUploadSize` in *LocalSettings.php* to the same amount, in bytes:

```
$wgMaxUploadSize = 1024*1024;  // 1 megabyte
```

and the MediaWiki configuration setting `$wgUpload SizeWarning` to the size (in bytes) for which users will see a warning message:

```
$wgUploadSizeWarning = 500 * 1024;  // Half a megabyte
```

The warning is configurable in the system message `Media Wiki:Large-file`.

File Location

The configuration setting `$wgUploadDirectory` in *LocalSettings.php* determines the directory to hold the uploaded files. This is usually the *images* directory, but you can change it:

```
$wgUploadDirectory = '/data/images/mediawiki';
```

Likewise, the URL path to the upload directory is held in `$wgUploadPath`. Other settings are derived from these two, including the path to the *math* directory (`$wgMathDirectory` and `$wgMathPath`) and the temporary directory (`$wgTmpDirectory`), though you can override each of these individually.

You can also set a second location for files from an external source, known as *shared uploads*. For example, your company might have several MediaWiki sites and you'd like a common image repository.* (This location is read-only; uploads are never placed there by MediaWiki.) When an [[Image:...]] tag appears in an article, if the image is not found among the standard uploads, MediaWiki looks for it next among the shared uploads.

To enable shared uploads, set:

```
$wgUseSharedUploads = true;
```

and define the URL path and directory path to the images:

```
$wgSharedUploadPath = 'http://images.example.com/shared/';
$wgSharedUploadDirectory = '/mnt/images/common';
```

Virus Scanning

MediaWiki can invoke an antivirus program to scan uploaded files. Just configure the following settings in *LocalSettings.php*:

$wgAntivirusSetup
> This is an array of supported virus scanners; see the default value in *includes/DefaultSettings.php*. At press time, only the programs *clamav* (*http://www.clamav.net/*) and *f-prot* (*http://www.f-prot.com/*) are supported. You can add others to the array, but you'll need to know the return codes produced by different scan results.

$wgAntivirus
> Set to the name of your desired antivirus scanner in $wgAntivirusSetup, such as f-prot or clamav.

$wgAntivirusRequired
> Set to true to reject uploads if they fail the virus scan, or false to permit them.

Search

MediaWiki's search engine can be tailored in behavior and scope, as discussed in the following sections.

---

* This is how Wikipedia uses the Wikimedia Creative Commons images at *http://commons .wikimedia.org*.

AJAX Search

Using an interactive technology called AJAX, the search box can automatically complete article titles as they are typed, as shown in Figure 12-2. To enable this feature, set this configuration setting in *LocalSettings.php*:

```
$wgUseAjax = true;
$wgEnableMWSuggest = true;
```

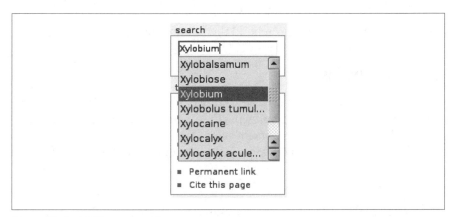

Figure 12-2. AJAX search with auto-suggest

Search Database Tuning

MediaWiki's built-in search uses the full-text search capabilities of your database (e.g., MySQL). In MySQL's case, only words of four characters or more are indexed. To adjust this limit, edit your MySQL initialization file (*mysql.ini*) and set the variable ft_min_word_len to the minimum word length to index, such as 3:

```
[mysqld]
ft_min_word_len=3
```

After this change, restart MySQL. Then rebuild your full-text index using MediaWiki's handy maintenance script, *maintenance/rebuildtextindex.php*:

```
php rebuildtextindex.php
```

This script is fairly heavy-handed, dropping not only MediaWiki's index but also MySQL's. To speed up the process greatly and rebuild only MediaWiki's index, run this SQL in database wikidb:

```
REPAIR TABLE searchindex QUICK;
```

More information is found at:

http://dev.mysql.com/doc/refman/5.1/en/fulltext-fine-tuning.html

MySQL also ignores a particular set of words, called *stopwords*, by default. A list is found at:

http://dev.mysql.com/doc/refman/5.1/en/fulltext-stopwords.html

To change the list, create your own stopwords file and point MySQL at it via the `ft_stopword_file` variable:

```
[mysqld]
ft_stopword_file=/path/to/your/file
```

As before, restart MySQL and rebuild the full-text index.

Special Page List

The list of special pages, `Special:SpecialPages`, can be modified in a few simple ways. By default, it groups pages by purpose, using groupings deemed important by the MediaWiki development team. You can change these groupings with the configuration array `$wgSpecialPageGroups` in *LocalSettings.php*.[†] An entry:

```
'X' => 'Y'
```

means that `Special:X` will be grouped under the *Y* category, whose subtitle is read from the system message `MediaWiki:Specialpages-group-Y`. See the default value in *includes/DefaultSettings.php* for a detailed example:

```
$wgSpecialPageGroups = array(
  'DoubleRedirects'         => 'maintenance',
  'Userlogin'               => 'login',
  ...
  'Recentchanges'           => 'changes',
  ...
  'BrokenRedirects'         => 'maintenance',
  ...
  );
```

If you prefer an alphabetical listing with no subtitles, just set:

```
$wgSpecialPageGroups = false;
```

Database Configuration

When you install MediaWiki, its database settings are configured for you based on your choices. A typical setup in *LocalSettings.php* might include:

```
$wgDBtype = "mysql";          // Type of database
$wgDBserver = "localhost";    // Hostname of database server
```

[†] New in MediaWiki 1.13.

```
$wgDBname = "wikidb";              // Database name containing wiki data
$wgDBuser = "wikiuser";            // Database user for running the wiki
$wgDBpassword = "********";        // Password for database user
$wgDBprefix = "mw_";               // Prepended to all table names
$wgDBTableOptions = "TYPE=InnoDB"; // Use InnoDB table type
```

You can modify these settings later (as long as they're consistent with your actual database setup, of course).

Email Configuration

MediaWiki's primary email settings are described in "LocalSettings.php mail settings" on page 189.

JavaScript Configuration

As a sysop, you can create custom JavaScript to run on all wiki pages. Media-Wiki provides several locations for JavaScript code, much as it does for cascading stylesheets (see "CSS for All Pages" on page 267):

Global JavaScript
> `MediaWiki:Common.js` affects all skins.

Per-skin JavaScript
> `MediaWiki:Monobook.js` affects only the MonoBook skin, and `MediaWiki:Modern.js` affects only the Modern skin. Each overrides `MediaWiki:Common.js`.

Per-user JavaScript
> `User:`*Yourname*`/monobook.js` is included only for the given user when logged in, as we saw in "User CSS and JavaScript" on page 43. It overrides the preceding JavaScript locations.

After any change to these JavaScript-related system messages, force-refresh your browser to clear its cache and pick up your changes.

All of these JavaScript locations work only if the configuration setting `$wgUseSiteJs` is true (the default), so you can disable them in *LocalSettings.php* with:

```
$wgUseSiteJs = false;
```

Likewise, per-user JavaScript works only if it's enabled with the configuration setting `$wgAllowUserJs`:

```
$wgAllowUserJs = true;
```

Logging and Debugging

When monkeying with MediaWiki, you might want additional insight into what's going on internally. Here are some handy logging features to try.

 Some log messages display sensitive or private information that can put your wiki at risk! For features that log to files, be sure that the files are not publicly accessible. For those that log to the browser, do not leave this logging enabled while other users have access to the wiki. Don't compromise your wiki: practice safe logging!

Where to Log?

To send log messages to a file, use the configuration setting $wgDebugLogFile in *LocalSettings.php*:

```
$wgDebugLogFile = '/path/to/your/file';
```

To disable this logging, set the value to the empty string:

```
$wgDebugLogFile = '';  // disabled
```

You can also log to the browser in HTML comments with the setting:

```
$wgDebugComments = true;
```

Logging Database Queries

Want to see every SQL operation executed by MediaWiki? Simply set:

```
$wgDebugLogFile = '/path/to/your/file';
$wgDebugDumpSql = true;
```

and the SQL will be logged in the given file.

Detailed Exceptions

If MediaWiki is throwing PHP errors (exceptions), you can display them in more detail by setting:

```
$wgShowExceptionDetails = true;
```

which provides a stack trace of the exception. Additionally, if the error message states that a SQL query is involved:

(SQL query hidden)

the setting $wgShowSQLErrors will cause these queries to be displayed:

```
$wgShowSQLErrors = true;
```

Be warned that the SQL code might contain sensitive information and should not be displayed to other users.

## CHAPTER 13

Changing Appearances

MediaWiki's default look and feel is familiar to any Wikipedia visitor. All the same, you might want to change it for various reasons: reflecting the theme of the wiki, matching your corporate branding, or simple personal preference. Fortunately, the look is highly configurable, although the means for changing it is spread across cascading stylesheets, configuration settings, system messages, and more. This chapter will guide you through the maze of changing your wiki's appearance. (Read Chapter 11 first to learn about configuration in general.) For CSS changes, it's assumed that you're using the default Mono-Book skin or another skin derived from it.

After any CSS change, force-refresh your browser to clear its cache and pick up your changes.

If an article does not change as expected, try *purging* the page from MediaWiki's cache by appending the query parameter `action=purge` onto the URL. (This should rarely be needed, however.)

The Basics

Let's start by configuring your wiki name, logo, and home page.

Wiki Name

The name of your wiki is stored in the configuration setting `$wgSitename`, in the file *LocalSettings.php*:

```
$wgSitename = 'BongoWiki';
```

This name is also available within wikitext as the variable `SITENAME`:

```
Welcome to {{SITENAME}}!
```

Logos and Icons

The graphical logo on every page is determined by the configuration setting $wgLogo in *LocalSettings.php*. Any 135×135 pixel image will do, ideally with a transparent background. You can point to a URL:

```
$wgLogo = 'http://images.example.com/logo.png';
```

or use an uploaded image within the wiki, by this process:

1. Upload an image, say, *mylogo.png*, via Special:Upload.
2. Determine the URL to *mylogo.png* by any means:
   - Find the image in Special:FileList and examine the "file" link
   - Visit Image:mylogo.png and examine the "Full resolution" link
   - Create a [[Media:mylogo.png]] link and examine the result
   - Enter "mylogo.png" on the Special:FilePath page and look in the browser's address bar
3. From the URL (say, *http://wiki.example.com/w/images/8/85/mylogo.png*), extract the path after the domain name (*/w/images/8/85/mylogo.png*). This is not required—the full URL will work, too—but it's recommended, so the image location is independent of your wiki's domain name or file paths, either of which might change someday.
4. Set $wgLogo to this path:

   ```
   $wgLogo = '/w/images/8/85/mylogo.png';
   ```

If you don't want any logo, set:

```
$wgLogo = false;
```

Speaking of icons, you can also change your wiki's favicon from the default (*/favicon.ico*) to an uploaded icon with $wgFavicon:

```
$wgFavicon = '/w/images/8/85/mylogo.png';
```

Home Page

One wiki article is designated as the home or "main" page, accessible by:

- Hitting the wiki at its base URL
- Clicking its link in the Navigation menu
- Clicking the logo

You can set the main page by placing its article title in the system message MediaWiki:Mainpage. The default value is Main Page.

Messages for Every Page

To place a custom message above the title of every page, edit `MediaWiki:Site notice`. Any wikitext will work, whether simple text:

```
Welcome to my '''wonderful wiki'''!
```

or a navigation bar for your company's department home pages:

```
{| border="1" align="center"
| [[Home]]
| [[Sales]]
| [[Marketing]]
| [[Operations]]
| [[Finance]]
| [[Legal]]
|}
```

You could even replace all article titles by hiding them with CSS:

```
h1.firstheading { display:none; }
```

and add a `MediaWiki:Sitenotice` value instead, such as:

```
<big>'''{{FULLPAGENAME}} on {{SITENAME}}'''</big>
```

which displays the article name and the wiki name in large, bold type.

Below the title, you can also display a custom subtitle, which is the contents of `MediaWiki:Tagline`. It is hidden by default, but you can unhide it via CSS:

```
#siteSub { display:block; }
```

and even make it fancy:

```
#siteSub { display:block; font-style:italic; font-size:12px; }
```

Login Messages

To place a custom message on the login page, just edit the system message `MediaWiki:Loginprompt`. To place a custom message on the logout page, use `MediaWiki:Logouttext`.

Article Content

The text of each article is contained in a `<div>` with ID `bodyContent`, so modify it however you like:

```
#bodyContent {
  font-size: 14px;
  color: blue;
}
```

Of course you can style individual HTML elements inside this `<div>`, such as `<code>` blocks:

```
#bodyContent code {
  color: green;
}
```

Preformatted Text Boxes

When you begin a line with a space character, or surround text with `<pre>` tags, the text appears in a box. Unfortunately, if the text is wider than the browser, it runs past the right margin and disappears. Add horizontal scroll bars to these boxes with the following CSS swiped from MediaWiki.org:

```
pre { overflow: auto; }
```

This trick works for Firefox and Internet Explorer 7, but not Internet Explorer 6 and earlier.

Menus

The menus on each MediaWiki page (see "Menu Reference" on page 23) can be modified, though each requires a different technique.

General Changes

Most menus are in `<div>` tags with CSS class `portlet`, so you can change their look consistently by overriding this class. For example, to turn menu links green:

```
div.portlet a {
  color: green !important;
}
```

Class `portlet` refers to the menu title and body together. The bodies are also enclosed in `<div>` tags of class `pBody`, so you can tailor them as well:

```
div.portlet div.pBody { ... }
```

Each menu also has a unique ID, so you can tailor each individually via CSS (as we'll do in a later section).

Changing the Navigation Menu

The Navigation menu is controlled by the system message `MediaWiki:Sidebar` that contains a two-level bulleted list like this:

```
* navigation
** mainpage|mainpage-description
```

```
** portal-url|portal
** currentevents-url|currentevents
** recentchanges-url|recentchanges
** randompage-url|randompage
** helppage|help
** sitesupport-url|sitesupport
```

(These are the default contents in MediaWiki 1.13.0.) Each line contains the names of other system messages. The top line, `navigation`, is the menu title ("navigation") stored in `MediaWiki:Navigation`. Each second-level bullet is a menu item with two system messages, separated by a pipe symbol:

1. The menu item link (either an article name or a URL)
2. The menu item text

In the fourth menu item, for example, `MediaWiki:Recentchanges-url` contains the page name "Special:RecentChanges", and `MediaWiki:Recentchanges` contains the text "Recent Changes".

The CSS ID to change the Navigation menu's look is `p-navigation`. Here we make the title background pink and the menu background yellow:

```
#p-navigation {
  background-color: pink;
}

#p-navigation div.pBody {
  background-color: yellow;
}
```

Each menu item also has a CSS ID. Its name is the system message for the item preceded by "n-". For example, the Current Events item, found in the system message `MediaWiki:Currentevents`, has the ID `n-currentevents`, so you could make it bold with:

```
#n-currentevents { font-weight: bold; }
```

Changing the Toolbox Menu

The Toolbox menu is controlled programmatically. To add a menu item, write a wiki extension as shown in "Adding a Toolbox Link" on page 309. To change the text of a menu item, edit the appropriate system message (see Table 13-1).

Table 13-1. Configuring the Toolbox menu

Menu item	System message
Block user	MediaWiki:Blockip
E-mail this user	MediaWiki:Emailuser

Menu item	System message
Logs	MediaWiki:Log
Permanent link	MediaWiki:Permalink
Printable version	MediaWiki:Printableversion
Related changes	MediaWiki:Recentchangeslinked
Special pages	MediaWiki:Specialpages
Upload file	MediaWiki:Upload
User contributions	MediaWiki:Contributions
What links here	MediaWiki:Whatlinkshere

To change the Toolbox's look, use the CSS ID p-tb:

```
#p-tb div.pBody {
  background-color: #eeeeee;
}
```

As in the Navigation menu, each Toolbox menu item has an ID for CSS. Its name is the system message for the item preceded by t-, such as t-special pages. This is true for standard items only; if you add custom items to the Toolbox via extension, there won't be a similar ID unless you create one.

Changing the User Options Menu

To add, change, or remove items from the user options menu, write a wiki extension that uses the hook PersonalUrls. (See "Hooks and Callbacks" on page 286 to learn about hooks.) To change the text of a menu item, edit the appropriate system message (see Table 13-2), which changes depending on whether the user is logged in or not.

Table 13-2. Configuring the user options menu

Menu item	System message for logged-in users	... for anonymous users
username linking to the user page	MediaWiki:Userpage	MediaWiki:Anonuserpage
My talk	MediaWiki:Mytalk	MediaWiki:Anontalk
My preferences	MediaWiki:Mypreferences	(not displayed)
My watchlist	MediaWiki:Mywatchlist	(not displayed)
My contributions	MediaWiki:Mycontris	(not displayed)
Log in / create account	(not displayed)	MediaWiki:Anonlogin
Log out	MediaWiki:Logout	(not displayed)

The CSS ID for the user options menu is `p-personal`:

```
#p-personal { font-size: 18px; }
```

and each link has an ID for CSS. Its name is *usually* the system message for the item preceded by `pt-`, such as `pt-userpage`, but some are slightly different: "My watchlist" is `pt-watchlist` (not `pt-mywatchlist`) and "My preferences" is `pt-preferences`.

Changing the Top Tabs

To add or remove top tabs, there are two approaches:

- Write an extension that uses the hook `SkinTemplateContentActions`. See "Hooks and Callbacks" on page 286 to learn about hooks.
- Allow or deny certain rights to users so only the permissible tabs appear. For example, denying the `edit` right will suppress the edit tab. See "Assigning Users to User Groups" on page 234 to learn how to set rights.

To change the text of a menu item, edit the appropriate system message (see Table 13-3).

Table 13-3. Configuring the top tabs

Menu item	System message
namespace	nstab-*namespace* (e.g., nstab-main, nstab-help)[a]
Discussion	MediaWiki:Talk
Edit	MediaWiki:Edit
History	MediaWiki:History
Delete	MediaWiki:Delete
Move	MediaWiki:Move
Protect	MediaWiki:Protect
Unprotect	MediaWiki:Unprotect
Watch	MediaWiki:Watch
Unwatch	MediaWiki:Unwatch

[a] True for custom-defined namespaces as well as system-supplied ones.

The CSS ID for the top tabs menu is `p-cactions`:

```
#p-cactions { font-family:courier; }
```

and each link has an ID for CSS. Its name is the system message for the item preceded by `ca-`, such as `ca-history`. If you add custom items via extension, there won't be a similar ID unless you create it yourself.

Changing the Footer Menu

The footer content is set in the current skin, usually MonoBook, and changing it might require you to edit its PHP source code. At press time, most of Mono-Book's footer links are hardcoded into *skins/MonoBook.php*. (See "Creating a Skin" on page 313 for more on editing skins.) But some changes don't require programming.

To change the text of a menu item, edit the appropriate system message (see Table 13-4).

Table 13-4. Configuring the footer menu

Menu item	System message	To remove	CSS ID
Privacy policy	MediaWiki:Privacy	Set to - (dash)	privacy
About {{SITENAME}}	MediaWiki:Aboutsite	Set to -	about
Disclaimers	MediaWiki:Disclaimers	Set to -	disclaimer
This page was last modified...	MediaWiki:Lastmodifiedat	Set to	lastmod
This page has been accessed...	MediaWiki:Viewcount	Set to [a]	viewcount
"Powered by MediaWiki" icon		Use CSS, display:none	f-powered byico

[a] Alternatively, set the configuration setting $wgDisableCounters = true in *LocalSettings.php*, which disables page counts altogether.

The footer can optionally contain copyright or licensing information for the wiki's content. The message is controlled by three configuration settings in *LocalSettings.php*:

$wgRightsText
: The name of the license, such as "Creative Commons License". This text appears in the footer in a message such as, "Content is available under Creative Commons License." The format of this message is controlled by the system message MediaWiki:Copyright, which of course can be modified. (Default value: Content is available under $1.)

$wgRightsIcon
: URL of a graphical icon to appear in the footer. Provide a value just as we did for $wgLogo (see "Wiki Name" on page 257). For CSS purposes, the icon appears inside a <div> with ID f-copyrightico.

$wgRightsUrl
: URL to visit when the icon is clicked.

For CSS changes, the ID `footer` refers to the entire footer, and the ID `f-list` to the list of links. Some individual links also have IDs for CSS, as shown in Table 13-4. For example:

```
#footer { background-color:red; }
#f-list { border:1px solid black; }
#privacy { font-weight:bold; }
```

Search Box

The search box draws its text from three system messages:

`MediaWiki:Search`
> The search heading

`MediaWiki:Searcharticle`
> The Go button

`MediaWiki:Searchbutton`
> The Search button

For CSS changes, the entire box has the ID `p-search`, and the individual parts have IDs as well, shown in Table 13-5.

Table 13-5. CSS for the search box

Item	CSS ID	CSS class
`<div>` surrounding the form	searchBody	pBody
The form		searchform
The input	searchInput	
Go button	searchGoButton	searchButton
Search button	mw-searchButton	searchButton

You can also change the appearance of search results via CSS. The list of results is a `<ul>` tag containing list items (`<li>`) roughly like the following, ready for CSS styling:

```
<ul class='mw-search-results'>
 <li>
  <a href="...">Name of article</a>
  <div class='searchresult'>
   <span class='searchmatch'>Matching line from article here</span>
  </div>
  <div class='mw-search-result-data'>
   83 B (12 words) - 01:37, 31 March 2008
  </div>
 </li>
 ...more results...
</ul>
```

Tables of Contents

As we saw in "Miscellaneous Preferences" on page 41, a table of contents appears automatically in articles with enough headings. By default, all headings, subheadings, sub-subheadings, and so on appear. You can limit the depth of these tables—say, to only top-level headings—with the configuration setting $wgMaxTocLevel in *LocalSettings.php*.

For example, to permit only level-one headings (=like this=) in the table of contents, set:

```
$wgMaxTocLevel = 1;
```

To permit level-two headings as well (==like this==), set:

```
$wgMaxTocLevel = 2;
```

and so on.

External Link Appearance

External links, by default, have a little icon on the end indicating they are external. For a single link, if you want to remove the icon, wrap it in a <span> of class plainlinks:

```
<span class="plainlinks">http://example.com</span>
```

To change all external links, modify the CSS for a.external. The icon is located in *skins/monobook/external.png*.

Page Credits

To find out who wrote a wiki page, you can view its history. Alternatively, you can configure the wiki to display authorship information within the article, using the configuration setting $wgMaxCredits in *LocalSettings.php*:

```
$wgMaxCredits = 3; // or other number
```

The value is the number of authors to display, as most wiki articles have multiple contributors. The value -1 displays all authors.

 This feature may slow your wiki's performance, so test it carefully.

Overall Look and Feel

The look and feel of a MediaWiki site is set by its skin and its stylesheets.

Default Skin

Each registered user can select their preferred skin on `Special:Preferences`, as we saw in "Skin Preferences" on page 37. The wiki administrator sets the default skin for the wiki—for anyone who has not overridden it in their preferences—with the configuration setting `$wgDefaultSkin` in *LocalSettings.php*:

```
$wgDefaultSkin = 'standard';
```

To switch all current users to a particular skin, except those users who have overridden the default in their preferences, run the *userOptions.php* maintenance script, described in "Setting User Preferences" on page 331:

```
php userOptions.php skin --old '' --new standard
```

Users can change their skin afterward in `Special:Preferences`, but this would be a quick way to (say) migrate people to a new, custom skin.

CSS for All Pages

MediaWiki provides many stylesheets, some as files in the *skins* directory and some as system messages within the wiki. Because the system messages override the files, there is almost never a reason to modify the files.

Global stylesheet
> `MediaWiki:Common.css` affects all skins.

Per-skin stylesheet
> `MediaWiki:Monobook.css` affects only the MonoBook skin, and `MediaWiki:Modern.css` affects only the Modern skin. Each stylesheet overrides `MediaWiki:Common.css`.

Per-user stylesheet
> `User:`*Yourname*`/monobook.css` is included only for the given user (*Yourname*) when logged in, as we saw in "User CSS and JavaScript" on page 43. It overrides the preceding stylesheets.

 After any change to these CSS-related system messages, force-refresh your browser to clear its cache and pick up your changes.

All these stylesheets work only if the configuration setting $wgUseSiteCss is true, which is the default. You can disable this in *LocalSettings.php* with:

```
$wgUseSiteCss = false;
```

Likewise, per-user stylesheets work only if they're enabled with the configuration setting $wgAllowUserCss:

```
$wgAllowUserCss = true;
```

For more information on CSS files and articles within MediaWiki, see:

http://en.wikipedia.org/wiki/Wikipedia:Catalogue_of_CSS_classes

CSS for Particular Pages

Want to give each namespace in your wiki a different look and feel? Perhaps the various departments in your company want their wiki pages to have customized layouts. To do this, you could assign a custom namespace to each department and tailor the CSS for each separately.

MediaWiki enables this customization by tagging each <body> tag with a CSS class specific to the namespace. The class name is ns-*N*, where *N* is the integer ID of the namespace, which you can find by this method:

1. Read the file *includes/Defines.php*.
2. Locate the section where namespaces are defined. You'll see PHP constants with names like NS_MAIN and NS_HELP, e.g.:

    ```
    define('NS_HELP', 12);
    ```
3. Take note of the integer, in this case, 12 (for the Help namespace).
4. The CSS class is ns-12.

Now define your style for body.ns-12. For example, to underline all links on Help pages:

```
body.ns-12 #bodyContent a {
  text-decoration: underline;
}
```

Individual pages can also be styled distinctively because MediaWiki inserts a unique CSS class in the <body> tag of each page:

```
page-namespace-article_title
```

As an example, for the article Help:Creating a category, the CSS class would be page-Help-Creating_a_category. Here's an instance that hides the page title (h1.firstheading) on the wiki's home page, Main Page:

```
body.page-Main_page h1.firstheading {
  display:none;
}
```

 If you rename a page that has custom CSS like this, the CSS will no longer work because the class will no longer match the article name. You'll need to update the stylesheet.

Another approach is to use the Page CSS extension to add CSS styles directly in an article, as described in "Installation Example" on page 274.

CSS for Printing

To tailor CSS for printing, edit an appropriate stylesheet article and use the @media keyword:

```
@media print {
  ...
}
```

For example, to hide the page footer when printed:

```
@media print {
  #footer { display:none; }
}
```

Note that styles within the @media section apply only to printed output, not to the onscreen display of printed output (e.g., the "printable version" link in the Toolbox menu).

International Support

The default language of your wiki is controlled by the configuration setting $wgLanguageCode in *LocalSettings.php*:

```
$wgLanguageCode = 'de';  // German
```

This is usually set by the MediaWiki installation procedure. Users can set their preferred language in Special:Preferences (see "User Profile Preferences" on page 35). Additionally, you can let users choose a language at login time via the configuration setting $wgLoginLanguageSelector:

```
$wgLoginLanguageSelector = true;
```

which causes MediaWiki to display a list of common language choices on the login page:

Language: Deutsch | English | Esperanto | Français | Español | ...

To change the list of languages, you can simply edit the system message MediaWiki:Loginlanguagelinks. This contains a bulleted list of language names and two-letter language codes (as defined in the *languages/Names.php* file), separated by a pipe symbol:

```
* Deutsch|de
* English|en
* Esperanto|eo
* Français|fr
* Español|es
* Italiano|it
* Nederlands|nl
```

So to add Afrikaans, you'd insert:

```
* Afrikaans|af
```

## CHAPTER 14

Installing Extensions

Powerful as MediaWiki is, you can make it even more so by adding *extensions*: third-party plug-ins that provide additional features. Extensions cover a wide range of functionality, such as:

- Converting wiki articles to PDF format
- Inserting Google maps into an article
- Adding a CAPTCHA image to the login page
- Creating fill-in-the-blanks web forms
- Automatic syntax-highlighting of displayed source code
- Replacing the wiki's search engine

In this chapter, we'll install extensions and survey some recommended ones. And in Chapter 15, you'll see how you can create your own extensions (programming is required).

Obtaining Extensions

Apart from ordinary Googling, here are two effective ways to learn about and locate extensions:

- Examining your favorite MediaWiki sites to see which extensions they have installed
- Visiting MediaWiki.org's catalog of extensions

Viewing Extensions on a Wiki

While working on a MediaWiki site such as Wikipedia, you might see a feature that other MediaWiki sites don't have. Suppose you notice an article with an image link: that is, a graphical image that is a link to another page, produced by the tag `<imagemap>`. Image links are not built into MediaWiki. What is this feature, and how can you obtain it for your own wiki?

To locate the origin of an extension, visit the `Special:Version` page, which lists all extensions installed on a wiki (see "Version" on page 158). Among the many entries on *http://www.wikipedia.org/wiki/Special:Version*, you'll see a "parser hook" extension called ImageMap with the description, "Allows client-side clickable image maps using `<imagemap>` tag." Bingo!

As is standard on the `Special:Version` page, the extension name (ImageMap) is a link to the official web page for that extension, in this case *http://www .mediawiki.org/wiki/Extension:ImageMap*. Visit that page, read the instructions, download the extension, and you're ready to install it.

The MediaWiki Catalog of Extensions

Most MediaWiki extensions are documented at:

> *http://www.mediawiki.org/wiki/Extension:Contents*
> *http://www.mediawiki.org/wiki/Extension_Matrix*

Starting from these articles, you can browse the catalog of extensions by name, category, extension type (parser hook versus special page, etc.), and more. At press time, nearly 1,000 extensions are documented on this site. (This chapter recommends some favorites.) Each extension has not only an article page, but also a talk page, which is often a good place to provide feedback to the extension author.

Installing an Extension

Most MediaWiki extensions are installed in the same manner:

1. Obtain the extension.
   - If the extension is contained in one or more files on the Web, download them using your browser's standard "save link to file" feature.
   - If the extension is presented as PHP source code on a web page, copy and paste it from the browser into a file. Make sure the destination filename is reasonably descriptive and ends with *.php*.

Copying and pasting PHP code from a browser window into a file is unreliable. If the PHP code contains HTML tags—a common occurrence—the browser might interpret them rather than display them literally. Consider this line of PHP that displays an HTML message in italics:

```
print "<i>Woof!</i>\n";
```

In a browser window, this line might be shown literally (and correctly), or the italics tag might be interpreted by the browser and displayed as:

```
print "Woof!\n";
```

If you copy and paste this line into a file, the code is missing the italics tag and is incorrect. Serious and subtle bugs/omissions can arise this way.

To get around this problem, view the code literally before copying. If the PHP code is on a MediaWiki page (say, on MediaWiki.org), click the Edit tab (or "View Source" if Edit is unavailable) and copy and paste the code from the edit box.

- If the extension is in a Subversion repository and you have the *svn* program, run an *svn checkout* command to copy the extension to your local machine. (If you don't know Subversion, you can learn it at *http:// svnbook.red-bean.com*.)

2. Copy the extension to your wiki's *extensions* subdirectory.

3. Append a line to *LocalSettings.php* to make MediaWiki load the extension:

```
require_once( "$IP/extensions/path-to-extension-file" );
```

Some extensions are contained in a single file:

```
require_once( "$IP/extensions/FunkyExtension.php" );
```

while others comprise a directory or folder full of files:

```
require_once( "$IP/extensions/FunkyExtension/FunkyExtension.php" );
```

4. Verify that the extension is installed by trying out the new feature or, for most extensions, by hitting your Special:Version page and looking for its name. (Some less well-behaved extensions do not add an entry to Special:Version.)

Usually, that's all you need to do: the extension is ready for action. A small number of extensions, however, have more complicated installation steps, including:

- Installing other third-party PHP code
- Modifying a skin file
- Adding JavaScript or cascading stylesheet code to a wiki page such as `MediaWiki:Monobook.js` or `MediaWiki:Monobook.css` (explained in "CSS for All Pages" on page 267)
- Running a SQL script to create or modify database tables on your wiki server
- Modifying core MediaWiki source code files (generally frowned upon)

In these cases, the extension will have more detailed installation instructions.

Installation Example

The Page CSS extension permits any article to define its own cascading stylesheet (CSS) styles to modify the look and feel of the page. Let's install it and try it out. First, download the extension from:

http://www.mediawiki.org/wiki/Extension:PageCSS

Follow the download link to copy the extension file *PageCSS.php* to your local machine. Then, visit the root of your MediaWiki installation and store the file as *extensions/PageCSS/PageCSS.php*. Finally, just append a line to *LocalSettings.php*:

```
require_once( "$IP/extensions/PageCSS/PageCSS.php" );
```

Next, edit any page on your wiki and insert the lines:

```
<css>
h1.firstHeading { color:green; }
</css>
```

Now, save the article, force-refresh your browser, and presto, the title appears in green.

Recommended Extensions

As mentioned earlier, MediaWiki has hundreds of extensions. It's fun to wade through them, but to save you time, here are a few that have proven highly useful.

Extensions for Readers

Some extensions add convenient features to the site, and you don't need any technical knowledge to use them.

PDF Export

The PDF Export extension (*http://www.mediawiki.org/wiki/Extension:Pdf_Export*) adds a Toolbox link to convert the current article to Adobe PDF format. It requires the *htmldoc* program (*http://www.htmldoc.org/*), so read the installation instructions carefully.

Download the extension's files into the directory *extensions/PdfExport* and append this line to *LocalSettings.php*:

```
require_once( "$IP/extensions/PdfExport/PdfExport.php" );
```

Hit any wiki article and click the new "PDF Export" link in the Toolbox. Your browser will either display the page as a PDF (assuming you have Adobe Reader or other plug-in installed in your browser) or offer you a PDF file to download.

CategoryTree

The CategoryTree extension (*http://www.mediawiki.org/wiki/Extension:CategoryTree*) modifies all category pages to display subcategories dynamically with AJAX. If your category page for Animals has subcategories for Dogs, Cats, and Iguanas, each subcategory appears with a "+" sign next to it, which you click to expand the subcategory. Additionally, for authors, this extension provides the <categorytree> tag to produce an expandable, collapsible list of categories and pages in any article.

Download the extension's files into the directory *extensions/CategoryTree* and append this line to *LocalSettings.php*:

```
require_once( "$IP/extensions/CategoryTree/CategoryTree.php" );
```

Then, hit any category page on your wiki (provided it has subcategories) to see the extension in action.

Lucene search

Lucene is a popular search engine that many MediaWiki sites, including Wikipedia, install in place of the standard one, as it has a more powerful search syntax. The Lucene extension makes this engine available to MediaWiki.

This extension has a long installation procedure and several prerequisites (Java™, Ant), so it's recommended for advanced wiki administrators only. Instructions are at *http://www.mediawiki.org/wiki/Extension:Lucene-search*.

Extensions for Writers

Some extensions are mainly for writers. They usually provide new magic words that produce interesting or complex effects.

Cite

The Cite extension (*http://www.mediawiki.org/wiki/Extension:Cite*) places footnote symbols in desired locations and generates a list of references. It's used throughout Wikipedia for reference sections of articles.

Download the extension's files into the directory *extensions/Cite* and add this line to *LocalSettings.php*:

```
require_once( "$IP/extensions/Cite/Cite.php" );
```

Now you can use the extension's two custom tags, `<ref>` and `<references>`. The `<ref>` tag replaces itself with a numbered footnote, so a citation like this:

```
Mount Everest is the world's tallest mountain.<ref>John Smith, ''The
Observer's Book of Mountains'', page 72</ref>
```

becomes:

Mount Everest is the world's tallest mountain.[1]

The footnote numbers are consecutive, beginning with 1. Finally, to produce the list of references, simply add anywhere within the article:

```
<references/>
```

to produce:

1. John Smith, *The Observer's Book of Mountains*, page 72
2. ...

If you want a "References" heading, you must add it yourself:

```
== References ==
<references/>
```

ImageMap

The ImageMap extension (*http://www.mediawiki.org/wiki/Extension:Image Map*), creates image links in wiki articles. These links can be simple (the entire image links to one article), or they can be image maps in which different parts of the image link to different articles.

Download the extension's files into the directory *extensions/ImageMap* and add this line to *LocalSettings.php*:

```
require_once( "$IP/extensions/ImageMap/ImageMap.php" );
```

Now, upload an image into the wiki (say, *Baboon.jpg*, 200 pixels wide), edit the desired article where the image should appear, and insert an image link:

```
<imagemap>
Image:Baboon.jpg|200px|Learn about baboons
default [[Baboon]]
</imagemap>
```

Now the entire image links to the article Baboon. To make parts of the image link to different articles, define rectangles or other shapes using the syntax described at *http://www.mediawiki.org/wiki/Extension:ImageMap*.

RSS with WikiArticleFeeds

The WikiArticleFeeds extension (*http://www.mediawiki.org/wiki/Extension: WikiArticleFeeds*) turns any article into an RSS feed. Some MediaWiki pages are already RSS feeds, such as Special:RecentChanges and Special:NewPages, but now you can make your own. The extension places RSS-related links (labeled "RSS" and "Atom" for two different formats) in the Toolbox.

Download the extension file (*WikiArticleFeeds.php*) into the directory named *extensions/WikiArticleFeeds* and add this line to *LocalSettings.php*:

```
require_once( "$IP/extensions/WikiArticleFeeds/WikiArticleFeeds.php" );
```

Now, use its special syntax, documented on its download page, to turn the article into an RSS feed. For example, create a new article and add:

```
<startFeed />
Jim Wilson's amazing animal circus!
== News flash ==
We just got a new elephant. See our [[elephant video]]!
--~~~~
== Performances coming up ==
We'll be appearing in [[Kansas City]] in August.
--~~~~
<endFeed />
```

Save the article, and you'll see several RSS-related links in the Toolbox. Right-click a link, and copy its URL into your favorite RSS reader. The two headings "News flash" and "Performances coming up" become two news headlines.

Extensions for Advanced Authors and Programmers

Here are some more complex extensions. It might take a while to learn to use them effectively, but the results are worth the effort.

Dynamic Page List

Dynamic Page List, or DPL (*http://www.mediawiki.org/wiki/Extension:Dynamic icPageList*), is an extremely powerful, multipurpose extension for generating wiki content. It has so many uses, as demonstrated in "Dynamic Page List" on page 124, that you'll wonder how you ever got along without it. In short, it can query the MediaWiki database at your command and display the results in wikitext. For example, to display a bulleted list of links to all articles in the Animals category, simply enter:

```
<dpl>
category = Animals
</dpl>
```

Would you prefer your list in three columns, excluding all articles whose titles begin with "D" or whose contents contain the string "tooth"? Just write:

```
<dpl>
category = Animals
nottitlematch = D%
includenotmatch = tooth
columns = 3
</dpl>
```

This is just the tip of the iceberg. DPL can produce tables, include excerpts from articles, display page authors and timestamps, sort data in various ways, and much more. It reduces the need to hardcode things in articles, making your wiki more consistent and maintainable. DPL is truly the "Swiss army knife" of extensions, with a million household uses.

DPL installs in the usual manner: download the files into the directory named *extensions/DynamicPageList* and append to *LocalSettings.php*:

```
require_once( "$IP/extensions/DynamicPageList/DynamicPageList.php" );
```

SyntaxHighlight GeSHi

The SyntaxHighlight GeSHi extension (*http://www.mediawiki.org/wiki/Extension:SyntaxHighlight_GeSHi*) displays source code listings with color highlights appropriate to the syntax of the language. Its <source> tag is much better than indenting your code listings by one space to typeset them in a box. This extension is a wrapper around GeSHi (*http://qbnz.com/highlighter/*), a general-purpose syntax-highlighting toolkit written in PHP, so you'll need to install that first.

To install SyntaxHighlight GeSHi, download the files into *extensions/SyntaxHighlight_GeSHi*, and within this directory, install GeSHi into a *geshi* subdirectory. Then append to *LocalSettings.php*:

```
require_once("$IP/extensions/SyntaxHighlight_GeSHi/SyntaxHighlight_GeSHi.php");
```

Now, test it by editing a page and entering (say) some C code:

```c
<source lang="c">
int main(int argc, char *argv[]) {
  printf("Hello, world!");  /* Display a message */
  exit(0);
}
</source>
```

Its syntactic parts should be highlighted in different colors.

Parser function extensions

Template programmers will appreciate the parser functions provided by the parser function extensions (*http://www.mediawiki.org/wiki/Extension:Parser _function_extensions*). These include:

- if/then/else conditionals
- switch statements
- for loops
- string functions
- mathematical functions
- variable definitions

and more. See "Logical Parser Functions" on page 122 for detailed examples.

ExpandTemplates

As you become more adventurous in creating complex templates, try the ExpandTemplates extension (*http://www.mediawiki.org/wiki/Extension:Ex pandTemplates*) as a programming and debugging aid. It creates the special page "Expand templates" (`Special:ExpandTemplates`) that presents a window for entering wikitext, particularly template transclusions {{`like this`}}. Click the Submit button, and you're shown what the wikitext will look like after templates are expanded.

This extension is installed in the usual way: download the files to *extensions/ ExpandTemplates*, and append to *LocalSettings.php*:

```
require_once( "$IP/extensions/ExpandTemplates/ExpandTemplates.php" );
```

Web forms in wiki articles

Several extensions add the capability to embed web forms in a wiki page. For example:

InputBox (http://www.mediawiki.org/wiki/Extension:Inputbox)
> Produces web forms of a few preset types, including search boxes, "add a wiki page" boxes, and "add a wiki comment" boxes

Simple Forms (http://www.mediawiki.org/wiki/Extension:Simple_Forms)
> A more flexible extension that defines parser functions to produce more customized forms

Each of these installs easily in the standard way.

Extensions for Administrators

Here are a few extensions that wiki administrators will appreciate.

LDAP Authentication

The LDAP Authentication extension (*http://www.mediawiki.org/wiki/Extension:LDAP_Authentication*) integrates MediaWiki with an LDAP or Active Directory server to authenticate wiki users. It works great, as long as you have enough LDAP knowledge to configure it properly. Download and install it in the *extensions/LdapAuthentication* folder, then add to *LocalSettings.php*:

```
require_once( "$IP/extensions/LdapAuthentication/LdapAuthentication.php" );
$wgAuth = new LdapAuthenticationPlugin();
```

From here, you must configure many PHP variables defined by the extension. This requires detailed knowledge of LDAP or Active Directory. The extension's web page provides full documentation and much advice on this.

Semantic MediaWiki

Semantic MediaWiki (*http://semantic-mediawiki.org/*) is an enhanced MediaWiki that can model stronger relationships between pieces of information. If a wiki is devoted to animals, for example, the information about dogs, cats, baboons, and so on is contained in articles. Semantic MediaWiki goes a step beyond articles and "models" those dogs, cats, and other animals as classes with properties. This permits intricate queries against the wiki, such as, "How many species of dogs are found in North America?" or "On average, are dogs larger than cats?"

Sounds intriguing, right? Semantic MediaWiki is a significant departure from standard MediaWiki, and you can read up on it at *http://semantic-mediawiki.org/*.

## CHAPTER 15

Creating Extensions

MediaWiki has hundreds of third-party extensions, but sometimes you need something new. Perhaps you'd like to integrate MediaWiki with custom applications or databases on your corporate intranet. Or maybe you want the first vowel in each article to be blue. Whatever it is, MediaWiki's *extension architecture* makes it is easy to add features to MediaWiki in a maintainable manner that doesn't change the supplied "core" MediaWiki code.

To write extensions, you'll need to know, at minimum, the PHP programming language. (This chapter assumes you know it.) For anything complicated, you'll also need to become familiar with MediaWiki's PHP code—particularly its classes, constants, and global variables—and its database schema. Your primary references are:

- The MediaWiki technical manual, *http://www.mediawiki.org/wiki/Manual:Contents*
- The extension documentation, *http://www.mediawiki.org/wiki/Extension:Contents*
- The core MediaWiki code in the *includes* directory
- The PHP manual, *http://www.php.net/manual/*

A full exploration of MediaWiki's PHP classes and database tables is beyond the scope of this book. This chapter will only skim the surface of the power of extensions, but it should give you a healthy background to build on.

All code in this chapter was confirmed to work properly in MediaWiki 1.13.0, the most recent version at press time.

 All extension code in this chapter is downloadable from:

> *http://www.oreilly.com/catalog/9780596519797*

Overview of Extension Types

There are three general ways to extend MediaWiki:

1. *Creating magic words* for wiki authors. This includes:
   - *Variables* that simply stand for values
   - *Parser functions* that perform arbitrary computations and emit wikitext
   - *Tag extensions* that perform arbitrary computations and emit HTML
2. *Changing MediaWiki's overall behavior.* This can be done with:
   - *Callback functions* that run at designated times
   - Custom *hooks* of your own creation
   - *AJAX extensions* that communicate with the web server dynamically
   - *Skins* that determine MediaWiki's look and feel
3. *Creating special pages.* Those are complete web applications with access to MediaWiki's internals.

So, which type of extension should you create? If you need one at all (see the sidebar "Do You Really Need an Extension?"), the best type depends on the context in which you'll be using it:

- For accessing an internal value, a variable might be your best bet.
- Features for authors are usually tags or parser functions. A tag is usually sufficient for general use, while parser functions may be preferable when mixed with other "double curly brace" features (templates and other parser functions). For manipulating text in simple ways, a template might be sufficient: no extension required.
- New functionality is usually implemented with hooks and callbacks.
- Independent web applications are usually created as special pages. However, there are third-party extensions that embed special features, such as HTML forms, into ordinary wiki articles.

Do You Really Need an Extension?

Before writing an extension, think about whether your task can be accomplished by other means that don't involve programming:

- Templates (see "Templates and Transclusion" on page 112)
- Dynamic Page List (see "Dynamic Page List" on page 124)
- Setting the many MediaWiki configuration settings (see "Configuration Settings" on page 224)

- Adding wikitext to existing system messages just above or below the things you want to change (see "System Messages" on page 218)

And of course, don't forget the hundreds of existing extensions found at *http://www.mediawiki.org/wiki/Category:Extensions*.

Follow the Standards

MediaWiki is just a big PHP program, so in theory, PHP programmers can modify it any way they want. Nevertheless, the MediaWiki team provides guidance and standards for doing it right. This means:

- Don't change the core source code unless you have no alternative. Limit your changes to the file *LocalSettings.php*. Never change *includes/Default Settings.php* (as covered in Chapter 11); instead, override its values in *LocalSettings.php*.
- Follow the programming standards for extensions documented on *www.mediawiki.org*.

Doing it the "right" way might require extra planning and effort and might even seem unnecessary, especially for small extensions. For instance, Example 15-1 is a complete extension in just six lines that prints the small message "Share and enjoy!" in small type at the top of every wiki article.

Example 15-1. Nonstandard extension

```php
<?php
$wgHooks['OutputPageBeforeHTML'][] = 'wfHello';
function wfHello($out, &$text) {
  $text = '<small>Share and enjoy!</small>' . $text;
  return true;
}
```

This extension works perfectly, but it is written in a nonstandard manner. The "right" way requires three separate files, a class definition, and support for foreign languages. Is the extra infrastructure worthwhile? From the perspective of the wiki community, yes, because little extensions tend to grow into big ones later, and then you'll wind up reimplementing it the "right" way anyway.

A properly developed extension is:

- Less likely to interfere with (or be affected by) other extensions
- Less likely to break in future versions of MediaWiki
- Easier to install for other MediaWiki administrators (if you share it)
- A candidate to be incorporated into the official MediaWiki repository

Best Practices for Writing Maintainable Extensions

Don't reinvent the wheel

Before writing an extension, check the list of existing extensions at *http://www.mediawiki.org/wiki/Category:Extensions* to see if someone else has written something similar.

Don't modify core code; create extensions instead

If you have no alternative but to modify core code, limit your changes to inserting custom hooks, and put the rest of the functionality in extensions that use the hooks. If your hook seems generally useful, submit it to the MediaWiki developers for inclusion in the core code.

Follow the standards

Use MediaWiki's recommended structure for writing extensions, documented at *http://www.mediawiki.org/wiki/Extensions*.

Encapsulate

Program with classes, rather than global variables and functions, to avoid name clashes with core MediaWiki code and other extensions.

Use good names

Global variable names for MediaWiki begin with `$wg` and global function names with `wf`. To avoid clashes with present and future MediaWiki code, append the name of your extension or its class: if your class is `SuperExtend`, begin your global variable names with `$wgSuperExtend` and global function names with `wfSuperExtend`. Also, be sure to name your classes so that they don't clash with MediaWiki's, perhaps prefixing them with something unique (say, your company's name), at least until PHP 6 namespaces are widespread.

Use APIs

Rely on public interfaces of MediaWiki classes, not their internals.

No terminating ?> marker

Do not place a terminating `?>` at the end of your PHP files: the file end itself will be sufficient. Accidental whitespace after `?>` is responsible for various subtle bugs, particularly in RSS processing.

Be multilanguage

Don't hardcode English (or other) text; define system messages instead.

Avoid MediaWiki's globals when possible

When writing callbacks for hooks, if the callback function passes you a system object (say, a `Parser` object), use that object rather than any global object (e.g., the global parser `$wgParser`).

Share it

Make your extension freely available to others; see "Publishing an Extension" on page 316.

The Three Extension Files

Store an extension's code in a subdirectory of the *extensions* directory, e.g., *extensions/NameOfExtension*. This subdirectory should contain up to three files:

NameOfExtension.php
> A *setup file* that gets things ready, performing only efficient, lightweight operations, such as:
>
> - Defining global PHP variables ($wg...) that control your extension
> - Defining global PHP variables ($wg...) that control your extension
> - Registering the extension on the Special:Version page
> - Setting up hooks
>
> For small, simple extensions with no displayed text, this might be the only file you need.

NameOfExtension_body.php
> An *implementation file* containing the code of your extension. Typically, the class name matches the filename, e.g., *NameOfExtension*.
>
> For small, simple extensions, the implementation can go in the setup file instead.

NameOfExtension.i18n.php
> A *messages file* or *internationalization file* containing any hardcoded text your extension will display. When properly set up, this text defines custom system messages (Chapter 11), giving your extension:
>
> - Multilanguage support
> - The ability for sysops to override the text in the MediaWiki namespace, like any other system messages
> - The chance to be accepted as an "official" MediaWiki extension by the MediaWiki development team, earning a place in the source code repository

When writing extensions, consider the performance of your PHP code. The setup file should get everything ready, but *not load the implementation class* nor do other time-consuming operations. A good way to ensure this is to use the PHP autoloader (*http://www.php.net/autoload*), which has a simplified API in MediaWiki, using the $wgAutoloadClasses configuration array:

```
$wgAutoloadClasses['NameOfExtensionClass'] = path to body file;
```

This locates the implementation, but doesn't load it until a caller requests it. (If the implementation file contains several classes, load them all this way in the setup file.) You'll see this technique in several of our example extensions.

If you aren't careful, your extensions will run on every page load, even on pages that don't use the extension, slowing down your wiki.

In our examples, we'll use the three-file system when it makes sense, but fewer files when the extension is simple or we want to improve performance.

If your extension is properly set up, a wiki administrator can install it merely by adding a single line to *LocalSettings.php*:

```
require_once("$IP/extensions/NameOfExtension/NameOfExtension.php");
```

Hooks and Callbacks

Most extensions connect to MediaWiki by a system of hooks and callbacks. A *hook* is an entry point in MediaWiki's code that, on request, will run custom code supplied by others. For example, there's a MediaWiki hook that runs whenever an article is saved. By submitting your custom code to be run by that hook, you can extend the capabilities of MediaWiki.

Every hook has a name. For instance, the hook that runs before any article is saved is called `ArticleSave`. Common hooks are documented at *http://www .mediawiki.org/wiki/Hooks* and in the file *docs/hooks.txt*. Each hook is listed with its purpose (i.e., when and why it is called) and the required parameters for attaching to it.

To make a hook call your custom code:

- Write a *callback* function: a PHP function that passes the correct information to and from the hook
- Create an entry in the global `$wgHooks` array that associates your callback with the desired hook

Callback functions return true or false, and this value controls what the hook does next. A true value tells the hook to run any other callback functions attached to it, whereas a false value causes the hook to terminate without processing its other callbacks. In other words, a true value *preserves* the functionality it extends, whereas a false value *overrides* it. True values are more common because most extensions don't want to disable standard wiki functionality. If a callback returns no value, MediaWiki throws a fatal error when the extension is active. (Older MediaWiki versions do not throw errors; they just silently malfunction.)

For example, if your callback function is:

```
function NameOfCallbackFunction($a, $b) {
  doSomethingExciting($a);
  anotherThing($b);
  return true;
}
```

you'd connect it to a hook like so:

```
$wgHooks['NameOfHook'][] = 'NameOfCallbackFunction';
```

This assumes *NameOfCallbackFunction* is a global function. For a callback that's a static method in a class, write:

```
$wgHooks['NameOfHook'][] = 'ClassName::MethodName';
```

For a callback within an object, write:

```
$obj = new ClassName();
$wgHooks['NameOfHook'][] = array($obj, 'MethodName');
```

but beware of instantiating a class too early, lest your class run on every page load, hurting performance. Some extensions set up their callbacks inside the implementation class, which looks like:

```
$wgHooks['NameOfHook'][] = array($this, 'MethodName');
```

We'll see other ways of setting up hooks and callbacks for parser functions ("Creating a Parser Function" on page 291) and tag extensions ("Creating a Tag Extension" on page 294) using methods on `Parser` objects (`setHook` and `setFunctionHook`).

To take full advantage of hooks, you'll need to read MediaWiki's PHP classes. For example, callbacks for the `ArticleSave` hook require an `Article` object and a `User` object as parameters. Unless you understand the `Article` and `User` classes by reading *Article.php* and *User.php* in the *includes* directory, you're limited in what you can do.

Custom Hooks

An extension can define its own hooks to permit other extensions to control it. Simply call the MediaWiki function `wfRunHooks`:

```
if (! wfRunHooks('NameOfHook', array($parameter1, $parameter2,
  ...))) {
  // something bad happened
  return false;
}
```

`wfRunHooks` returns true or false, as noted earlier, depending on whether the callback permits further callbacks to run (true) or overrides them (false). You

---

can also add hooks to the core MediaWiki code in this manner, though you should avoid modifying core code whenever possible.

Giving Credit

Whenever you create an extension, tell the world (or at least your wiki) you wrote it by appending a description to the $wgExtensionCredits array:

```
$wgExtensionCredits['parserhook'][] = array(
    'name' => 'My Wacky Extension',
    'author' =>'Vicky Wiki',
    'url' => 'http://www.example.com/wiki/wacky',
    'version' => '1.2',
    'description' => 'This extension prints random, wacky text'
);
```

This creates an entry for your extension on your wiki's Special:Version page. You'll need to know two sets of array keys to make this work. First, you have the fields specific to your extension, shown in Table 15-1.

Table 15-1. Extension credits

Field	Required?	Description
name	Yes	The name of the extension
author	Yes	Author's name
description	Yes	A brief explanation of the extension's purpose
url	No	Web address where the extension is documented
version	No	Version number of the extension

Second, the $wgExtensionCredits array has keys for the four kinds of extensions shown in Table 15-2. Our extension is a parserhook.

Table 15-2. $wgExtensionCredits elements

Array key	Description
parserhook	A tag extension or parser function
specialpage	A special page
variable	A MediaWiki variable
other	Anything else

Debugging Extensions

You develop an extension, deploy it, and boom, your wiki stops working. What now? If you see a blank page or tiny messages at the top of the page, this usually means a PHP error. Read the PHP log file (usually your web server log file) for error messages.

To make MediaWiki print a detailed message on fatal errors, set the global variable $wgShowExceptionDetails in *LocalSettings.php*:

```
$wgShowExceptionDetails = true;
```

To display any SQL database errors, also add:

```
$wgShowSQLErrors = true;
```

Be aware that this may display sensitive information, so don't leave it enabled for unwanted users to see. For even more detailed debug information, install the XDebug DLL (*http://xdebug.org/*), which prints a stack dump in the web server log file when PHP runtime errors occur.

 If a bug prevents an article from displaying when you're testing an extension, you can jump directly to the edit page by adding the query parameter action=edit to the article URL.

Also, make sure that PHP error reporting is enabled by placing at the top of *LocalSettings.php*:

```
error_reporting(E_ALL);
ini_set("display_errors", 1);
```

For more information, see:

http://www.mediawiki.org/wiki/How_to_debug

Creating a Variable

Let's create our first extension. Variables are the simplest magic words: just a name surrounded by double curly braces, (see "Variables" on page 109):

```
{{PAGENAME}}
```

To create a custom variable, the steps are:

1. Invent a variable name.
2. Invent an internal ID for the variable (never seen by users).
3. Create simple callback functions for three hooks:
   - To declare your variable as a magic word (hook LanguageGetMagic)
   - To declare it as a variable (hook MagicWordwgVariableIDs)
   - To set its value (hook ParserGetVariableValueSwitch)
4. Load your code in *LocalSettings.php*.

Let's create a variable USER that holds the MediaWiki username of the currently logged-in user (or the user's IP address if not logged in). In this short example, we use a single file, *UserVariable.php* (Example 15-2). If the code were larger, we would define a `UserVariable` class in a separate implementation file *UserVariable_body.php*, and if we needed internationalization—for instance, naming the USER variable differently in each language—we'd also have a *UserVariable.i18n.php* file.

Our code defines constants for the variable name, NAME_USER, and the internal ID, MAG_USER, then sets up the three required hooks pointing to three callback functions. Function `wfUserVariable_Magic` creates an entry in a "magic words" array, function `wfUserVariable_Var` creates an entry in a "variables" array, and function `wfUserVariable_Set` obtains the value we want (`$wgUser->getName()`) and assigns it to the variable.

Example 15-2. UserVariable.php

```php
<?php

# Credits
$wgExtensionCredits['variable'][] = array(
  'name' => 'USER',
  'author' =>'Interstellar Stella',
  'url' => 'http://wiki.example.com/wiki/User_variable',
  'description' => 'Username of the current user.',
  'version' => '1.0');

# Set up hooks
$wgHooks['LanguageGetMagic'][] = 'wfUserVariable_Magic';
$wgHooks['MagicWordwgVariableIDs'][] = 'wfUserVariable_Var';
$wgHooks['ParserGetVariableValueSwitch'][] = 'wfUserVariable_Set';

# Define constants
define('NAME_USER', 'USER');
define('MAG_USER', 'uservariable');

# Callback functions
function wfUserVariable_Magic(&$magicWords, &$langID) {
  // Declare that USER is a magic word by adding it to the
  // magic words array.
  $magicWords[MAG_USER] = array(0, NAME_USER);
  return true;
}

function wfUserVariable_Var(&$variables) {
  // Declare that USER is a variable by adding it to the
  // variable array
  $variables[] = MAG_USER;
  return true;
}
```

```
function wfUserVariable_Set(&$parser, &$cache, &$id, &$returnValue) {
  global $wgUser;

  if ($id == MAG_USER) {
    // Disable cache so current username is displayed
    $parser->disableCache();

    // Associate a value with USER
    $returnValue = $wgUser->getName();
  }
  return true;
}
```

In almost every case, the callback for the `ParserGetVariableValueSwitch` hook should return true, as this return value unfortunately has two overloaded meanings for variables. True means not only that future callbacks for this hook should run (the traditional meaning), but also that the function found a value for the variable. You cannot separate these two meanings of true for variable extensions. If you return false, it means not only that future callbacks for the hook should be suppressed, but also that no value was found for the variable, and the variable will be set to null. Strange but true.

To test the extension, edit a wiki article and insert:

```
{{USER}}
```

When rendered, this should produce your username as desired.

Creating a Parser Function

Parser functions are similar to variables, but are much more powerful. They can accept parameters (supplied in the wiki article), perform arbitrarily complicated tasks, and display any wikitext. We saw several parser functions in "Logical Parser Functions" on page 122 that added if/then/else logic to an article:

```
{{#ifexist:My article
| The article exists
| No it doesn't
}}
```

Here, we'll create a simple parser function that capitalizes all words in a string. This is normally done in PHP with the standard function ucwords (*http://www .php.net/manual/en/function.ucwords.php*), which we can expose as a MediaWiki parser function. In this case we'll expose a MediaWiki-specific version of this function, $wgContLang->ucwords()$, which deals better with Unicode text.

Here are the steps to create a parser function:

1. Invent a name for your parser function.

2. Associate the name with a callback function. The method depends on the version of MediaWiki, either using the hook `ParserFirstCallInit` (MediaWiki 1.12 and later) or the global array `$wgExtensionFunctions`.

3. Create a callback function to declare your variable as a magic word (hook `LanguageGetMagic`).

4. Create a callback function that runs the "real work" of your extension, and tell the MediaWiki parser (global variable `$wgParser`) to run it via the `setFunctionHook` method.

5. Load your code in *LocalSettings.php*.

In this example, we use a single file *Capitalizer.php* (Example 15-3), which begins by setting up two callbacks declaring that our class represents an extension and a magic word. The function `wfCapitalizer_Setup` tells the MediaWiki parser to associate the name `caps` with its implementation, `wfCapitalizer_Render`. Function `wfCapitalizer_Magic` declares that `caps` is a magic word. `wfCapitalizer_Render` does the real work, capitalizing all words in the string. The returned value is emitted by the parser function into the article.

Example 15-3. Capitalizer.php

```php
<?php

# Credits
$wgExtensionCredits['other'][] = array(
  'name' => 'Capitalizer',
  'author' =>'Ron Nibbly',
  'url' => 'http://wiki.example.com/wiki/Caps',
  'description' => 'Capitalize all words in a string.',
  'version' => '1.0');

# Set up the hook, using different logic depending
# on the version of MediaWiki
if (defined('MW_SUPPORTS_PARSERFIRSTCALLINIT')) {
  $wgHooks['ParserFirstCallInit'][] = 'wfCapitalizer_Setup';
} else {
  $wgExtensionFunctions[] = 'wfCapitalizer_Setup';
}

# Set up magic word hook
$wgHooks['LanguageGetMagic'][] = 'wfCapitalizer_Magic';
```

```
# Name the magic word
define('CAPITALIZER_NAME', 'caps');

function wfCapitalizer_Setup($parser) {
  // Associate the parser function name with its implementation.
  $parser->setFunctionHook(CAPITALIZER_NAME, 'wfCapitalizer_Render');
  return true;
}

function wfCapitalizer_Magic(&$magicWords, $langID) {
  // Declare that your parser function name is a magic word.
  $magicWords[CAPITALIZER_NAME] = array( 0, CAPITALIZER_NAME );
  return true;
}

function wfCapitalizer_Render(&$parser, $text) {
  // All the action happens here.
  // For more complicated behavior, define some PHP classes and
  // use them here.
  global $wgContLang;
  return $wgContLang->ucwords($text);
}
```

Test the parser function with:

```
{{#caps:my dog has fleas}}
```

to produce:

My Dog Has Fleas

There's a lot going on in this small amount of code, but this example can form the basis for any parser function.

Parser functions can accept more than one parameter. Let's modify the rendering function to accept another parameter, a color, and render the resulting text in that color. Just for fun, we'll declare a default color, green, using the standard PHP mechanism:

```
function wfCapitalizer_Render( &$parser, $text, $color = 'green' ) {
  return sprintf("<span style=\"color:%s\">%s</span>",
            wfEscapeWikiText($color),
            ucwords($text));
}
```

Now the preceding "My Dog Has Fleas" will display in green, whereas the following example will display in purple:

```
{{#caps:my dog has fleas
| purple
}}
```

A few closing notes:

- Parameters, when passed from an article to the parser function, are separated by vertical pipe symbols.
- Parser functions can have any number of parameters. You can declare them statically (as we did) as arguments to the hook function (in our case, it's `wfCapitalizer_Render`). To permit a variable or unknown number of arguments, use the standard PHP function `func_get_args` to process them, skipping the first argument (the `Parser` object).
- Parser functions produce wikitext, not HTML.* The `<span>` tag is permissible in wikitext.

Creating a Tag Extension

A tag extension lets you define a custom tag, like `<wacky/>` or `<kangaroo/>`, that does anything you like. Generally a tag will produce HTML, but it could also perform more sophisticated actions or side-effects: query a database, grab user data from an LDAP server, send email, modify MediaWiki's internals, and so on.

Tag extensions produce HTML. Parser functions produce wikitext.

Here is a simple tag extension that merely displays "Hello, world" in an article. The code consists of two files: a setup file that does lightweight operations to get things ready, and an implementation file containing the class `HelloTag`. The setup file in Example 15-4 points to the implementation file via the configuration array `$wgAutoloadClasses`, which causes the class to load automatically only when needed. It then sets up the required hook in two ways, depending on which version of MediaWiki is running. We create the callback function as a static method in the implementation class `HelloTag`.

Example 15-4. HelloTag.php: setup

```
<?php

# Credits
$wgExtensionCredits['other'][] = array(
  'name' => 'HelloTag',
```

---

* This behavior is configurable. For a meticulous discussion, see *http://jimbojw.com/wiki/index.php?title=Raw_HTML_Output_from_a_MediaWiki_Parser_Function*.

```
    'author' =>'Snortygord Zonkerdoodle',
    'url' => 'http://wiki.example.com/wiki/HelloTag',
    'description' => 'Print a hello message.',
    'version' => '1.0');

# Set up the hook, using different logic depending
# on the version of MediaWiki
if (defined('MW_SUPPORTS_PARSERFIRSTCALLINIT')) {
    $wgHooks['ParserFirstCallInit'][] = 'HelloTag::setup';
} else {
    $wgExtensionFunctions[] = 'HelloTag::setup';
}

# Autoload the implementation class
$wgAutoloadClasses['HelloTag']
    = dirname( __FILE__ ) . "/HelloTag_body.php";
```

The HelloTag class in Example 15-5 contains two methods: render, which does
the work (emits the message), and setup, which associates the <hello/> tag
and the render function.

Example 15-5. HelloTag_body.php: implementation

```php
<?php

class HelloTag {
  const NAME = 'hello';

  static function setup() {
    // The entry point. Associates the tag with a function.
    global $wgParser;
    $wgParser->setHook(self::NAME, array('HelloTag', 'render'));
    return true;
  }

  static function render($input, $argv, &$parser) {
    // The function that does the work.
    return 'Hello, world';
  }
}
```

The render function has three important parameters, though in this simple
case it uses none of them. The first, which we call $input, contains any text
passed by the containing wiki article. If we write:

```
<hello>This is some text</hello>
```

then $input is "This is some text". The second parameter, which we name
$argv, is an associative array of named parameters that were passed to the tag
as attributes (in the wiki article). If we write:

```
<hello id="me" color="red" dog="woof">...
```

then $argv contains three elements:

- $argv['id'], with value 'me'
- $argv['color'], with value 'red'
- $argv['dog'], with value 'woof'

The third argument, $parser, is a MediaWiki Parser object (see *includes/ parser/Parser.php*) that you should use instead of the global $wgParser. Our example extension does not need it.

 Remember that tags and templates do not work together (see the sidebar "Parsing Order and #tag" within "Basic DPL Lists" on page 125). If you plan to mix them, consider implementing your tag as a parser function instead.

Let's make a more complex tag, <extimg>, that displays an external image by its URL. It simply constructs an HTML <img> tag, accepting some of its attributes: src (the URL of the image), width, and height. Just for fun, we'll accept any text between <extimg> and </extimg> as a caption preceding the image. For example:

```
<extimg src="http://example.com/picture.jpg" height="100" width="30">
My picture</extimg>
```

produces the image *http://example.com/picture.jpg* in the dimensions given (30×100 pixels), preceded by the caption "My picture".

The setup file, *ExternalImage.php* (Example 15-6), associates the name extimg with a callback function in class ExternalImage.

Example 15-6. ExternalImage.php: setup

```
<?php
# Credits
$wgExtensionCredits['other'][] = array(
  'name' => 'ExternalImage',
  'author' =>'Bobby Blazebleeder',
  'url' => 'http://wiki.example.com/wiki/ExternalImage',
  'description' => 'Display an external image by URL.',
  'version' => '1.0');

# Set up the hook, using different logic depending
# on the version of MediaWiki
if (defined('MW_SUPPORTS_PARSERFIRSTCALLINIT')) {
  $wgHooks['ParserFirstCallInit'][] = 'wfExternalImage';
} else {
  $wgExtensionFunctions[] = 'wfExternalImage';
}
```

```
# Autoload the implementation class
$wgAutoloadClasses['ExternalImage']
  = dirname( __FILE__ ) . "/ExternalImage_body.php";

# Callback
function wfExternalImage($parser) {
  $parser->setHook('extimg', array('ExternalImage', 'render'));
  return true;
}
```

The implementation file, *ExternalImage_body.php* (Example 15-7), contains
the ExternalImage class, which has the same basic form as HelloTag. Its
render method iterates through the tag attributes, validating them, and constructing an <img> tag using MediaWiki's Xml class. Finally it prints $input,
sanitized for malicious characters, as an image caption.

Example 15-7. ExternalImage_body.php: implementation
```
<?php
class ExternalImage {
  static function render($input, $argv, $parser) {
    global $wgUrlProtocols;

    // Build array of valid attributes passed to us
    $validAttributes = array();

    foreach ($argv as $attribute => $value) {
      $error = false;

      // Check attributes for validity and security
      switch ($attribute) {
      case 'src':
        // Make sure it's an acceptable URL for this wiki
        $regex = sprintf("/^%s/", wfUrlProtocols());
        if (!preg_match($regex, $value)) {
          error_log("Skipping Illegal src = '$value'");
          $error = true;
        }
        break;

      case 'height':
      case 'width':
        // Make sure value is an integer
        if (!preg_match('/^\d+$/', $value)) {
          error_log("Skipping attribute $attribute = '$value'");
          $error = true;
        }
        break;

      default:
        error_log("Skipping unknown attribute $attribute = '$value'");
        $error = true;
      }
```

```
      // If we got here, we have a valid attribute and value
      if (! $error) {
        $validAttributes[$attribute] = $value;
      }
    }

    // Use MediaWiki's Xml class to generate the
    // img tag and sanitize/escape all values
    $imgTag = Xml::element('img', $validAttributes);

    // Sanitize and prepend the caption ($input).
    return sprintf("%s: %s", htmlspecialchars($input), $imgTag);
  }
}
```

Multilanguage Tag Extension

Our HelloTag example printed a phrase in English. Let's make the tag international by adding an *internationalization file* and loading multilanguage text into system messages. Our HelloTag class can then invoke the wfMsg function to print the appropriate message for the current language. The internationalization file, *HelloTag.i18n.php*, is shown in Example 15-8.

Example 15-8. HelloTag.i18n.php: internationalization

```php
<?php
$messages = array(
  'en' => array(
    'hello-message' => 'Hello, world',
    'some-other-text' => 'My dog'
  ),

  'es' => array(
    'hello-message' => 'Buenos dias',
    'some-other-text' => 'Mi perro'
  ),

  'fr' => array(
    'hello-message' => 'Bonjour',
    'some-other-text' => 'Mon chien'
  ),
);
```

HelloTag.i18n.php defines an associative array of arrays to hold the system messages. The outer array, which *must* be named $messages, contains one element per language ('en' for English, 'fr' for French, etc.), and the inner arrays are the system messages in each language. In our example, we include translations for English, French, and Spanish.

Class `HelloTag` now needs to load the system messages into MediaWiki, which requires two steps:

1. In the setup file, *HelloTag.php*, add an entry to the global configuration array `$wgExtensionMessagesFiles`, pointing to your messages file:

   ```
   $wgExtensionMessagesFiles['HelloTag'] =
       dirname(__FILE__) . '/HelloTag.i18n.php';
   ```

2. In the implementation file, call `wfLoadExtensionMessages` as in Example 15-9. Call this function as late as possible, only when it's needed, for performance reasons.

Example 15-9. HelloTag_body.php that loads system messages

```php
<?php
class HelloTag {
  const NAME = 'hello';

  function __construct() {
    // The entry point. Associates the tag with a function.
    global $wgParser;
    $wgParser->setHook(self::NAME, array($this, 'render'));
  }

  function render($input, $argv) {
    // Load system messages
    wfLoadExtensionMessages('HelloTag');
    // Print the system message, escaping any special characters
    // since the text may be user-provided.
    return htmlspecialchars(wfMsg('hello-message'));
  }
}
```

For more information on internationalization, see:

> *http://www.mediawiki.org/wiki/Internationalisation*
> *http://meta.wikimedia.org/wiki/Help:System_message*

Behavior Changes

Extensions such as variables, parser functions, and tags are usually designed for authors. Other extensions can change MediaWiki's behavior in more "global" ways. This is accomplished with a callback function, attached to a hook, that loads and runs under certain conditions. It could run on:

- Every page
- One particular page (say, the edit page)
- Every article in a particular namespace

and so on. Because PHP is such a flexible language, there are many ways to add global functionality to MediaWiki. We'll look at a typical example that changes the display of category links in all articles. Normally, category links display in the same order that their tags appear in the article. Our extension sorts them alphabetically.

The single file *CategoryTagSorter.php* (Example 15-10) associates a callback method, wfCategoryTagSorter, with a conveniently placed MediaWiki hook, ParserLimitReport. Our callback simply runs the standard PHP function ksort to sort the array of categories.

Example 15-10. CategoryTagSorter.php

```php
<?php
# Credits
$wgExtensionCredits['other'][] = array(
  'name' => 'CategoryTagSorter',
  'author' =>'Ivan Knackerthrasher',
  'url' => 'http://wiki.example.com/wiki/CategoryTagSorter',
  'description' => 'Sort category tags displayed in an article.',
  'version' => '1.0');

# Set up hook
$wgHooks['ParserLimitReport'][] = 'wfCategoryTagSorter';

function wfCategoryTagSorter($parser, $text) {
  $cats = $parser->mOutput->getCategories();
  ksort($cats);
  $parser->mOutput->setCategoryLinks($cats);
  return true; // Required return value for hook callback functions
}
```

Now, test your extension by creating a wiki article like this:

```
[[Category:Banana]]
[[Category:Dog food]]
[[Category:Cherry]]
[[Category:Apple]]
```

and it should display the category links in alphabetical order:

Categories: Apple | Banana | Cherry | Dog food

To make the extension run only for certain articles—say, all articles in the Help namespace—use the $wgTitle global variable to test this condition and change the wfCategoryTagSorter method:

```php
function wfCategoryTagSorter($parser, $text) {
  global $wgTitle;
  if ($wgTitle && ($wgTitle->getNamespace() == NS_HELP)) {
    $cats = $parser->mOutput->getCategories();
    ksort($cats);
    $parser->mOutput->setCategoryLinks($cats);
```

```
    }
        return true; // Required return value for hook callback functions
    }
```

Creating a Special Page

Special pages are full-fledged PHP web applications with access to MediaWiki's internals. You can create your own special page that appears on Special:SpecialPages and does whatever you like.

Starting a Special Page

MediaWiki provides three files to be used as a starting point for a special page. Download them from:

> *http://svn.wikimedia.org/viewvc/mediawiki/trunk/extensions/examples/ ThreeFileTemplate/*

 This is a view of a Subversion repository. If clicking on a filename does not produce the behavior you expect, try clicking a revision number instead.

The three files are named *MyExtension.php*, *MyExtension_body.php*, and *MyExtension.i18n.php*, with purposes similar to those in "The Three Extension Files" on page 285.[†] Once you've downloaded them, do the following:

1. Pick a unique string to represent your special page, such as TrulyExciting.
2. Rename the three files, replacing MyExtension with TrulyExciting, and put them in a new subdirectory, *extensions/TrulyExciting*.
3. Within the three files, change every occurrence of "MyExtension" to "TrulyExciting" (in mixed case), and every occurrence of "myextension" to "trulyexciting" (in lowercase).
4. Add a line to *LocalSettings.php*:

   ```
   require_once("$IP/TrulyExciting/TrulyExciting.php");
   ```

   and you'll have a working—though trivial—special page to build on, available directly at Special:TrulyExciting and as well in the list on Special:SpecialPages.

[†] At press time, these files do internationalization with an outdated technique, so we present the current best practice instead.

A Closer Look

Let's take a closer look at the three files, beginning with the setup file, *TrulyExciting.php* (Example 15-11). The code begins with a statement that exits immediately if run outside of MediaWiki, which is a recommended step. Next, it autoloads the implementation class by assigning a value as shown to the array $wgAutoloadClasses, and sets up its system messages as we saw in "Multilanguage Tag Extension" on page 298.

Example 15-11. TrulyExciting.php: setup

```php
<?php
# Not a valid entry point, skip unless MEDIAWIKI is defined
if (!defined('MEDIAWIKI')) {
        echo <<<EOT
To install my extension, put the following line in LocalSettings.php:
require_once( "\$IP/extensions/TrulyExciting/TrulyExciting.php" );
EOT;
        exit( 1 );
}

$wgAutoloadClasses['TrulyExciting']
  = dirname(__FILE__) . '/TrulyExciting_body.php';
$wgExtensionMessagesFiles['TrulyExciting']
  = dirname(__FILE__).'/TrulyExciting.i18n.php';
$wgSpecialPages['TrulyExciting'] = 'TrulyExciting';
```

The unique ID you created previously, TrulyExciting, is then used as a key in the global array $wgSpecialPages, which contains callback functions for all special pages. The value of element $wgSpecialPages['TrulyExciting'] is the name of the class you'll create in your implementation file, also TrulyExciting.

The implementation file, *TrulyExciting_body.php* (Example 15-12), defines a class that must inherit from the standard MediaWiki class SpecialPage.

Example 15-12. TrulyExciting_body.php: implementation

```php
<?php
class TrulyExciting extends SpecialPage {
  function __construct() {
    SpecialPage::SpecialPage('TrulyExciting');
    wfLoadExtensionMessages('TrulyExciting');
  }

  function execute( $par ) {
    global $wgRequest, $wgOut;
    $this->setHeaders();
    // Always escape unknown HTML to prevent malicious tricks
    $wgOut->addWikiMsg('very-special-message');
  }
}
```

The class's methods are:

- A constructor, which calls the parent constructor, passing in the name of the class as a parameter, and loads the system messages.

- `execute`, which does the "real work" of the extension. Ours calls the (inherited) `setHeaders` method, which sets the page title and does other bookkeeping, then displays the text of a system message. The global object `$wgOut` (of class `OutputPage`) is, among other things, a container for output. You can append HTML (`addHTML` method), wikitext (`addWikiText`), JavaScript (`addInlineScript`), and other strings to be rendered in the page; see "Useful Tasks for Extension Writers" on page 307 for more details. The `$par` argument to `execute` holds any parameters appearing after the page name in the URL. These are not query string parameters, but URL parameters separated by slashes. If you hit [[`Special:TrulyExciting/one/two`]], then `$par` is "one/two", which you can break into an array with the PHP `split` function.

You can override other methods from the `SpecialPage` class: read *includes/SpecialPage.php* for details.

Finally, the internationalization file, *TrulyExciting.i18n.php* (Example 15-13), is just like the one we saw in "Multilanguage Tag Extension" on page 298: a nested, associative array of multilanguage strings.

Example 15-13. TrulyExciting.i18n.php: internationalization

```php
<?php
$messages = array(
  'en' => array(
    'trulyexciting' => 'My Very Exciting Special Page',
    'very-special-message' => "Aren't I special?"
  )
);
```

One message is mandatory, `trulyexciting`, which is the same as our unique ID but all in lowercase. This message determines the description of the special page as it appears in `Special:SpecialPages`. We also define a second system message for fun, giving our special page something to display.

> If your special page's description appears wrong in the list on `Special:SpecialPages`—perhaps it appears just like `<trulyexciting>`—then you did not properly define the mandatory system message (`trulyexciting`) in *TrulyExciting.i18n.php*.

That's it! Your special page is now available as `Special:TrulyExciting` and appears in the list on `Special:SpecialPages`.

A More Interesting Special Page

Let's make a special page with a form, called FancyForm. The setup file named *FancyForm.php* (Example 15-14) is the usual.

Example 15-14. FancyForm.php: setup

```php
<?php

# Not a valid entry point, skip unless MEDIAWIKI is defined
if (!defined('MEDIAWIKI')) {
        echo <<<EOT
To install my extension, put the following line in LocalSettings.php:
require_once( "\$IP/extensions/FancyForm/FancyForm.php" );
EOT;
        exit( 1 );
}

$dir = dirname(__FILE__) . '/';
$wgAutoloadClasses['FancyForm'] = $dir . 'FancyForm_body.php';
$wgExtensionMessagesFiles['FancyForm'] = $dir . 'FancyForm.i18n.php';
$wgSpecialPages['FancyForm'] = 'FancyForm';
```

For our implementation in *FancyForm_body.php* (Example 15-15), let's create a form that accepts a MediaWiki username and displays facts about the user. Our execute method checks whether a POST request has been received, and if so, processes the form. Likewise, if a username has been passed in the URL as a special page parameter (e.g., [[Special:FancyForm/Jsmith]]), we'll run the same form-processing logic. Otherwise, we just display the form.

Example 15-15. FancyForm_body.php: implementation

```php
<?php
class FancyForm extends SpecialPage {
  const PARAM_USER = 'user';

  function __construct() {
    SpecialPage::SpecialPage('FancyForm');
    wfLoadExtensionMessages('FancyForm');
  }

  function execute( $par ) {
    global $wgRequest;

    $this->setHeaders();

    $results = '';
    if ($wgRequest->wasPosted()) {
      // Form POST
      $username = $wgRequest->getText(self::PARAM_USER);
      $this->processForm($username);
    } elseif ($par) {
```

```
    // Parameter passed in the URL
    $this->processForm($par);
  } else {
    // Just display the form
    $this->displayForm();
  }
}

function processForm($username) {
  global $wgOut;
  $error = false;

  // Create a user object
  $user = User::newFromName($username);
  if (is_null($user)) {
    // Invalid username
    $wgOut->addWikiMsg('fancyform-error-invalid',
                       wfEscapeWikiText($username));
    $error = true;
  } elseif ($user->idForName() == 0) {
    // No such user in database
    $wgOut->addWikiMsg('fancyform-error-none',
                       wfEscapeWikiText($username));
    $error = true;
  } else {
    // Display info in a bulleted list.
    // Xml class automatically sanitizes/escapes the input.
    $html = Xml::element('h2',
                         null,
                         wfMsg('fancyform-hello', $username))
      . Xml::openElement('ul')
      . Xml::element('li',
                     null,
                     wfMsg('yourrealname') . ' ' . $user->getRealName())
      . Xml::element('li',
                     null,
                     wfMsg('youremail') . ' ' . $user->getEmail())
      . Xml::closeElement('ul')
      ;
    $wgOut->addHTML($html);
  }

  // On error, repeat the form
  if ($error) {
    $this->displayForm();
  }
}

function displayForm() {
  global $wgOut, $wgScript, $wgTitle;

  $html = Xml::openElement('form',
                           array(
                               'method' => 'post',
```

```
                            'action' => $wgScript
                        ))
    . Xml::element('p', null, wfMsg('fancyform-prompt'))
    . Xml::input(self::PARAM_USER)
    . Xml::submitButton(wfMsg('fancyform-submit'))
    . Xml::hidden('title', $wgTitle->getPrefixedDBkey())
    . Xml::closeElement('form')
    ;

    $wgOut->addHTML($html);
  }
}
```

The form is produced by the `displayForm` method, which simply emits an HTML `<form>` tag. For convenience, we use MediaWiki's `Xml` class, which generates XHTML tags and automatically escapes and sanitizes the input for security. The `processForm` method makes use of MediaWiki's `User` class (*includes/User.php*) to obtain user information and print it. The technique we use is standard:

1. Allocate a `User` object via the `newFromName` method.
2. If it's null, the username is syntactically invalid.
3. Otherwise, we get a `User` object. The user might not exist in the MediaWiki database, however, so we must check that as well.
4. Assuming all went well, we call a few `User` methods to get the user's real name and email address and print them with the `Xml` class. (The system messages `MediaWiki:yourrealname` and `MediaWiki:youremail` already exist in MediaWiki; they're used on the Preferences page.)

Finally we have an internationalization file, *FancyForm.i18n.php* (Example 15-16), defining the system messages for the special page.

Example 15-16. FancyForm.i18n.php: internationalization

```
<?php
$messages = array(
  'en' => array(
    'fancyform' => 'My Fancy Form',
    'fancyform-prompt' => "Please enter a username:",
    'fancyform-submit' => 'Submit',
    'fancyform-error-invalid' => "Sorry, '''$1''' cannot be a username.",
    'fancyform-error-none' => "Sorry, no user '''$1''' was found.",
    'fancyform-hello' => "Facts about $1",
  )
);
```

To explore more possibilities for special pages, read a few of them in the MediaWiki source code *include/specials* directory. Their filenames usually begin with "Special", e.g., *SpecialRecentchanges.php* is the Recent Changes page (`Special:RecentChanges`).

Useful Tasks for Extension Writers

The following operations commonly need to be performed by extension writers.

Rendering Wikitext

To display wikitext in a special page extension, use the `addWikiText` method on the global `OutputPage` object:

```
global $wgOut;
$wgOut->addWikiText("How about a nice '''bold''' message?");
```

In tag extensions, you should parse wikitext before displaying it by calling the `recursiveTagParse` method on your `Parser` object (passed into the extension's callback function automatically as the third parameter). See *http://www.mediawiki.org/wiki/Manual:Tag_extensions* for more details.

```
function tagExtensionHook($input, $args, &$parser) {
    $output = $parser->recursiveTagParse($input);
    // continue using $output...
    // ...
}
```

For displaying system messages, which often contain wikitext, use `addWikiMsg`:

```
$wgOut->addWikiMsg('mymessage', $param1, $param2, ...);
```

Rendering HTML

To insert HTML into a wiki page, just use the `addHTML` method on the global `OutputPage` object:

```
global $wgOut;
$wgOut->addHTML("<p>This is a paragraph</p>");
```

Again, if the HTML comes from another source (user input, a database), always escape it with PHP's `htmlspecialchars` function before emitting it to the browser. Otherwise, someone could inject malicious code and you'll blindly run it.

Getting the Text of an Article

Sometimes, an extension needs wikitext from an article. Some hooks will provide it to you in a parameter, but if not, you can get to the text programmatically from the article's title. Example 15-17 demonstrates this technique, thanks to Rob Church and his Preloader extension (*http://www.mediawiki.org/wiki/Extension:Preloader*).

Example 15-17. Obtaining article text

```
$text = '';  // Will contain the article text

// Get title object
$title = Title::newFromText('My article');
if ($title && $title->exists()) {
  // Get revision object
  $revision = Revision::newFromTitle($title);
  if ($revision) {
    // Obtain the text
    $text = $revision->getText();
  }
}
```

In the end, the variable $text contains the article's wikitext.

Accessing Query String Parameters

To retrieve query string parameters passed to the current page, use the global $wgRequest object and its "get" methods:

```
global $wgRequest;
$value = $wgRequest->getText('stringParameterName');
$value = $wgRequest->getInt('numericParameterName');
```

You can tell if a form was posted (say, on a special page) using:

```
if ($wgRequest->wasPosted()) { ... }
```

If your form writes data or performs other critical actions, you should also protect it from cross-site request forgery by constructing an edit token, placing it as a hidden parameter in your form, and, after submission, checking it against the login session. Edit tokens are created with:

```
$token = $wgUser->editToken('some string');
```

placed as a hidden parameter in your form:

```
<input type="hidden" name="token" value="$token">
```

and checked after submission with:

```
$token = $wgRequest->getVal('token');
$success = $wgUser->matchEditToken($token, 'some value');
```

See *http://www.mediawiki.org/wiki/Manual:Edit_token* for details.

Adding a Toolbox Link

To add a link to the Toolbox menu on each wiki page, attach a callback function to the skin hook MonoBookTemplateToolboxEnd, as in Example 15-18. Here, we'll append the link "My silly link" to the Toolbox menu, pointing to *example.com*.

Example 15-18. ToolboxLink.php

```php
<?php
# Set up hook
$wgHooks['MonoBookTemplateToolboxEnd'][] = 'wfToolboxLink';

# Set up system messages
$wgExtensionMessagesFiles['ToolboxLink']
  = dirname(__FILE__) . '/ToolboxLink.i18n.php';

function wfToolboxLink(&$monobook) {
  // Optional: Restrict the link only to certain pages here.
  // ...

  // Load system messages
  wfLoadExtensionMessages('ToolboxLink');

  // Print a bulleted link
  echo sprintf("<li> <a href=\"%s\">%s</a></li>",
               'http://example.com',
               wfMsg('toolboxlink-text'));
  return true;
}
```

The system message MediaWiki:toolboxlink-text is defined in a traditional internationalization file, as shown in Example 15-19.

Example 15-19. ToolboxLink.i18n.php: internationalization

```php
"<?php
$messages = array(
  'en' => array(
    'toolboxlink-text' => 'My silly link'
  )
);
```

Adding a Preferences Checkbox

To add a checkbox to Special:Preferences under the Misc tab, attach a callback function to the hook UserToggles. You add the checkbox to a special array, then create a system message to hold the preference description. The name of the message must be tog- followed by the preference's ID. To test the checkbox's value, use the getOption method of MediaWiki's User class.

In Example 15-20 we add a checkbox to disable our CategoryTagSorter extension (see "Behavior Changes" on page 299) so category links appear in their natural order in articles. We define a constant CATEGORY_SORT_PREF for the preference's ID, and a system message category-sort-preference for the preference's description. The callback function wfCategoryTagSorterPref creates the preference, and the callback wfCategoryTagSorter tests the preference.

The internationalization file is shown in Example 15-21.

Example 15-20. CategoryTagSorter.php with preference checkbox

```php
<?php
# Credits
$wgExtensionCredits['other'][] = array(
  'name' => 'CategoryTagSorter',
  'author' =>'Ivan Knackerthrasher',
  'url' => 'http://wiki.example.com/wiki/CategoryTagSorter',
  'description' => 'Sort category tags displayed in an article.',
  'version' => '1.2');

# Set up hooks
$wgHooks['ParserLimitReport'][] = 'wfCategoryTagSorter';
$wgHooks['UserToggles'][] = 'wfCategoryTagSorterPref';

# Locate system messages
$wgExtensionMessagesFiles['CategoryTagSorter']
  = dirname(__FILE__) . '/CategoryTagSorter.i18n.php';

# Define a constant for the preference
define('CATEGORY_SORT_PREF', 'nocategorysort');

function wfCategoryTagSorter($parser, $text) {
  global $wgUser;
  if ($wgUser->getOption(CATEGORY_SORT_PREF) != 1) {
    ksort($parser->mOutput->getCategories());
  }
  return true; // Required return value for hook callback functions
}

function wfCategoryTagSorterPref($toggles) {
  global $wgMessageCache;

  // Load our custom system messages
  wfLoadExtensionMessages('CategoryTagSorter');

  // Set up the preference
  $toggles[] = CATEGORY_SORT_PREF;
  $wgMessageCache->addMessage('tog-' . CATEGORY_SORT_PREF,
                              wfMsg('category-sort-preference'));

  return true; // Required return value for hook callback functions
}
```

Example 15-21. CategoryTagSorter.i18n.php: internationalization

```php
<?php
$messages = array(
  'en' => array(
    'category-sort-preference' => 'Do not sort category links in articles'
  )
);
```

Visit `Special:Preferences` to see the new checkbox in action on the Misc tab. Try selecting and deselecting it, viewing wiki articles and watching the category sort order change. (You might need to force-refresh your browser to see the change take effect.)

Running JavaScript

To emit JavaScript in extensions that run on every page load, simply use the `addOnloadHook` function found in *skins/common/wikibits.js*:

```javascript
addOnloadHook(function() {
    ... put your JavaScript here ...
});
```

Build a JavaScript string in your extension (say, storing it in a variable named `$js`):

```
$js = <<< _END_OF_JS_
addOnloadHook(function() {
    ... put your JavaScript here ...
});
_END_OF_JS_;
```

then, insert the JavaScript into the article with:

```php
global $wgOut;
$wgOut->addInlineScript($js);
```

 wikibits.js is recommended reading for extension developers and contains many highly useful functions. Check out the other *.js* files in that directory, too.

Variables, tags, and parser functions cannot use the preceding method because their output gets cached and you won't get the dynamic behavior you desire. Instead, use the `addHeadItem` method of the `OutputPage` class, accessible from your local `Parser` object:

```php
$parser->mOutput->addHeadItem("<script>JavaScript code here</script>")
```

A JavaScript extension

Here's an extension that gives focus to the search box via JavaScript when the wiki's home page is displayed. Example 15-22 is the usual setup file, instantiating a Focus object and setting up a hook.

Example 15-22. Focus.php: setup

```php
<?php
# Credits
$wgExtensionCredits['other'][] = array(
  'name' => 'Focus',
  'author' =>'Bing Bongo',
  'url' => 'http://wiki.example.com/wiki/Focus',
  'description' => 'Focus the search box on the wiki home page.',
  'version' => '1.0');

# Autoload the implementation class
$wgAutoloadClasses['Focus'] = dirname( __FILE__ ) . "/Focus_body.php";

require_once("Focus_body.php");

# Hook and callback
$wgHooks['OutputPageBeforeHTML'][] = 'Focus::setup';
```

Example 15-23 is the implementation, which compares the current page title to the home page and adds the JavaScript with addInlineScript. The JavaScript itself is an anonymous function added to the page's onload handler via addOn loadHook from *wikibits.js*.

Example 15-23. Focus_body.php: implementation

```php
<?php
class Focus {
  static function setup() {
    global $wgOut;
    global $wgTitle;

    // Check if we're on the main page
    if ($wgTitle->getPrefixedText() == wfMsgForContent('mainpage')) {
      // If so, define JavaScript...
      $js = <<< END_JS
        addOnloadHook(function() {
          var searchBox = document.getElementById('searchInput');
          if (searchBox) {
            searchBox.focus();
          }
        });
END_JS;

      // ...and add it to the page
      $wgOut->addInlineScript($js);
    }
```

```
    return true;
  }
}
```

Disabling the Parser Cache

Some extensions produce dynamic output that should not be cached. For example, you might create an extension that queries an external database and prints the results. In these cases, disable the parser cache within the extension, using the available `Parser` object (a parameter for many callback functions) or `$wgParser`:

```
$parser->disableCache();
```

Creating a Skin

A MediaWiki *skin* is a description, in code, of the look and feel of MediaWiki web pages. Skins are found in the *skins* subdirectory of the MediaWiki tree. To create or modify skins, you'll need knowledge of cascading stylesheets (CSS), HTML, and PHP.

Of all the ways to configure MediaWiki, skinning is one of the most complicated, mainly because the code is not well-factored. From the supplied skin files, it's nontrivial to understand which parts are required to write a skin and what are the best practices. (In contrast, the rest of the MediaWiki code base is quite reasonable.)

As a result, the easiest way to create a skin is to base it on the default, Mono-Book. This can be done in several ways:

Copy it
> Copy the MonoBook files and hand-edit them, as recommended in the official documentation at *http://meta.wikimedia.org/wiki/Skins*

Reference it
> Incorporate MonoBook by reference; this is done by several of the supplied skins, such as Simple and MySkin

The main difference between these two methods is maintainability:

- If MonoBook is changed in a subsequent MediaWiki release, the "copy" technique will not incorporate the changes, while the "reference" technique will. Either may be good or bad depending on your purposes.

- The "copy" technique forces you to deal with MonoBook's source code, whereas the "reference" technique will probably keep your code cleaner (though you'll need to read the MonoBook code for guidance).

A Simple Skin

Let's make a trivial skin, named "OReilly", by the reference technique.

In the *skins* directory, create a file *OReilly.php* that contains:

```
<?php
if( !defined( 'MEDIAWIKI' ) )
  die( -1 );

require_once( dirname(__FILE__) . '/MonoBook.php' );

class SkinOReilly extends SkinTemplate {
  function initPage( &$out ) {
    SkinTemplate::initPage( $out );
    $this->skinname  = 'oreilly';
    $this->stylename = 'oreilly';
    $this->template  = 'MonoBookTemplate';
  }
}
```

Next, create a subfolder *oreilly* containing an empty file, *main.css*, to be included automatically by the skin. Now hit your wiki and force a browser refresh to clear out any cached styles. Visit "my preferences" and click the Skins tab and you should see the new skin "OReilly" as a choice. If you click the Preview link, you'll see that the skin is very plain: the traditional MediaWiki links on a nondescript white background. If you like, select "OReilly" as your skin and save your preferences.

Now let's play with CSS. In the *main.css* file, define some styles to make things look the way you want, such as changing the text color:

```
body {
 color: sienna;
}
```

You can also define MediaWiki-specific styles by viewing the HTML source of wiki pages and overriding the style names you find. For example, the user options menu links (user, user talk, preferences, watchlist, etc.) are in a <div> identified by the name p-personal. To make the links italic and place them horizontally in a green box surrounded by a thick black border, write:

```
#p-personal {
  border: 3px solid black;
  background-color: lightgreen;
}
#p-personal a {
  font-style: italic;
}
#p-personal ul {
  list-style: none;
}
```

```
#p-personal li {
  display: inline;
  padding-left: 10px;
}
```

From here you can get as complex as you like, limited only by your imagination and your patience in staring at the HTML page source. Table 15-3 lists some identifiers to get you started.

Table 15-3. Useful CSS IDs and classes for skins

Name	Type	Description
content	ID	Entire content area
bodycontent	ID	Article text area
p-logo	ID	Logo area
siteSub	ID	Site subtitle (hidden by default)
p-cactions	ID	Article action menu (article, edit, my preferences, etc)
p-navigation	ID	Navigation menu
p-search	ID	Search box
searchGoButton	ID	"Go" button
mw-searchButton	ID	"Search" button
p-personal	ID	User menu
p-tb	ID	Toolbox menu
footer	ID	Footer area
f-list	ID	Footer menu
page-*TITLE*	ID	A particular article page, e.g., page-Main_Page or page-Dogs
catlinks	ID	List of category links
h1.firstHeading	class	Article title
portlet	class	All menus
pBody	class	Menu bodies
mediawiki	class	Entire page body

Set the Default Skin

To make your skin the default for new users, set the variable `$wgDefaultSkin` in *LocalSettings.php*, providing the lowercase name of the *oreilly* subdirectory:

```
$wgDefaultSkin = 'oreilly';
```

This will not change the preferences set by existing users. To do that, use the userOptions.php maintenance script from "Setting User Preferences" on page 331. For example:

```
php userOptions.php skin --old monobook --new oreilly
```

Publishing an Extension

Please share your extensions freely with other MediaWiki administrators. To do this best:

- Write your extension following MediaWiki's guidelines so administrators will have an easy time installing it.
- Document it at *www.mediawiki.org*, where administrators look for extensions. See *http://www.mediawiki.org/wiki/Template:Extension* for instructions on creating a standard article about extensions. At press time, this page has a simple form to help you create this article.

Other Extension Topics

In case you still don't have enough choices for programming with MediaWiki, here are pointers to a few capabilities we haven't covered. See *http://www.mediawiki.org/wiki/Category:MediaWiki_Development* for a full list.

Database Access

Your extensions can run queries against the MediaWiki database using the Database class, documented at:

> *http://www.mediawiki.org/wiki/Manual:Database_access*

and in the file *includes/db/Database.php*. This class properly escapes and sanitizes the SQL for security, among other things. If for some reason you must use handcrafted SQL:

- Use the Database object's addQuotes function to sanitize the SQL
- Deallocate properly by calling the Database object's freeResult method

The MediaWiki database schema is described at:

> *http://www.mediawiki.org/wiki/Manual:Database_layout*

 Before writing an extension that queries the MediaWiki database, see if "Dynamic Page List" on page 124 can accomplish what you need.

AJAX Extensions

MediaWiki has special support for extensions that use AJAX, documented at *http://www.mediawiki.org/wiki/Manual:Ajax*. These extensions work as long as your *LocalSettings.php* file doesn't disable AJAX:

```
$wgUseAjax = false; // AJAX is disabled
```

Examples of AJAX extensions can be found at *http://www.mediawiki.org/wiki/ Category:Ajax_extensions*.

The MediaWiki API

MediaWiki has an API (application programming interface) to perform wiki operations programmatically by HTTP request. It's a relatively recent feature that is quite usable as of MediaWiki 1.13. This is not an extension, but a channel for third-party applications to read and write wiki data and metadata.[‡] Operations include:

- Retrieving articles, categories, images, users, recent changes, etc.
- Creating, modifying, and deleting articles
- Performing revision-control operations

and much more. Operations are performed by hitting MediaWiki URLs with GET or POST requests, sending required parameters, and retrieving results in XML or other formats. The full specification and manual are available at:

http://www.mediawiki.org/wiki/API

The API is a convenient platform for creating bots that operate on the wiki.

Finding a MediaWiki Programmer

If you need a custom extension but cannot write it yourself, try asking in one of the MediaWiki mailing lists for developers and administrators. Be brief and polite to increase your chances of getting a response:

> Looking for a programmer to integrate MediaWiki with our company's search engine. This is a paying job. Please contact mike@example.com, 717-555-1234.

Mailing lists are described at:

http://www.mediawiki.org/wiki/Mailing_lists

[‡] Writing is disabled by default. To enable it, set `$wgEnableWriteAPI = true` in *LocalSettings.php*.

The mediawiki-l list will likely be your best bet, but check the descriptions in case another is more appropriate for your purposes. You'll have to subscribe to the list to post your request.

## CHAPTER 16

Wiki Administration

A *wiki administrator* is a system administrator who installs and maintains the MediaWiki software and associated infrastructure. This is different from a sysop, a wiki user with special rights and privileges within the wiki. MediaWiki sites don't need much day-to-day maintenance, but wiki administrators should:

- Set up regular processes, such as backups and upgrades
- Improve performance as needed
- Be prepared for emergencies, such as vandalism
- Know the maintenance scripts supplied with MediaWiki

We'll cover these topics briefly, enough to get you started, and supply pointers to further information. These kinds of topics require experience not only with MediaWiki, but also with system administration and security, as well as thorough knowledge of your wiki server's operating system and application programs. This chapter assumes you are already a competent system administrator for your host operating system of choice.

In addition to the topics in this chapter, many wiki administration tasks are described at:

http://meta.wikimedia.org/wiki/Help:System_admin
http://www.mediawiki.org/wiki/Manual:FAQ
http://www.mediawiki.org/wiki/Manual:Administration

 Many tasks that seem "administrative" can be accomplished more simply within MediaWiki by a sysop, as discussed in Chapter 12.

Maintenance Scripts

The MediaWiki distribution includes a *maintenance* directory full of useful scripts. Their purposes include changing passwords, deleting uploaded files, running administrative SQL queries, dumping and restoring all wiki content, and more. We'll discuss specific scripts as they come up in this chapter.

AdminSettings.php

Some maintenance scripts require root access to the MediaWiki database, so you must set up database authentication before you run them. This is done conveniently by creating a file *AdminSettings.php* in the top-level MediaWiki directory, containing the username and password for the scripts to access the MediaWiki database. The supplied file *AdminSettings.sample* serves as a guide.

Because *AdminSettings.php* contains a password, you should protect it from unauthorized users. If you do this, though, remember to run the maintenance scripts as a user who is authorized to read *AdminSettings.php*, since the scripts need to access it.

 A properly configured MediaWiki site has plaintext passwords in two files, *AdminSettings.php* and *LocalSettings.php*. "Protecting the Database Password in Subversion" on page 201 has tips for reducing this exposure to a single file.

Backups

Make sure to back up your wiki regularly in case disaster strikes. Don't let MediaWiki's version-control features lull you into a false sense of security: even though all old versions of articles are saved, this means nothing if your database disk dies. Perform frequent backups.

A full MediaWiki backup consists of three separate parts:

* MediaWiki source code, stored in the filesystem
* Wiki content, stored in a database
* Uploaded files, stored in the filesystem (in the *images* folder)

Source Code Backups

If you're running a typical MediaWiki site and have not modified its source code, the only source files you need to back up are:

* *LocalSettings.php* and *AdminSettings.php*

- The *extensions* directory
- The *skins* directory

Rather than just performing ordinary backups, however, it's recommended that you maintain these files with a version-control system such as Subversion so you can track changes and roll back to previous versions easily (see "Maintenance with Version Control" on page 197). Then, back up your version-control repository by whatever means you like.

Database Backups

There are two ways to back up the wiki content stored in the database:

Database backup
Use the backup features of your database software, such as the *mysql-dump* program supplied with MySQL. This backs up the entire state of the wiki: not only the articles but also the users, preferences, watchlists, and so on, as is necessary for a full, administrative backup.

XML export
This backs up only the content and revision history of the wiki in a format easily importable into another wiki.

To perform a database backup, if your database administrator login is root and your database is wikidb, run:

```
mysqldump -u root -p****** -r backupfile.sql wikidb
```

which creates the file *backupfile.sql.*

 No space is permitted between -p and the password. To be prompted for the password instead of supplying it on the command line, supply -p without the password.

To restore this file, overwriting everything else in the wiki, run:

```
mysql -u root -p****** < backupfile.sql
```

These are bare-bones backup and restore commands that may or may not be appropriate for your wiki. The previous *mysqldump* command, for instance, may lock database tables and render the wiki unusable while backups are running. You can add the `--single-transaction` flag to avoid this performance problem:

```
mysqldump --single-transaction ...
```

Read the manual page for *mysqldump* carefully to evaluate the most appropriate options for your site and situation.

The second backup method is to perform a MediaWiki XML export. The wiki page `Special:Export` can back up portions of the content, and the script *maintenance/dumpBackup.php* can back up all content:

```
cd maintenance
php dumpBackup.php --full > backupfile.xml
```

To restore an XML dump, use *maintenance/importDump.php*:

```
cd maintenance
php importDump.php < backupfile.xml
```

or for smaller XML files, use the wiki page `Special:Import`. (Large imports on this page might fail if your PHP initialization file, *php.ini*, has low values for its variables `max_execution_time`, `max_input_time`, and `memory_limit`.)

Uploaded File Backups

Uploaded files are found in the *images* directory on your MediaWiki server. Use your favorite file backup program to keep safe copies elsewhere.

Upgrades

New versions of MediaWiki are released about four times per year at MediaWiki.org.[*] Each release includes a file *UPGRADE* with instructions, or you can read them on the Web at *http://www.mediawiki.org/wiki/Manual:Upgrading_MediaWiki*. Here is the usual method for upgrading:

1. Back up your wiki.
2. Copy the latest files on top of your MediaWiki installation.
3. Run the script *maintenance/update.php*.

but always read the *UPGRADE* file first to make sure.

> Join the `mediawiki-announce` mailing list to hear about new releases (see *http://www.mediawiki.org/wiki/Mailing_lists*).

Whenever you upgrade MediaWiki, consider also upgrading your third-party extensions. Many extensions work fine from one MediaWiki version to the

---

[*] Details at *http://www.mediawiki.org/wiki/Version_lifecycle*.

next, but others are targeted to specific MediaWiki versions. In any event, take the opportunity to check for updates. Visit your `Special:Version` page to find each extension's official web page to download its latest release.

Read-Only Wiki

To make the wiki read-only during maintenance operations, you have several options. The configuration setting `$wgReadOnly` in *LocalSettings.php* will reject changes by users:

```
$wgReadOnly = 'Routine maintenance until midnight.';
```

and display the message you specify. (Actually it displays the system message `MediaWiki:Readonlytext`, incorporating your `$wgReadOnly` string, so you can tailor it further.)

This technique will serve most purposes, but it's not perfect because the database is still writable, so someone with sufficient privileges could still modify the wiki data. You might want to place the database into read-only mode, assuming this won't interfere with your maintenance. Here is the command for MySQL:

```
SET GLOBAL read_only = ON;
```

To make the database writable again, run:

```
SET GLOBAL read_only = OFF;
```

> When the database is read-only, you must also disable MediaWiki's page counters in *LocalSettings.php* with:
>
> ```
> $wgDisableCounters = true;
> ```
>
> or MediaWiki will still attempt to write to the "page hits" table. Additionally, logins are not possible because they write to the user table.

Performance and Scaling

MediaWiki software is generally quite efficient, but as your wiki gets larger, you might need to improve performance. As a rule, performance optimization is part art, part science, and depends heavily on your setup. We'll get you started with a few pointers.

Measuring Page Times

Every MediaWiki page contains a performance measurement in an HTML comment:

```
<!-- Served in 0.168 secs. -->
```

Example 16-1, *timer.php*, is a simple PHP script that hits random articles in your wiki and prints their page-serving times. It requires the program *wget*, supplied with Linux and available for most other operating systems at *http://www.gnu.org/software/wget/*.

Example 16-1. timer.php

```php
<?php
# Your wiki's base URL: change as appropriate
$wikiUrl = 'http://localhost/wiki';
# Command to run
$cmd = "wget --quiet -O - $wikiUrl/Special:Random";
# Regular expression to test
$regex = '<\!-- Served in ([0-9]+\.[0-9]+) secs\. -->';
# How many times to repeat
$repeat = isset($argv[1]) ? $argv[1] : 1;

$sum = 0.0;
for ($i=0; $i < $repeat; $i++) {
  if (preg_match("/$regex/", `$cmd`, &$matches)) {
    print "$matches[1]\n";
    $sum += $matches[1];
  }
}
print sprintf("Average time: %0.3f secs\n", $sum / $repeat);
```

Time a single page with:

```
php timer.php
```

or, provide an argument specifying the number of times to run:

```
php timer.php 250
```

At the end, the script prints the average (mean) page serving time. Use a method like this to monitor the average time as your wiki gets larger.

Also check out *ab*, the Apache HTTP server benchmarking tool that displays statistics of your web server performance. It ships with Apache and can be found at *http://httpd.apache.org/docs/2.0/programs/ab.html*.

PHP Acceleration

If your wiki gets too slow at serving pages, consider installing a *PHP accelerator* to speed up PHP processing via bytecode caching. This can give your wiki a 2–10 times speed boost with virtually no effort. Several popular, free accelerators are APC (*http://pecl.php.net/package/APC*), Zend Optimizer (*http://www.zend.com/*) and this author's favorite, eAccelerator (*http://eaccelerator.net/*).

 Check out *http://www.mediawiki.org/wiki/User:Robchurch/Performance_tuning* for tips on accelerating a small wiki.

Apache and MySQL Performance

A discussion about tuning Apache and MySQL for performance could occupy an entire book. Here are some good starting points:

Apache
   http://httpd.apache.org/docs/2.0/misc/perf-tuning.html

MySQL
   http://dev.mysql.com/doc/refman/5.0/en/optimizing-the-server.html

Proxy Servers

Another approach to increasing performance is to use proxy servers to cache whole copies of wiki articles so they needn't be regenerated on every hit. Squid (*http://www.squid-cache.org/*) is a well-known proxy server compatible with MediaWiki. For more information see:

   http://meta.wikimedia.org/wiki/Squid_caching
   http://meta.wikimedia.org/wiki/As_your_Site_Grows

Scaling the Database

MediaWiki can scale to multiple database servers. If you've got a master MySQL server for writes and multiple slave servers for reads, a MediaWiki site can load-balance among these servers fairly transparently. The key is to modify *LocalSettings.php*, removing the single-database configuration based on the $wgDBserver variable and replacing it with $wgDBservers, an array of arrays that specifies a set of load-balanced servers.

Given this old configuration for a single server:

```
$wgDBserver = "myserver.example.com";
$wgDBtype = "mysql";
$wgDBname = "wikidb";
$wgDBuser = "wikiuser";
$wgDBpassword = "******";
```

convert it to use $wgDBservers like this:

```
$wgDBservers = array(
    array(
        'host' => "myserver.example.com",
        'type' => "mysql",
        'dbname' => "wikidb",
        'user' => "wikiuser",
        'password' => "******",
        'load' => 0,
    )
);
```

Then, add however many slave servers you like, making sure that the master remains the first array element:

```
$wgDBservers = array(
    array(
        'host' => "myserver.example.com",
        'type' => "mysql",
        'dbname' => "wikidb",
        'user' => "wikiuser",
        'password' => "******",
        'load' => 0,
    ),
    array(
        'host' => "slave1.example.com",
        'type' => "mysql",
        'dbname' => "wikidb",
        'user' => "wikiuser",
        'password' => "******",
        'load' => 1,
    ),
    array(
        'host' => "slave2.example.com",
        'type' => "mysql",
        'dbname' => "wikidb",
        'user' => "wikiuser",
        'password' => "******",
        'load' => 1,
    ),
    ...
);
```

The load values represent the proportional traffic to route to each slave. To route twice as much traffic to slave2 as slave1, set slave2's load value to 2. See *http://www.mediawiki.org/wiki/Manual:$wgDBservers* for more information on this setup. Also, see *http://dev.mysql.com/doc/refman/5.0/en/replication .html* to set up MySQL replication.

Wiki Families

A *wiki family* (or "wiki farm") is a single server for multiple wikis. Families are not hard to set up, but have several styles with different advantages and disadvantages. Comprehensive advice is available at:

http://www.mediawiki.org/wiki/Manual:Wiki_family

Security

MediaWiki security encompasses network and server security. These are complex subjects best handled by an expert at your location, but here's a list of issues to consider:

Filesystem security
> Make sure the MediaWiki source tree and uploaded files on all web servers (including development, testing, and public use) and in your revision-control system (if any) are accessible only by authorized personnel. Remember that MediaWiki keeps plaintext passwords in its source files *AdminSettings.php* and *LocalSettings.php*.

PHP scripting
> Ensure that PHP files within the MediaWiki source tree cannot be directly executed via the Web, unless they are intended to be (*index.php*, *api.php*, and others in the root).

Authentication
> MediaWiki's login page is not secure, as it does not use SSL (https). Examples 16-2 and 16-3 provide an extension to secure the login page by redirecting it to a secure page. You'll first need to configure your web server to serve https pages via the same hostname and path (i.e., Special:UserLogin must be reachable by the identical URL with only "http" changed to "https").[†]

> If your wiki uses a third-party authentication plug-in, make sure (via packet sniffer) that plaintext passwords are not being transmitted over the network. Do likewise for the connection between MediaWiki and your database server if they reside on separate hosts.

[†] This extension secures only the login page and is not a complete solution to password security on the network. MediaWiki has other pages that transmit passwords, such as the password-change feature on Special:Preferences. Also, an attacker could sniff a user's session cookie from a nonsecured page and take over his login session. You'd need to run the whole session over SSL to secure it.

Network access

Obviously, you'll want to protect your wiki by firewall if it's not for public access. MediaWiki's user rights system can control logins, but it's best to have more than one layer of security for authentication.

Database backups

Keep your database backups in a secure location where unauthorized people cannot read, delete, or modify them.

Within MediaWiki

Give sysop privileges only to trusted, responsible people.

For more information, see:

http://www.mediawiki.org/wiki/Manual:Security

Example 16-2. SecureLogin.php

```php
<?php
$wgExtensionCredits['other'][] = array(
  'name' => 'Secure login',
  'author' =>'Dan Barrett',
  'url' => 'http://example.com/wiki/Secure_login',
  'description' => 'Secure the wiki login page with SSL');

if (isset($_SERVER['REQUEST_METHOD'])) {
  $wgAutoloadClasses['FancyForm']
    = dirname(__FILE__) . '/SecureLogin_body.php';
  $wgHooks['UserLoginForm'][] = 'SecureLogin::secureLogin';
  $wgHooks['BeforePageDisplay'][] = 'SecureLogin::otherPage';
}
```

Example 16-3. SecureLogin_body.php

```php
<?php
class SecureLoginPage {
  // On the login page, if nonsecure, flip to secure
  function secureLogin($junk) {
    global $wgCookieSecure;

    // Login cookies must be nonsecure so other pages see them
    $wgCookieSecure = false;

    // Secure the login page
    if ( ! self::isSecurePage() ) {
      self::flipProtocol('https');
    }
    return true;
  }

  // For all other pages, if secure, flip to nonsecure
  function otherPage($out) {
    global $wgTitle;
    if (! $wgTitle->isSpecial('Userlogin') && self::isSecurePage()) {
```

```
    self::flipProtocol('http');
  }
  return true;
}

// Are we on a secure page or not?
private static function isSecurePage() {
  return isset($_SERVER['HTTPS'])
    && ($_SERVER['HTTPS'] == 'on');
}

// Switch from http to https or vice-versa
private static function flipProtocol($protocol) {
  $domain = $_SERVER['HTTP_HOST'];
  $uri = $_SERVER['REQUEST_URI'];
  header("Location: $protocol://$domain$uri");
  }
}
```

Vandalism

In "Block User" on page 150, we discussed how to ban users from the wiki. Administrators have other tools at their disposal. If your wiki is a victim of spam user accounts created by bots, considering adding a CAPTCHA to the create account page. The ConfirmEdit extension, *http://www.mediawiki.org/ wiki/Extension:ConfirmEdit*, is one of the most popular. It installs in the standard manner for extensions (see "Installing an Extension" on page 272), and configuration is documented on the web page.

If a vandal manages to create a large number of useless pages before you catch on, consider installing and running the Nuke extension, *http://www.mediawiki .org/wiki/Extension:Nuke*. It mass-deletes articles that were recently created by a single author or IP address. A similar extension is NukeDPL (*http://www .mediawiki.org/wiki/Extension:NukeDPL*), which mass-deletes articles that match a DPL query (see "Dynamic Page List" on page 124). This extension requires DPL.

Another approach is to prevent suspicious content from being added to articles in the first place. The SpamBlacklist extension (*http://www.mediawiki.org/ wiki/Extension:SpamBlacklist*) prevents edits that include links to known spammer sites, and MediaWiki's title protection (see "Protecting titles" on page 243) blocks users from creating articles with unwanted titles. For more tips on vandalism and spam, see:

http://www.mediawiki.org/wiki/Manual:Combating_spam

Common Maintenance Tasks

As mentioned earlier, the *maintenance* directory in the MediaWiki distribution is full of helpful scripts. Wiki administrators should review them all to get familiar with their capabilities. We'll cover a few favorites.

 Read scripts before you use them. Their purposes are so diverse, from simple queries to destructive batch deletions, that you should not run a script without understanding it. When run without arguments, some scripts print a help message (*change Password.php*) while others take irreversible actions (*up date.php*). Some scripts respect the --help option to print a usage message, but many do not. It's a disorganized state of affairs, so you need to be careful. Still, some scripts are so critically useful that they're worth getting to know.

Uploading Files

To upload many files into the Image namespace with a single command, use the *importImages.php* script. Place all images into a directory and run:

```
php importImages.php directoryName --user username --comment "my comment"
```

The --user and --comment flags are optional but recommended. For full usage, run:

```
php importImages --help
```

Creating and Editing Articles

In "Import Pages" on page 162, we saw that the Special:Import page can create and modify wiki articles from an XML file. You can also create an article from a wikitext file using the *importTextFile.php* script:

```
php importTextFile.php filename --title "my title" --user username \
    --comment "my comment"
```

The --title, --user, and --comment flags are optional but recommended. For full usage, run:

```
php importTextFile.php --help
```

Similarly, the *edit.php* script will modify an article interactively from the command line. Simply run:

```
php edit.php -u username -s "my comment" "my title"
```

and enter text afterward. The article "my title" will be replaced by that text.

Deleting Multiple Articles

The script *deleteBatch.php* deletes a set of articles by their titles. List the titles in a text file, one per line, and run:

```
php deleteBatch.php -u username -r "my comment" -i secs filename
```

This deletes all articles whose titles are in file *filename*, crediting the deletions to user *username* with the comment "my comment", pausing for *secs* seconds between deletions.

For the complete usage information, run:

```
php deleteBatch --help
```

Setting User Preferences

Want to change a preference for all wiki users? Use the *userOptions.php* script. To see a list of available preferences, run:

```
php userOptions.php --list
```

To change a preference—say, the `rows` preference that controls the number of lines in the edit box on the edit page—run:

```
php userOptions.php rows --old 24 --new 50
```

This means "For all users that currently have `rows` set to 24, change the value to 50." The command ignores users who have `cols` values other than 24.

To create a preference that users have not already configured, set `--old` to the empty string:

```
php userOptions.php myNewPref --old '' --new 1
```

This sets all accounts to have the preference *myNewPref* with value 1, if those accounts have not selected a value for *myNewPref*.

Resetting Passwords

A user who forgets his or her password can reset it from the login page by clicking "E-mail password." If for some reason this won't work, a wiki administrator can reset a password with the *changePassword.php* script:

```
php changePassword.php --user username --password "new password"
```

You can give this capability to sysops within the wiki, so you don't need to rely on a maintenance script. To do this, install the Password Reset extension at *http://www.mediawiki.org/wiki/Extension:PasswordReset*.

Creating Interwiki Links

Interwiki links are created by the wiki administrator using SQL and are stored in the database. The table name will be the database table prefix you chose in "Database setup" on page 185 (say, mw_), followed by `interwiki`:

```
REPLACE INTO mw_interwiki  -- use correct table prefix
(iw_prefix, iw_url, iw_local)
VALUES
('name', 'http://www.example2.com/wiki/$1', 0)
```

The `iw_prefix` value is the interwiki link name, and `iw_url` is the URL of the remote website, with $1 substituted for the article name. For instance, to create an interwiki link [[smart:...]] that points to Wikipedia, you'd run this SQL statement:

```
REPLACE INTO mw_interwiki  -- use correct table prefix
(iw_prefix, iw_url, iw_local)
VALUES
('smart', 'http://www.wikipedia.org/wiki/$1', 0)
```

Now [[smart:dog food]] will resolve to *http://www.wikipedia.org/wiki/ Dog_food* automatically.

Interwiki sites are not necessarily wikis: they just need to have a predictable URL pattern so the $1 substitution works. For instance, a bug-tracking system with URLs of the form:

```
http://bugs.example.com/?id=12345
```

where 12345 is the bug ID, can be represented by an interwiki link like this:

```
REPLACE INTO mw_interwiki  -- use correct table prefix
(iw_prefix, iw_url, iw_local)
VALUES
('bug', 'http://bugs.example.com/?id=$1', 0)
```

and inserted into articles as [[bug:12345]]. Just keep in mind the following:

- The `iw_url` value must be 127 characters or less; this is a database column limit.

- Spaces in the interwiki link [[like this]] will be converted to underscores in the URL like_this, so $1 values without spaces are most effective.

Enabling Interlanguage Link Support

Making your wiki support interlanguage links (see "Interlanguage Links" on page 84) takes several steps:

1. Set up a wiki for each language: Wikipedia has *en.wikipedia.org* for English, *fr.wikipedia.org* for French, etc. Mimicking this behavior requires a subdomain per language, so ideally your web provider permits you this capability (see "Hosting Prerequisites" on page 174).

    If your provider does not support subdomains, set up separate directories per language:

    > *http://wiki.example.com/en/*
    > *http://wiki.example.com/fr/*
    > ...

2. Set up a family of wikis (see "Wiki Families" on page 327) and configure your web server to make each URL work as desired.

3. In each wiki, add interwiki table entries for each language code: `es` for Spanish, `fr` for French, etc. For example:

    ```
    REPLACE INTO mw_interwiki  -- use correct table prefix
    (iw_prefix, iw_url, iw_local)
    VALUES
    ('es', 'http://es.example.com/wiki/$1', 0),
    ('fr', 'http://fr.example.com/wiki/$1', 0)
    ```

4. Start linking.

The configuration settings `$wgHideInterlanguageLinks` and `$wgInterwikiMagic` control the interlanguage features and are set properly by default. To disable them, set in *LocalSettings.php*:

```
$wgHideInterlanguageLinks = true;
$wgInterwikiMagic = false;
```

For More Information

This ends our tour of MediaWiki. For more information, visit:

> *http://www.mediawiki.org/*
> *http://meta.wikimedia.org/*

and join the official MediaWiki mailing lists of interest:

> *http://meta.wikimedia.org/wiki/Mailing_list*

The `mediawiki-l` is of particular interest if you are technically inclined.

Index

Symbols

!
    table heading, 69
    unpatrolled edit, 244

#
    anchors, 80
    numbered lists, 64
    parser function syntax, 123
        (see also parser functions)
    REDIRECT, 101
$1 (system message parameter), 219, 220
$wgAutoloadClasses, 285
$wg... configuration settings (see wg...)
$wgTitle, 300
%20 (encoded space character), 77
'' (italics), 54
''' (bold), 54
''''' (bold italics), 54
*
    bulleted list, 61
    user group, 230
+ tab, 17
    configuring, 241
..
    transcluding subpages, 120
/ (subpage), 99
64-bit Windows server, 178
:
    after namespace, 16, 96
    in category link, 80, 95
    in definition lists, 65
    in image link, 80
    in image tags, 57
    in lists, 63
    indenting paragraphs, 54
    transclusion, 120
; (definition list), 65
= (heading), 52
?> (PHP terminator), 284
{| (begin table), 68
|
    image options, 59
    internal links, 55, 77
    language selector on login page, 270
    parser functions, 294
    tables in wikitext, 68
    template parameters, 116
|- (table row), 68
|| (inline table cell), 69
|} (end table), 68
~ (signatures), 33

A

ab, 324
about link
    configuring, 264
access control, 229
    (see also user rights)
    anonymous users, 232
    limitations, 204
    lists, 151, 209
    logins required, 232
    models, 209
    per namespace, 247
    private namespace, 233
accessibility links, 42

We'd like to hear your suggestions for improving our indexes. Send email to *index@oreilly.com*.

action=credits, 20
action=edit, 289
action=purge, 257
Active Directory, 175
add pages to watchlist automatically, 40
addHeadItem, 311
addHTML, 304
addInlineScript, 223, 311, 312
addOnloadHook, 311, 312
addQuotes, 316
addWikiMsg, 307
addWikiText, 307
administration, 319
    (see also governance)
administrator, 216
    (see also sysop)
AdminSettings.php, 193, 226, 320
    passwords, 327
AdminSettings.sample, 193, 320
AJAX, 163, 251, 282
    extensions, 317
alerts on user talk page, 31
    (see also email notifications)
aliases (see redirects)
all pages, 147
AlternateEdit hook, 234
anchors, 53
    linking to, 80
anonymous users, 29, 209
    restricting logins, 232
        except for Talk pages, 232
    talk pages, 25
    user pages, 25
antivirus scanning, 250
Apache, 174
    configuring, 181
    on Linux, 176
    on Macintosh, 179
    on Windows, 177
    performance, 325
        measurement, 324
    short URLs, 191
APC, 325
API, 317
api.php, 195
Apple Macintosh, 179
    socket file problem, 180
archival (see backups)

arguments (see parameters)
arithmetic operations, 124
Article class, 287
article namespace, 16
article tab, 26
article titles, 10, 12
    case-sensitivity, 76
    prefix search, 149
    protecting, 243, 329
    standards, 211
    underscores, 76
Article.php, 287
articles, 10, 12
    body, 10, 12
    configuration settings, 236
    creating, 13, 51
    credits, 266
    dead-end, 141
    deleted, restoring, 162
    deleting, 106
    editing, 47
    existence test, 123
    exporting, 161
    highly active, 159
    HTML forms, 279
    HTML header, 237
    least revised, 142
    list of all, 147
    longest, 142
    metadata, 129
    most categorized, 160
    most linked-to, 160
    most revised, 161
    newest, 153
    organizing, 89, 108
    orphaned, 142
    ownership, 208
    patrolling, 243
    popular, 164
    protected, 143
    purging from the cache, 257
    random, 158
    redirects (see redirects)
    renaming, 26, 104, 164
        reverting a rename, 105
    reverting edits, 20
    sample, 10
    shortest, 143

size limit, 236
splitting, 135
statistics, 157, 165
titles (see article titles)
uncategorized, 144
undeleting, 106, 162
unwatched, 146
wanted, 146
XML export, 161
ArticleSave hook, 286
ARTICLESPACE, 112
asterisk (see *)
Atom, 213
authentication, 175, 327
auto-number headings, 42
automatic watchlist, 40
autopatrol right, 244

B

backups, 320
database, 321, 328
security, 328
source code, 320
uploaded files, 322
XML, 322
backward links, 162
banning (see blocking users)
base URL, 82
BASEPAGENAME, 111, 120
BASEPAGENAMEE, 111
behavior changes, 299
big tag, 55
bin directory, 195
blank lines, 52
blank slate approach, 206
blocking users, 150, 228
block log, 152
configuring, 261
standards, 212
blue links (see links, colors)
bold, 21, 47, 54
bold italics, 54
book sources, 163
Boolean logic in articles (see
        ParserFunctions extension)
border (image tag option), 59
bots, 94
(see also pywikipedia)

bot user group, 230
creating, 317
watchlist, 40
br tag, 62
branching, 200
broken links, 42
broken redirects, 140
browser refresh, 43
bulleted lists, 22, 61
fixing broken, 63
nested, 62
bureaucrats, 229, 230
(see also user rights)
assigning user rights, 151
bureaucrat user group, 230, 234
extending privilege to other user
        groups, 234
button bar, 50
button labels, 218

C

caching, 184
browser, 43, 257
page, 42
parser, 313
purging, 257
callback functions, 282, 286, 299
return value, 286
Cancel link, 51
capitalizing titles (see case-sensitivity)
CAPTCHA, 329
cascading stylesheets, 223, 257, 267
article content, 259
enabling, 268
global, 267
help with, 44
list of styles, 315
Page CSS extension, 274
per namespace, 268
per page, 268, 274
per skin, 267
per user, 43, 267
printing, 269
tables in wikitext, 70
case conversion, 124
case-sensitivity, 76, 204
redirects to work around it, 102
categories, 11, 14, 90

adding articles to, 90
articles with most, 160
child, 16
   (see also subcategory)
creating, 91
deleting, 94
Dynamic Page List, 125
hidden, 94
list of all, 148
listing members, 91
most linked-to, 159
parent, 16
   (see also supercategory)
preplanned, 206
redirects, 103
renaming, 93
subcategories, 16
   (see also subcategory)
supercategories, 16
   (see also supercategory)
taxonomy, 206
templates, categorizing, 119, 144
tree view, 163
uncategorized, 144
unused, 145
uploaded files, 144
versus category page, 90
versus namespaces and subpages, 99
wanted, 147
Category namespace, 16, 17, 90, 97
category page, 15, 90
creating, 92
linking to, 80, 95
sorting, 95
versus category, 90
category tag, 90
sort key, 95
transcluding, 119
Category talk namespace, 17, 97
CategoryTree extension, 163, 275
center (image tag option), 59
change comment, 22, 50
blank, 39
configuring, 240
uploads, 58
changing a username, 37
child category (see subcategory)
Cite extension, 276

clamav, 250
clashing edits (see conflicts)
clearing browser cache, 43
code formatting, 54, 55
code tag, 55
coding extensions, 281
colon (see :)
columns (edit box), 38
Common.css (see
   MediaWiki:Common.css)
Common.js (see MediaWiki:Common.js)
community portal link, 23
compare selected versions, 19
comparing revisions (see diffs)
compress, 180
conditional statements in articles (see
   ParserFunctions extension)
conditional transclusion, 116
config directory, 195
configuration settings, 224
   (see also settings by name, wg...)
reference manual, 224, 227
configuring MediaWiki settings, 215, 227
ConfirmEdit extension, 329
conflicts, 51, 72
configuring, 241
consistency maintenance, 108
content management, 6
context per line (search), 41
contributions, 25, 32, 35, 150
configuring, 262
cookies, 30, 36
copyright notice, 240
corporate wiki, 207
interwiki links, 84
navigation bar, 259
create tab, 26
createaccount right, 230
createpage right, 229
creating
accounts, 30
permission, 230
articles, 13, 51
permission, 229
interwiki links, 332
Creative Commons, 250, 264
credits
article authors, 266

credits page, 36
extension writers, 288
CSS (see cascading stylesheets)
css tag, 274
cur link, 19
curly braces, 47
current events link, 23

D

database, 185
(see also SQL programming)
backups, 321, 328
configuration, 252
logging SQL operations, 254
master and slave, 325
protecting passwords, 201
reference manual, 226
scaling, 325
search tuning, 251
setup, 185
SQL, 225
errors, 255, 289
superuser account, 178, 186, 225
table prefix, 186
wiki user, 186, 225
Database.php, 316
date format, 38
days to show in
recent changes, 40
watchlist, 40
dead-end pages, 141
debugging, 254
extensions, 288
PHP exceptions, 254
DefaultSettings.php, 224, 231, 249, 250
never modify, 224, 283
Defines.php, 246, 268
definition lists, 65
deleteBatch.php, 331
deleted pages, 162
deleting articles, 106
batch deletes, 331
configuring, 242
delete right, 229
delete tab, configuring, 263
deletion log, 106, 153
list of reasons, 242
permission, 229

standards, 212
versus redirects, 106
diffs, 19, 51
conflicts, 73
patrolling, 244
preferences, 42
directories in MediaWiki source code, 193
disable page caching, 42
disambig template, 104, 148
disambiguation pages, 103, 211, 237
creating, 104
detection, 148
initial setup, 104
list of links to, 148
disaster recovery (see backups)
disclaimers link, 26
configuring, 264
discussion page (see talk pages)
discussion tab (see talk pages)
div tag, 55
docs directory, 193
donations link, 23
double quotes in search, 13
double redirects, 103, 141
due to double moves, 105
downloading MediaWiki, 180
DPL (see Dynamic Page List)
dummy template, 129
dumpBackup.php, 245, 322
dumps (see backups)
duplicate files, 156
dvipng, 191
Dynamic Page List, 124, 217, 245, 278
basics, 125
category processing, 125
dpl tag, 125
format option, 128
generating lists of links, 134
glossary building, 135
include option, 129
metadata, 129

E

eAccelerator, 325
edit box, 49
configuring, 240
has full width, 39

edit conflict (see conflicts)
edit links, 38, 48
   configuring, 241
edit page, 20, 49
   buttons, 50, 240
      adding, 43, 239
   configuring, 238
   help with, 51
   preferences, 38
   toolbar, 43, 50
edit pages on double-click, 39
edit raw watchlist, 35
edit right, 229
edit tab, 26
   configuring, 263
edit token, 308
edit.js, 223
edit.php, 330
editing, 20, 47
   (see also edit page; wikitext)
   canceling, 51
   conflicts (see conflicts)
   introduction to, 48
   minor edits, 51
   permission, 229, 242
   preferences, 38
   previewing, 50
   saving, 22, 50
   statistics, 157
   wikitext (see wikitext)
editinterface right, 230
email
   cc-ing, 37
   installing software, 188
   preferences, 37
   setup, 184, 189
   within wiki, 37, 152
email address
   preferences, 36
email notifications
   user talk page, 32, 37
   watchlist, 34, 37
email this user link, 32, 36, 152
   configuring, 261
emailconfirmed user group, 230
embedding articles in other articles (see
      transclusion)
enable jump-to links, 42

enable section editing by right-click, 38
equals sign (see =)
error message text, 218
escaping wikitext, 71
example code, downloadable, 281
exceptions thrown, 254
exclamation point (see !)
expand watchlist, 40
ExpandTemplates extension, 279
expiration date for article protection, 242
exporting pages as XML, 161, 245
#expr parser function, 122
extensions, 225
   Capitalizer, 292
   CategoryTagSorter, 300
   CategoryTree, 163, 275
   Cite, 276
   ConfirmEdit, 329
   creating, 281
      AJAX, 317
      behavior changes, 299
      best practices, 284
      choosing a type, 282
      credits, 288
      database access, 316
      disabling parser cache, 313
      form posts, 308
      getting article text, 307
      HTML rendering, 307
      implementation file, 285
      JavaScript, 311
      messages file, 285, 298
      nonstandard, 283
      parser functions, 291
      preferences checkbox, 309
      reference manual, 281
      setup file, 285
      skins, 313
      special pages, 301
      standards, 283
      tag extensions, 294
      three files for, 285
      toolbox links, 309
      variable argument lists, 294
      variables, 289
      wikitext rendering, 307
   debugging, 288
   do you need one?, 282

download example code, 281
Dynamic Page List, 124, 278
ExpandTemplates, 279
ExternalImage (extimg), 296
FancyForm, 304
finding, 271
ForcePreview, 240
Hello World tag, 294
hiring a programmer, 317
ImageMap, 272, 276
InputBox, 280
installing, 271, 272
    example, 274
LDAP Authentication, 280
LinkSearch, 164
list of all, 158, 271
loading, 225
Lucene Search, 275
MediaWiki+FCKeditor, 204
Newuserlog, 153
Nuke, 329
NukeDPL, 329
Page CSS, 269, 274
parser functions, 279
ParserFunctions, 122
PDF Export, 275
preferences, 42
Preloader, 308
publishing, 316
recommended, 274
RSS, 214
SecureLogin, 328
Semantic MediaWiki, 280
Simple Forms, 280
SpamBlacklist, 329
SubPageList2, 100
SyntaxHighlight GeSHi, 278
upgrading, 322
user rights, 235
UserVariable, 290
WikiArticleFeeds, 214, 277
extensions directory, 193, 273
external diff tool, 39
external editor, 39
external images, 56, 61
    embedding in articles, 61
    enabling, 236
external links, 18, 47, 55, 81

alternate text, 56, 81
configuring, 266
filepath, 60
icon, 81, 266
numbered, 82
protocols, 82
searching for, 164
to yourself, 82

F

f-prot, 250
factoring, 109
favicon, 258
FCKeditor, 204
file links, 86, 236
file list, 155
file path, 155
file uploads (see uploaded files)
filename extensions, 248
filepath parser function, 60
files in MediaWiki source code, 193
files you may modify, 194
Firefox, 43, 49, 87, 236, 260
firewall, 328
font tag, 55
fonts, 54
footer menu, 26
    configuring, 264
force paragraphs to be justified, 42
force-refreshing a web browser, 43, 257
ForcePreview extension, 240
__FORCETOC__, 53
formatting broken links, 42
forms
    in articles, 279
    posting, 308
    security, 308
frame (image tag option), 59
frameless (image tag option), 59
freeResult, 316
freeze, 200
ft_min_word_len, 251
ft_stopword_file, 252
FULLPAGENAME, 79, 111
FULLPAGENAMEE, 111
fullurl parser function, 83
functions (see parser functions)

G

gallery of new files, 152
GD2, 178
global variables, 224
GlobalFunctions.php, 222
glossary building, 135
Go button for search, 12, 51, 240
    configuring, 240, 265
governance, 212
graphical links, 86
    (see also image links; image tags)
graphics (see uploaded files)
groups (see user rights)

H

hash mark (see #)
headings, 22, 47, 52
    levels, 52
    numbering, 42
    tables, 69
height of edit box, 38
help, 7, 27
    MediaWiki.org, 27
    Wikipedia, 27
Help
    pages, installing, 190
help link, 23
Help namespace, 17, 97
Help talk namespace, 17, 97
__HIDDENCAT__, 94
hide bot edits from watchlist, 40
hide minor edits
    from watchlist, 40
    in recent changes, 40
hide my edits from the watchlist, 40
high use pages, 159
history, 18
    comparing revisions, 19
    date and time preferences, 38
    history page, 19
    history tab, 26
        configuring, 263
history page, 26
hit counter
    configuring, 264
    disabling during maintenance, 323
hits per page (search), 41

home page
    setting, 258
hooks, 282, 286, 299
    AlternateEdit, 234
    ArticleSave, 286
    hooks.txt documentation, 286
    LanguageGetMagic, 289, 292
    MagicWordwgVariableIDs, 289
    MonoBookTemplateToolboxEnd, 309
    ParserGetVariableValueSwitch, 289
    ParserLimitReport, 300
    PersonalUrls, 262
    SkinTemplateContentActionsz, 263
    UserToggles, 309
    wfRunHooks, 287
hostname, 82
.htaccess file, 192
HTML
    avoiding in articles, 53
    headers, 237
    rendering in extensions, 307
    tags, 53
        (see also parser tags; wikitext)
http links (see external links)
httpd.conf (see Apache)
https login page, 327
hyperlink (see links)

I

i18n file (see extensions, creating)
icon
    external link (see external links)
    favicon (see favicon)
    wiki logo (see logo)
#if parser function, 123
#ifeq parser function, 123
#iferror parser function, 122
#ifexist parser function, 123
#ifexpr parser function, 123
IIS, 177
image links, 57
    options, 59
Image namespace, 56, 59, 97
image page, 57, 60
    linking to, 57, 80
image tag, 56
Image talk namespace, 57, 97
Image talk page, 57

ImageMap extension, 272, 276
images (see uploaded files)
images directory, 193, 248, 322
   write access, 188
     (see also uploaded files)
img_auth.php, 195
import log, 153
importDump.php, 245, 322
importImages.php, 330
importing images in batch, 330
importing text files, 330
importing XML, 162, 245
   log, 153
importTextFile.php, 330
includeonly tag, 117, 118, 119
includes directory, 194, 287
   reference for creating extensions, 281
including articles in other articles (see
     transclusion)
indenting paragraphs, 54
index.php, 194
infinite protection, 242
initialization file (see mysql.ini)
InputBox extension, 280
installing MediaWiki, 173, 180
   Apple Macintosh, 179
   Help pages, 190
   Linux, 176
   Microsoft Windows, 177
   optional features, 187
   planning, 206
   prerequisites, 174
   web installer, 182
   with administrative access, 181
   without administrative access, 182
interlanguage links, 84
   configuring, 333
   maintenance, 143
interleaved edits (see conflicts)
internal links, 18, 47, 75
   alternate text, 55, 77
   anchors, 80
   cross-namespace, 78
   nonexistent articles, 76
   plural trick, 78
   wikitext, 22
international support, 269
   in extensions, 285, 298

internationalization file (see extensions,
     creating)
Internet Explorer, 43, 260
interwiki links, 84, 213
   configuring, 332
IP address, 25, 31
   blocked, 150
isAllowed, 234
ISBN, 163
italics, 21, 47, 54

J

JavaScript
   configuring, 253
   edit page buttons, 239
   editing pages by double-click, 39
   enabling, 253
   extensions, 311
   global, 253
   help with, 44
   per skin, 253
   per user, 43, 253
   programming, 223
   recent changes (enhanced), 40
   section editing by right-click, 38
   show edit toolbar, 39
   system-wide, 223
   toolbar buttons on edit page, 239
jump-to links, 42
justifying paragraphs, 42

K

Kerberos, 175

L

language
   configuring, 269
   HTML header, 238
   links, 143
   login page menu, 269
   preferences, 36
language menu, 24, 85
LanguageGetMagic hook, 289, 292
languages directory, 195
last change timestamp, 26
   configuring, 264
last link, 19

LaTeX, 71
  (see also mathematical formulas)
lazy linking, 76, 147
LDAP, 175, 178, 231
  LDAP Authentication extension, 280
leadership (see governance)
leading whitespace, 54
left (image tag option), 59
license, 193
  GNU, 4
  in footer, 264
limit images on file description pages, 38
line breaks
  in templates, 118
linebreaks, 62
lines in edit box, 38
lines per hit (search), 41
links, 18, 55, 75
  adjacent, 88
  broken (see broken links)
  colors, 18, 41
  external (see external links)
  file (see file links)
  image (see image links)
  interlanguage (see interlanguage links)
  internal (see internal links)
  interwiki (see interwiki links)
  mistakes, 83
  permanent, 24
  reverse, 162
  strategies, 87
  to category pages, 80
  to image pages, 80
  underlining, 42
  uploaded files, 60
Linux installation, 176
lists, 61
locale directory, 195
LocalSettings.php, 183, 187, 194, 227, 283, 286
  (see also configuration settings)
  editing, 187
  loading extensions, 273
  overriding configuration settings, 224
  passwords, 327
logging, 254
  PHP exceptions, 254
  SQL operations, 254

logging in, 25, 30, 149
  login link, configuring, 262
  login page message, 259
  requiring logins, 232
    except for Talk pages, 232
  securing the login page, 327
logging out, 25, 149
  log out link, configuring, 262
  logout page message, 259
logical parser functions, 122
login name (see username)
logo, 10, 258
logs, 152
  configuring, 262
  deletion, 106
  move, 105
logs link, 32
long pages, 142
look and feel
  configuring, 257
lower versus upper case (see case-sensitivity)
Lucene Search extension, 275

M

Macintosh (see Apple Macintosh)
macro expansion (see templates)
magic words, 108
  (see also parser functions; parser tags; templates; variables)
  creating, 282
MagicWordwgVariableIDs hook, 289
mailing list, 317, 322, 333
  mediawiki-l, 7, 333
main namespace, 16, 97
main page
  link, 23
  setting, 258
main.css, 314
maintenance directory, 194, 320
maintenance scripts, 226, 320
  (see also scripts by name)
mark as patrolled, 244
matchEditToken, 308
math directory, 195
mathematical formulas, 70, 71
  (see also LaTeX)
  alternative renderer, 191

calculating (#ifexpr), 124
configuring, 237
installing the software, 190
maximum number of changes in watchlist, 40
max_execution_time, 322
max_input_time, 322
@media, 269
media links, 57
Media namespace, 57, 60, 98
MediaWiki, 4
  administration (see administration)
  API, 195, 317
  configuration file (see LocalSettings.php)
  configuring, 215, 227
  downloading, 180
  extending, 281
  installing, 173, 180
    (see also installing MediaWiki)
  license, 4, 193
  limitations, 6, 203
  look and feel, 257
  performance, 323
  prerequisites, 174
  scaling, 323
  security, 327
  source code (see source code)
  stability, 6
  strengths, 5
  upgrading, 199, 322
  user interface, 257
  version, 158
MediaWiki namespace, 97, 215, 222
  (see also messages by name, MediaWiki:...; system messages)
MediaWiki talk namespace, 97
MediaWiki+FCKeditor, 204
mediawiki-l, 7, 333
MediaWiki.org, 7, 27, 333
  downloads, 180
  extension catalog, 271
  Manual namespace, 224, 227, 281
MediaWiki:Aboutsite, 264
MediaWiki:Anonlogin, 262
MediaWiki:Anontalk, 262
MediaWiki:Anonuserpage, 262
MediaWiki:Blockip, 261

MediaWiki:Common.css, 70, 223, 267
MediaWiki:Common.js, 223, 253
MediaWiki:Contributions, 262
MediaWiki:Copyright, 264
MediaWiki:Copyrightwarning, 240
MediaWiki:Copyrightwarning2, 240
MediaWiki:Delete, 263
MediaWiki:Deletereason-dropdown, 242
MediaWiki:Disambiguationspage, 237
MediaWiki:Disclaimers, 264
MediaWiki:Edit, 263
MediaWiki:Emailuser, 261
MediaWiki:Explainconflict, 241
MediaWiki:History, 263
MediaWiki:Large-file, 249
MediaWiki:Lastmodifiedat, 264
MediaWiki:Log, 262
MediaWiki:Loginlanguagelinks, 270
MediaWiki:Loginprompt, 259
MediaWiki:Logout, 262
MediaWiki:Logouttext, 259
MediaWiki:Longpageerror, 236
MediaWiki:Mainpage, 258
MediaWiki:Minoredit, 240
MediaWiki:Modern.css, 267
MediaWiki:Modern.js, 253
MediaWiki:Monobook.css, 223, 267, 274
MediaWiki:Monobook.js, 223, 253, 274
MediaWiki:Move, 263
MediaWiki:Mycontris, 262
MediaWiki:Mypreferences, 262
MediaWiki:Mytalk, 262
MediaWiki:Mywatchlist, 262
MediaWiki:Navigation, 261
MediaWiki:Newarticletext, 238
MediaWiki:Noarticletext, 240
MediaWiki:Noexactmatch, 240
MediaWiki:Permalink, 262
MediaWiki:Printableversion, 262
MediaWiki:Privacy, 264
MediaWiki:Protect, 263
MediaWiki:Readonlytext, 323
MediaWiki:Recentchanges-url, 261
MediaWiki:Recentchangeslinked, 262
MediaWiki:Savearticle, 240
MediaWiki:Search, 265
MediaWiki:Searcharticle, 265

MediaWiki:Searchbutton, 265
MediaWiki:Showdiff, 240
MediaWiki:Showpreview, 240
MediaWiki:Sidebar, 260
MediaWiki:Sitenotice, 259
MediaWiki:Specialpages, 262
MediaWiki:Summary, 240
MediaWiki:Tagline, 259
MediaWiki:Talk, 263
MediaWiki:Unprotect, 263
MediaWiki:Unwatch, 263
MediaWiki:Upload, 262
MediaWiki:Userpage, 262
MediaWiki:Viewcount, 264
MediaWiki:Watch, 263
MediaWiki:Watchthis, 240
MediaWiki:Whatlinkshere, 262
memory_limit, 322
menus, 23
    (see also menus by name)
    configuring, 260
    footer, 26
    language, 11, 85
    language menu, 24
    navigation, 11, 23
    text, 218
    toolbox, 11, 24, 32, 261
    top tabs, 11, 26
    user options, 25
message at the top of every page, 259
messages (see system messages)
messages file (see extensions, creating)
Meta-Wiki, 7, 27, 333
metadata, 129
Microsoft SQL Server, 178
Microsoft Windows, 177
    64-bit, 178
MIME
    article type, 238
    checking of uploaded files, 248
    JavaScript type, 238
    mime.info file, 248
    mime.types, 248
    search, 156
minor edit, 34
    default when editing, 39
    hiding from watchlist, 40
    hiding on recent changes page, 40

notification, 37
    saving, 51
Modern skin, 42
    JavaScript, 253
MonoBook skin, 37, 42, 257, 264, 313
    JavaScript, 253
    monobook.css, 43
    monobook.js, 43
MonoBookTemplateToolboxEnd hook,
        309
most linked-to
    categories, 159
    files, 159
    pages, 160
    templates, 160
move log, 105, 153
move right, 229
move tab, 26, 164
    configuring, 263
moving articles (see renaming articles)
msg, 222
mssql, 178
multilanguage tag extension, 298
mwCustomEditButtons, 43, 239
my contributions (see contributions)
my preferences (see preferences)
my watchlist (see watchlist)
MySQL, 174
    ft_min_word_len, 251
    ft_stopword_file, 252
    Linux, 177
    mysql.ini, 251
    mysqldump, 321
    on Macintosh, 180
    on Windows, 178
    performance, 325
    read-only database, 323
    setup, 186
    stopwords, 252

N

name of the wiki (see wiki, name)
Names.php, 270
NAMESPACE variable, 112
namespaces, 16, 96
    adding an article, 98
    ARTICLESPACE variable, 112
    Category, 17, 90, 97

Category talk, 17, 97
configuring, 245
creating, 98, 246
restricted to certain users, 233
Help, 17, 97
installing pages, 190
Help talk, 17, 97
IDs, 246, 268
Image, 56, 59, 97
Image talk, 57, 97
linking between, 78
pipe trick, 79
listing all articles, 98
main, 97
Media, 57, 60, 98
MediaWiki, 97
MediaWiki standard, 97
MediaWiki talk, 97
NAMESPACE variable, 112
Project, 97, 110
Project talk, 97
protecting, 247
read-only, 247
searching within, 13, 41, 247
security, 247
Special, 98
SUBJECTSPACE variable, 112
subpage support, 247
Talk, 17, 97
TALKSPACE variable, 112
TALKSPACEE variable, 112
Template, 97, 112
Template talk, 97
transcluding from, 119
preventing, 247
User, 17, 97
User talk, 17, 31, 97
variables, 112
versus categories and subpages, 99
virtual, 98
navigation menu, 11, 23
configuring, 260
nesting
categories, 93
(see also subcategory)
subpages, 99
templates, 115
new article message, 238

new pages, 153
patrolling, 244
new section tab, 17
configuring, 241
new uploaded files, 152
newFromName, 306
__NEWSECTIONLINK__, 241
__NOEDITSECTION__, 241
noinclude tag, 117, 118, 119
none (image tag option), 59
__NOTOC__, 42, 53
nowiki tag, 71
NS_HELP, 268
NS_MAIN, 268
Nuke extension, 329
NukeDPL extension, 329
number of edits to show in recent changes,
40
numbered lists, 22, 64
limitations, 64, 206
nested, 64

O

ocaml, 191
onlyinclude tag, 117, 118
OpenSearch, 195
opensearch_desc.php, 195
ordered list (see numbered lists)
organizing articles, 108
orphaned pages, 142
OS X (see Apple Macintosh)
OutputPage class, 303, 307
ownership of content, 208, 212

P

packet sniffer, 327
page (see articles)
page caching, 42
page credits, 266
Page CSS extension, 274
page statistics, 165
page tab, 26
page time, 324
PAGENAME, 111
as sort key for categories, 96
PAGENAMEE, 111
pages with the

fewest revisions, 142
  most categories, 160
  most revisions, 161
pages without language links, 143
paragraphs, 21, 52
  boxing, 54
  indenting, 54
  justifying, 42
parameters
  parser function, 294
  special page, 150
  system message, 220
  template, 113
parent category (see supercategory)
Parser class, 313
parser functions
  #dpl (see Dynamic Page List)
  #expr, 122
  #if, 123
  #ifeq, 123
  #iferror, 122
  #ifexist, 123
  #ifexpr, 123
  #rel2abs, 122
  #switch, 122
  #tag, 127
  #time, 122
  #titleparts, 122
  creating, 282, 291
  extensions, third-party, 279
  logical, 122
  parameters, 294
  parsing order, 127
  uc, 124
parser tags (see tags)
ParserFirstCallInit, 292, 294
ParserFunctions extension, 122
ParserGetVariableValueSwitch hook, 289
ParserLimitReport hook, 300
parsing order, 127
passwords, 327
  AdminSettings.php, 320
  changing, 36
  resetting, 331
patrolling, 243
  autopatrol right, 244
  log, 153, 244
  patrol right, 230, 244

permission, 244
  self-approval, 244
PDF Export extension, 275
PEAR, 189
permanent link, 24
  configuring, 262
permissions (see user rights)
PersonalUrls hook, 262
PHP, 5, 174
  (see also extensions; source code)
  acceleration, 324
  autoloading objects, 285
  avoid terminating ?>, 284
  errors, 254, 289
  extension programming, 281
  global variables, 224
  initialization file (see php.ini)
  Linux, 177
  max_execution_time, 322
  max_input_time, 322
  memory_limit, 322
  on Macintosh, 179
  on Windows, 178
  PEAR, 189
  reference manual, 281
  script path, 110
  test script, 178
  upload_max_filesize, 249
php.ini, 245, 249, 322
pictures (see uploaded files)
pipe symbol (see |)
pipe trick, 79
piped link, 77
plainlinks class, 81, 266
plurals, 102
  plural trick, 78
  standards, 211
policies
  standards, 212
popular pages, 164
positional parameters, 114
PostgreSQL, 174
  setup, 186
Powered By MediaWiki icon, 264
pre tag, 54
precedence in parsing, 127
preferences, 25, 35, 41, 150
  adding a checkbox, 309

configuring, 262
date and time, 38
diffs, 42
editing, 38
email, 36, 37
headings, 42
language, 36
links, 42
page caching, 42
paragraph justification, 42
recent changes, 40
search, 41
setting programmatically, 331
skin, 37
system messages, 309
table of contents, 42
text of preferences pages, 218
user profile, 35
watchlist, 40
prefix index, 149
preformatted text box, 54
configuring, 260
in bulleted list, 63
Preloader extension, 308
previewing, 22, 50
before edit box, 39
first edit, 39
printable version link, 24
configuring, 262
privacy, 31, 99
privacy policy link, 26
configuring, 264
processes
standards, 212
profileinfo.php, 195
programming extensions, 281
Project namespace, 97, 110
Project talk namespace, 97
protected titles, 143, 243
protecting articles
configuring, 242
expiration date, 242
list of protected pages, 143
namespace security, 247
protect right, 230
protect tab, configuring, 263
protection log, 153
standards, 212

user groups, 233
protocols for external links, 82
adding, 236
proxy server, 325
purging an article from cache, 257
pywikipedia, 94, 141

Q
query string parameters in extensions,
308
(see also $wgRequest)
quote marks (see "Symbols" section)
quoting wikitext (see escaping wikitext)

R
random page, 158
link, 23
random redirect, 159
read right, 229
read-only wiki, 323
real name, 36
rebuildtextindex.php, 251
recent changes, 152, 154
configuring, 261
date and time preferences, 38
enhanced (JavaScript), 40
link, 23
patrolling, 244
preferences, 40
red links (see specific link colors)
#REDIRECT, 101
redirects, 101
broken, 140
case-sensitivity approach, 102
categorizing, 103
double, 103, 105, 141
list of all, 148
loops, 103, 142
modifying, 102
random, 159
versus deletion, 106
redo, 49
refactoring, 109
techniques, 132
with DPL, 134
with subpages, 133
with templates, 133

references
   books, 163
refreshing your web browser, 43
registered users, 29, 35
   user group, 230
#rel2abs parser function, 122
related changes, 154
   configuring, 262
release process, 176, 199
   branching, 200
remember my login on this computer, 30
removing an article, 106
renaming articles, 26, 104
   log, 153
   permission, 229, 242
   reverting a rename, 105
   watching, 41
resetting passwords, 331
restoring a backup (see backups)
reverse links, 162
Revision class, 308
revision control, 18
   least-revised articles, 142
   most-revised articles, 161
   of MediaWiki source code, 176, 197
   Subversion, 197
   vendor branch, 197
REVISIONDAY, 109
REVISIONMONTH, 109
REVISIONYEAR, 109
right (image tag option), 59
rights, 229
   (see also user rights)
rollback, 245
root login for database, 178, 225
rows (edit box), 38
RSS, 213, 277
rsync, 199

S

sandbox (Wikipedia), 22
Save Page button, 22, 50
   configuring, 240
script path, 110
SCRIPTPATH, 110
scripts, 320
   (see also maintenance scripts)
search, 12, 159

AJAX suggest, 251
case-insensitive, 12, 76
   (see also case-sensitivity)
configuring, 240, 250
database tuning, 251
double quotes, 13
duplicate files, 156
Go versus Search button, 13
ignored search terms, 252
minimum length of search term, 251
namespace selection, 13, 41
phrases, 13
preferences, 41
results page, 13, 14, 159
search and replace, 245
search box, 11, 12
   configuring, 265
Search button, 12
   configuring, 265
search results page, 240
section edit links, 38, 49
   configuring, 241
secure logins, 328
security, 327
   patches, 199
see-also section, 88
Semantic MediaWiki, 280
semicolon (see ;)
serialized directory, 195
SERVER, 82, 110
server variables, 110
SERVERNAME, 82, 110
setFunctionHook, 292
setHook, 294, 297
settings, 215, 227
sharcd uploads, 250
SharePoint, 205
short pages, 143
short URLs, 176, 191
   with administrative access, 192
   without administrative access, 192
shortcuts (see redirects)
Show Changes button, 22, 51
   configuring, 240
show edit toolbar, 39
show preview
   before edit box, 39
   on first edit, 39

Show Preview button, 22, 50
(see also previewing)
configuring, 240
show table of contents, 42
sidebar, 11
configuring, 260
signatures, 32, 54
overriding, 36
raw, 36
signing in (see logging in)
signing out (see logging out)
Simple Forms extension, 280
simultaneous edits (see conflicts)
single quotes, 55
site notice, 259
SITENAME, 109, 110, 124, 257
size limits
articles, 236
uploaded files, 249
skins, 225
creating, 282, 313
default, 267, 315
Modern, 42
(see also Modern skin)
MonoBook, 37
(see also MonoBook skin)
preferences, 37
previewing, 37
skins directory, 194
SkinTemplate class, 314
SkinTemplateContentActions hook, 263
small tag, 55
SMTP server, 189
sortable tables, 70
source code, 281
backups, 320
files you may modify, 194
list of files, 193
local change maintenance (see vendor
branch)
maintenance, 196
space character
leading, 54
underscore conversion, 76
spam, 329
SpamBlacklist extension, 329
span tag, 55
Special namespace, 98

special pages, 15, 24, 139
(see also individual special pages by
title; Special:...)
alphabetical listing, 252
configuring, 262
creating, 282, 301
list of all
reordering, 252
names of, 218
parameters, 150, 242
reference, grouped by task, 165
access control, 169
adding content, 166
administration, 168
big picture, 168
browsing articles, 165
categories, 166
community, 167
current user, 167
infrastructure, 169
organizing, 168
popular content, 166
problem-solving, 168
pruning, 169
recent activity, 168
redirects, 166
searching, 165
templates, 167
topics for writing, 166
uploaded files, 165
watchlists, 167
restricted, 140, 218
Special:AllMessages, 157
Special:AllPages, 17, 96, 147, 246
Special:BlockIP, 228
Special:BookSources, 163
Special:BrokenRedirects, 140
Special:Categories, 148
Special:CategoryTree, 163
Special:Contributions, 150
Special:DeadendPages, 141
Special:Disambiguations, 148, 237
Special:DoubleRedirects, 141
Special:EmailUser, 152
Special:ExpandTemplates, 163, 279
Special:Export, 94, 161, 245, 322
Special:FewestRevisions, 142
Special:FileDuplicateSearch, 156

Special:FilePath, 155, 258
Special:ImageList, 155
Special:Import, 153, 162, 218, 245, 330
    limitations, 322
Special:IPBlockList, 150
Special:LinkSearch, 164
Special:ListGroupRights, 151, 230, 234
Special:ListRedirects, 148
Special:ListUsers, 151
Special:Log, 105, 106, 152, 244
Special:LonelyPages, 142
Special:LongPages, 142
Special:MIMEsearch, 156
Special:MostCategories, 160
Special:MostImages, 159
Special:MostLinked, 160
Special:MostLinkedCategories, 159
Special:MostLinkedTemplates, 160
Special:MostRevisions, 161
Special:MovePage, 141, 164
Special:MyPage, 151
Special:MyTalk, 152
Special:NewImages, 152
Special:NewPages, 153
    patrolling, 244
Special:PopularPages, 164
Special:Preferences, 150, 309
Special:ProtectedPages, 143
Special:ProtectedTitles, 143
Special:Random, 158
Special:RandomRedirect, 159
Special:RecentChanges, 23, 40, 154
    patrolling, 244
Special:RecentChangesLinked, 154
Special:ShortPages, 143
Special:SpecialPages, 140, 218
    extensions, 303
Special:Statistics, 157
Special:UncategorizedCategories, 144
Special:UncategorizedImages, 144
Special:UncategorizedPages, 144
Special:UncategorizedTemplates, 144
Special:Undelete, 106, 162, 242
Special:UnusedCategories, 145
Special:UnusedImages, 145
Special:UnwatchedPages, 146
Special:Upload, 57, 58, 157
Special:UserLogin, 30, 149, 227, 327

Special:UserLogout, 149
Special:UserRights, 151, 218, 234, 235
Special:Version, 158, 273, 323
Special:WantedCategories, 147
Special:WantedPages, 146
Special:Watchlist, 153
Special:WhatLinksHere, 162
Special:WithoutInterwiki, 143
SpecialPage.php, 303
spell-checking, 49
SQL programming, 225
SQL Server, 178
Squid, 325
SSL login page, 327
stack trace, 255
standards, 210
    content, 211
StartProfiler.php, 195
statistics, 157, 165
steward, 231
stopwords, 252
structuring a wiki, 206
stub link formatting, 18, 41
style attribute, 70
stylesheets (see cascading stylesheets)
subcategory, 16, 90, 93
subheadings, 22, 52
SUBJECTSPACE, 112
submit buttons, 240
SubPageList2 extension, 100
SUBPAGENAME, 111
SUBPAGENAMEE, 111
subpages, 99
    BASEPAGENAME variable, 111, 120
    limitations, 100
    listing, 100, 149
    namespace support, 99
        configuring, 247
    nested, 99
    strategies, 133
    SUBPAGENAME variable, 111
    transcluding, 120
    versus categories and namespaces, 99
    visibility, 100
subtitle, 259
subversion, 197
    (see also revision control)
Subversion

backups, 321
  extension downloading, 273
  externals feature, 201
  maintaining MediaWiki source code,
    197
  vendor branch, 197
summary line, 22, 50
  blank, 39
  configuring, 240
  uploads, 58
supercategory, 16, 93
superuser (see sysop)
svn (see subversion)
#switch parser function, 122
syndication (see RSS)
SyntaxHighlight GeSHi extension, 278
sysop, 5, 6, 18, 37, 94, 95, 97, 106, 215,
    216, 229, 230
  choosing, 212
  listing, 151
  user group, 230
system messages, 215, 218
  (see also MediaWiki namespace)
  creating, 221
  examples, 218
  in extensions, 222
  in skins, 222
  list of all, 157, 219
  list of overridden, 148, 158, 220
  loading in extension, 299
  locating, 219
  modifying, 219, 220
  overriding, 219
    permission, 230
  parameters, 220
  PHP programming with, 222
  preferences descriptions, 309
  source code, 219
  transcluding, 221, 222

T

t directory, 195
table of contents, 53
  anchors, 53
  configuring, 266
  hiding, 53
  position in article, 53
  preferences, 42, 53

tables
  database (see database)
  wikitext, 68
    borders, 68
    captions, 69
    headings, 69
    sortable columns, 70
    styles, 70
#tag parser function, 127
tag line for wiki, 259
tags, 47
  converting to parser functions, 127
  creating, 294
  evaluating in parser function context,
    127
  parsing order, 127
  tag extensions, 282
tailoring MediaWiki, 215, 227
Talk namespace, 17, 97, 98
talk pages, 17, 26, 98
  anonymous editing, 232
  configuring, 263
  indenting responses, 54
  signature, 32
TALKSPACE, 112
TALKSPACEE, 112
tar, 180
taxonomy, 206
Template namespace, 97, 112
Template talk namespace, 97
Template:Documentation, 121
templates, 112, 217
  (see also parser functions; transclusion)
  categorizing, 119
  disambig, 148
  documenting, 121
  dummy, 129
  expanding, 279
  list of all, 148
  metadata, 129
  most linked-to, 160
  nesting, 115
  parameters, 113, 133
    default values, 116
    metadata, 129
  parsing order, 127
  standards, 211
  uncategorized, 144

under construction, 95, 113, 121
   unused, 146
   whitespace problems, 118
temporary directory, 249
tests directory, 195
tetex, 191
text box, preformatted, 54
textarea on edit page, 240
this is a minor edit, 39
   configuring, 240
threshold for stub link formatting, 41
thumbnails, 38, 59, 152
   thumb (image tag option), 59
   thumbnail (image tag option), 59
#time parser function, 122
time format, 38
time zone, 38
timestamps, 38, 242
   XML export files, 245
title (see article titles)
Title class, 308
#titleparts parser function, 122
__TOC__, 42, 47, 53
toolbar on edit page, 50
toolbox menu, 11, 24
   configuring, 261
   creating links, 309
   on user page, 32
top tabs, 11, 26
   configuring, 263
transclusion, 112
   (see also templates)
   conditional, 116
   from all namespaces, 119
   subpages, 120
   system messages, 221
typestyles, 54

U

uc parser function, 124
UNC paths, linking, 86
uncategorized
   categories, 144
   files, 144
   pages, 144
uncategorized templates, 144
uncompress, 180
undeleting articles, 106, 162

permission, 230
   undelete right, 230
underlining links, 42
underlining text, 55
underscores
   converting to spaces, 76
   double (magic words), 47
   in article titles, 76
   in URLs, 76
undo, 19, 49, 245
undoing a move, 105
unprotect tab
   configuring, 263
untar, 180
unused
   categories, 145
   files, 145
   templates, 146
unwatch tab, 33
   configuring, 263
unwatched pages, 146
update.php, 322
upgrading MediaWiki, 199
uploaded files, 38, 56
   access control, 232
   backups, 322
   batch uploads, 330
   configuring, 248, 262
   destination directory, 249
   duplicates, 156
   embedding in articles, 56, 57, 59
   enabling, 188, 248
   limitations, 204
   linking to, 57, 60
   listing, 155
   MIME search, 156
   most linked-to, 159
   newest, 152
   restricting
      by file extension, 248
      by MIME type, 248
   scaling an image, 59
   setup, 188
   shared, 250
   size limit, 249
   special pages, 155
   statistics, 157
   thumbnails, 38

uncategorized, 144
unused, 145
upload log, 153
uploading, 56, 57, 157
URL path, 60, 155, 249
virus scanning, 250
upload_max_filesize, 249
upper versus lower case (see case-sensitivity)
uppercase conversion, 124
URL, 81
(see also external links)
of wiki, 82
short, 176, 191
special page parameters, 150
underscores, 76
User class, 287, 304, 306, 310
user CSS, 43, 267
(see also cascading stylesheets)
user group rights, 151
user groups (see user rights)
user interface
configuring, 257
user JavaScript, 43, 253
(see also JavaScript)
user list, 151
User namespace, 17, 97
user options menu, 11, 25
configuring, 262
user page, 17, 25, 31, 151
photograph, 31
privacy, 31
subpages of, 99
user profile, 35
user rights, 229, 328
bureaucrats, 229
creating, 234
examples, 229
extensions, 235
hiding top tabs, 263
isAllowed, 234
listing, 151
log, 153
management, 151
permission to assign, 230, 234
self-service, 235
special pages, 150
user groups, 230

assigning users to groups, 151, 231, 234
creating, 233, 242
examples, 230
listing, 151
protecting articles, 233
removing users from groups, 235
User talk namespace, 17, 31, 97
User talk page, 25
user talk page, 31, 152
browser alerts, 31
email notifications, 32, 37
User.php, 287, 306
username
changing, 37
userOptions.php, 267, 316, 331
userrights right, 230
users, 29
blocking (see blocking users)
configuring, 227
creating, 30, 227
in batch, 228
deleting, 228
fetching from database, 306
listing, 151
motivating, 210
renaming, 228
signatures, 32
statistics, 157
training, 210
UserToggles hook, 309
UTF-8, 238

V

Vandalism, 329
variable lists (see definition lists)
variables, 109
(see also individual variable names)
ARTICLESPACE, 112
BASEPAGENAME, 111, 120
BASEPAGENAMEE, 111
creating, 282, 289
FULLPAGENAME, 79, 111
FULLPAGENAMEE, 111
NAMESPACE, 112
PAGENAME, 111
PAGENAMEE, 111
REVISIONDAY, 109

REVISIONMONTH, 109
REVISIONYEAR, 109
SCRIPTPATH, 110
SERVER, 82, 110
SERVERNAME, 82, 110
SITENAME, 109, 110, 124, 257
SUBJECTSPACE, 112
SUBPAGENAME, 111
SUBPAGENAMEE, 111
TALKSPACE, 112
TALKSPACEE, 112
vendor branch, 197
version, 158
version control (see revision control)
view and edit watchlist, 35
view deleted pages, 162
view source, 26
virtual namespace, 98
virus scanning, 250

W

wanted categories, 147
wanted pages, 146
warning message text, 218
watchlist, 25, 33, 153
    adding from edit page, 51
    automatic watching, 40
    configuring, 262
    email notifications, 34, 37
    expanding, 40
    modifying, 35
    preferences, 40
    unwatched pages, 146
    viewing, 33
    watch tab, 26, 33
        configuring, 263
    watch this page checkbox, 51
        configuring, 240
web installer, 182
wfMsg, 222, 302, 304
wfMsgForContent, 222
wfRunHooks, 287
$wgAddGroups, 235
$wgAllowExternalImages, 236
$wgAllowExternalImagesFrom, 237
$wgAllowUserCss, 224, 268
$wgAllowUserJs, 253
$wgAntivirus, 250

$wgAntivirusRequired, 250
$wgAntivirusSetup, 250
$wgAutoloadClasses, 302
$wgCheckFileExtensions, 248
$wgDBadminpassword, 201
$wgDBname, 252
$wgDBpassword, 201, 252
$wgDBprefix, 252
$wgDBserver, 252, 325
$wgDBservers, 325
$wgDBTableOptions, 252
$wgDBtype, 224
$wgDBuser, 252
$wgDebugComments, 254
$wgDebugLogFile, 254
$wgDefaultSkin, 267, 315
$wgDisableCounters, 165, 323
$wgDocType, 238
$wgDTD, 238
$wgEmailConfirmToEdit, 190
$wgEmergencyContact, 189
$wgEnableEmail, 189, 224
$wgEnableMWSuggest, 251
$wgEnableUploads, 188, 248
$wgEnableUserEmail, 189
$wgEnableWriteAPI, 317
$wgExtensionCredits, 288
$wgExtensionFunctions, 292, 294
$wgExtraNamespaces, 246
$wgFavicon, 258
$wgFileBlacklist, 248
$wgFileExtensions, 224, 248
$wgGoToEdit, 241
$wgGroupPermissions, 231, 232, 233,
        235, 244
$wgGroupsAddToSelf, 235
$wgGroupsRemoveFromSelf, 235
$wgHooks, 286, 309, 310
$wgJsMimeType, 238
$wgLanguageCode, 238, 269
$wgLoginLanguageSelector, 269
$wgLogo, 224, 258
$wgMathDirectory, 237, 249
$wgMathPath, 237, 249
$wgMaxArticleSize, 236
$wgMaxCredits, 266
$wgMaxNameChars, 224
$wgMaxTocLevel, 266

$wgMaxUploadSize, 249
$wgMessageCache, 302, 304, 310
$wgMimeInfoFile, 248
$wgMimeType, 238
$wgMimeTypeBlacklist, 248
$wgMimeTypeFile, 248
$wgNamespacesToBeSearchedDefault, 247
$wgNamespacesWithSubpages, 121, 247
$wgNonincludableNamespaces, 247
$wgOut, 302, 303, 304, 307, 311
$wgOutputEncoding, 238
$wgParser, 284, 292, 294, 297, 313
$wgPasswordSender, 189
$wgReadOnly, 323
$wgRemoveGroups, 235
$wgRequest, 302, 304, 308
$wgRestrictionLevels, 233
$wgRightsIcon, 264
$wgRightsText, 264
$wgRightsUrl, 264
$wgScriptPath, 192
$wgSharedUploadPath, 250
$wgShowExceptionDetails, 254, 289
$wgShowSQLErrors, 255, 289
$wgSitename, 189, 257
$wgSMTP, 189
$wgSpecialPageGroups, 252
$wgSpecialPages, 302
$wgStrictFileExtensions, 248
$wgTmpDirectory, 249
$wgUploadDirectory, 249
$wgUploadPath, 249
$wgUploadSizeWarning, 249
$wgUrlProtocols, 236
$wgUseAjax, 251, 317
$wgUseNPPatrol, 244
$wgUser, 310
$wgUseRCPatrol, 244
$wgUseSharedUploads, 250
$wgUseSiteCss, 268
$wgUseSiteJs, 253
$wgUseTeX, 191, 237
$wgVerifyMimeType, 248
$wgVersion, 201
$wgWhitelistRead, 232
$wgXhtmlDefaultNamespace, 238
what links here, 106, 162

configuring, 262
whitelist, 232
whitespace
    in DPL format statement, 128
    in templates, 118
    leading, 54
who's in charge, 212
width of edit box, 38
wiki, 3
    administration (see administration)
    administrator (see administrator)
    family, 327
    farm, 327
    name, 110, 124, 183
        configuring, 257
    page (see articles)
WikiArticleFeeds extension, 214, 277
wikibits.js, 223, 311, 312
Wikimedia Foundation, 7
Wikipedia, xi, 7
    Help, 27
    policies, 213
    standards, 212
WikiSysop, 184
    (see also sysop)
wikitext, 21, 47
    (see also editing)
    (see also external links; internal links)
    blank lines, 52
    bold, 54
    bold italics, 54
    bulleted list, 61
    code formatting, 54
        inline, 55
    definition lists, 65
    escaping, 71
    fonts, 54
    headings, 52
    indenting, 54
    italics, 54
    linebreaks, 62
    lists, 61
        combining, 66
    math, 70
    monospaced, 55
    nowiki, 71
    numbered lists, 64
    ordered lists, 64

paragraphs, 52
quoting (see escaping wikitext)
rendering in extensions, 307
table of contents, 21
tables, 68
text box, preformatted, 54
text color, 55
text size, 55
typestyles, 54
underlined text, 55
uploaded files (see uploaded files)
variable lists, 65
wikiuser, 186, 225
Windows (see Microsoft Windows)
64-bit, 178
write-protected wiki, 323
WYSIWYG, 7, 21, 204

X

XDebug, 289
XML
dump and restore, 245, 322
export, 94, 161, 245, 322
import, 162, 245
rendering, 297, 306
tags, 47

Z

Zend Optimizer, 325

About the Author

Daniel J. Barrett has been immersed in Internet technology since 1985. Currently working in the software industry, Dan has also been a heavy metal singer, Linux system administrator, university lecturer, web developer, and humorist. He is the author of seven O'Reilly books, including *MediaWiki*, *Linux Pocket Guide*, and *SSH, The Secure Shell: The Definitive Guide*.

Colophon

The animals on the cover of *MediaWiki* are mimic butterflies. Several species of butterflies mimic other butterflies to protect themselves from predators or to gain an advantage over other insects.

Mimic butterflies often employ two types of mimicry: nonpoisonous (Batesian mimicry) and poisonous (Müllerian mimicry). Because predators will become sick (or, in some cases, die) after eating a poisonous insect, nonpoisonous butterflies benefit from mimicking their poisonous look-alikes. However, an advantage of poisonous mimicry is that fewer overall insects die as predators become skilled at avoiding both poisonous species.

For instance, the Ash Borer (*Podosesia syringae*) has markings that look strikingly like those of the paper wasp (*Polistes fuscatus*). As such, potential predators steer clear from the Ash Borer for fear of being stung, even though the butterfly has no ability to sting. The Queen butterfly (*Danaus gilippus*) is perhaps doubly protected, as it is poisonous, just like its twin, the Monarch butterfly (*Danaus plexippus*).

Some would also call the mimic butterfly a trickster. As a caterpillar, the Blue butterfly (*Everes comyntas*) will secrete skin molecules that are nearly identical to those of the fire ant. After secretion, an adult fire ant will usually find the butterfly and "adopt" it, bringing the larva back to its home, where it feeds the caterpillar until it is able to turn into a butterfly. The Blue butterfly repays the ant's kindness by eating the majority of its available food and also by devouring the ant's young.

The cover image is is from *Lydekker's Library of Natural History*. The cover font is Adobe ITC Garamond. The text font is Linotype Birka; the heading font is Adobe Myriad Condensed; and the code font is LucasFont's TheSansMonoCondensed.

Related Titles from O'Reilly

Web Authoring and Design

ActionScript 3.0 Cookbook

Ajax Hacks

Ambient Findability

Creating Web Sites: The Missing Manual

CSS Cookbook, *2nd Edition*

CSS Pocket Reference, *2nd Edition*

CSS: The Definitive Guide, *3rd Edition*

CSS: The Missing Manual

Dreamweaver 8: Design and Construction

Dreamweaver 8: The Missing Manual

Dynamic HTML: The Definitive Reference, *3rd Edition*

Essential ActionScript 3.0

Flex 8 Cookbook

Flash 8: Projects for Learning Animation and Interactivity

Flash 8: The Missing manual

Flash 9 Design: Motion Graphics for Animation & User Interfaces

Flash Hacks

Head First HTML with CSS & XHTML

Head Rush Ajax

Head First Web Design

High Performance Web Sites

HTML & XHTML: The Definitive Guide, *6th Edition*

HTML & XHTML Pocket Reference, *3rd Edition*

Information Architecture for the World Wide Web, *3rd Edition*

Information Dashboard Design

JavaScript: The Definitive Guide, *5th Edition*

JavaScript & DHTML Cookbook, *2nd Edition*

Learning ActionScript 3.0

Learning JavaScript

Learning Web Design, *3rd Edition*

PHP Hacks

Programming Collective Intelligence

Programming Flex 2

Web Design in a Nutshell, *3rd Edition*

Web Site Measurement Hacks

O'REILLY®

Our books are available at most retail and online bookstores.

To order direct: 1-800-998-9938 • order@oreilly.com • www.oreilly.com

Online editions of most O'Reilly titles are available by subscription at *safari.oreilly.com*

70502